# BUREAUCRATIC JUSTICE

# BUREAUCRATIC JUSTICE

## *Managing Social Security Disability Claims*

JERRY L. MASHAW

**YALE UNIVERSITY PRESS**
New Haven and London

Published with assistance from the Louis Stern Memorial Fund.

Designed by Nancy Ovedovitz and set in VIP Electra type by Ro-Mark Typographic Company, Inc. Printed in the United States of America by The Murray Printing Company, Westford, Mass.

**Library of Congress Cataloging in Publication Data**
Mashaw, Jerry L.
  Bureaucratic justice.

  Includes index.
  1. United States.    Social Security Administration.
2. Insurance, Disability—Law and legislation—United
States.    3. Administrative law—United States.
4. Administrative procedure—United States.    I. Title.
KF3650.5.M37    1983        344.73'023        82-17506
ISBN   0-300-02808-3          347.30423

10    9    8    7    6    5    4    3    2    1

*For my parents*

# Contents

# Preface and Acknowledgments

This book attempts to satisfy two converging personal curiosities. The first is concrete. In a study of hearings and appeals in the Social Security disability program, my colleagues and I repeatedly encountered statements from administrative law judges of the following form: "The real problem with this program is in the (a) poor development, (b) poor judgment, or (c) poor management of cases at the state agency level." Was this view correct or was it merely the conventional displacement of blame to the level below (or above) the level of the responding organizational actor?

The second curiosity is much more abstract. Is it possible to integrate the normative concerns of administrative law with the positive concerns of organizational theory? Could such an integration produce a revised vision of both—a law that is more than symbolic and a positive theory of organizational behavior driven by more than individual or organizational self-interest? Explaining whence this second curiosity arises would require more autobiography than even my parents would find interesting, and whether I have (or should have) satisfied either curiosity I will leave to be answered by the readers of the book that follows.

I would, however, be unforgiveably ungrateful were I not to give history enough to acknowledge the assistance of many who have made the effort to provide answers both feasible and personally rewarding. I owe a major intellectual debt to my colleagues Charlie Goetz, Frank Goodman, Warren Schwartz, and Paul Verkuil, who were my co-authors for *Social Security Hearings and Appeals* (Lexington, Mass.: Lexington Books, 1978). I have no way to determine how many of their good (and bad) ideas have been appropriated and employed here. Needed financial support has been provided at different times by the National Center for Administrative Justice, the Ford Foundation, and the Commonwealth Fund. I have benefited enormously from discussions with many of my colleagues at Yale. I am particularly grateful to Ted Marmor, Roy Schotland, and Peter Schuck, who gave me detailed comments on an earlier draft; to Dean Harry Wellington, who never asked when the book would be finished; and to Bruce Ackerman, who often did. Lorraine Nagle has typed three "final revisions" of the manuscript without commenting on my idiosyncratic use of "final."

My greatest appreciation must be reserved for the men and women at the Social Security Administration and six (known but unnamed) state disability determination services. I pestered them for a total of nearly thirty days of interviewing and observation. They responded with an openness and hospitability that made my work easy. Although all my SSA and state agency informants were promised anonymity, I must mention two whose assistance was critical: Stan Ross as commissioner both sustained my interest by his enthusiasm and opened many doors with keys only the commissioner holds. Alice Farley was an astonishing reservoir of information, documents, and people. Without her assistance I might still be wandering aimlessly on the outskirts of Baltimore.

# PART I · PERSPECTIVES

# 1 · The Quest for an Internal Administrative Law

## WHY THIS CRUSADE?

The search for a law within administration that aspires to something called "bureaucratic justice" may seem a doomed enterprise. In a legal culture largely oriented toward court enforcement of individual legal rights, "administration" has always seemed as antithetical to "law" as "bureaucracy" is to "justice." Law focuses on rights, administration on policy. Rights, if enforced, must limit policy, thereby stifling administration. When policy is wanted, the law's typical response is to create no-right, no-law policy enclaves where discretion can flourish. But permitting uncontrolled discretion generates a demand for law, and the competitive cycle of law and policy begins anew. Moreover, the usual image of routinized bureaucratic decisionmaking, based on typical or modal cases, seems to eliminate precisely the individual judgments essential to a sense of justice. The suggestion that positive administration, bureaucratically organized, can be combined with law in a unified vision—perhaps even a vision of justice—appears both historically implausible and conceptually muddled.

There is certainly force to these objections. For, to be blunt, the history of American administrative law is a history of failed ideas.[1] Administrative law's basic technique for formulating and implementing guiding legal norms—lawsuits asserting private rights and challenging the legality of official action—seems to have forced it to oscillate continuously between irrelevance and impertinence.

The early fault was impertinence. The Supreme Court attempted to

1. See generally, Stewart, *The Reformation of America Administrative Law*, 88 Harv. L. Rev. 1669 (1975).

use the due process clause and the notion that only Congress could "legislate" to protect private property and private markets from the emergence of positive government.[2] That attempt was crushed in the New Deal.[3] Accepting the bloodless revolution, the Court beat a hasty retreat. Indeed, it was routed. The history of administrative law from the thirties to the sixties is the history of the judicial development of technical defenses that prevented private plaintiffs from reaching the merits of their claims against government officials.[4]

But this phase too has passed. As the brave new agencies of the New Deal became creaky bureaucracies, the body politic and the courts began to lose faith in the administrative state. The civil rights movement and the war on poverty, joined later by the environmental, consumer, and women's rights movements, disclosed that minorities, the poor, indeed "people" in general, were being left out of the processes of governance. As the body politic embraced participatory governance, the technical barriers to judicial review came tumbling down.[5] The judiciary, assisted by congressional conferrals of broader and broader jurisdiction, became a hospitable forum for reform-minded bureaucracy fighters of every persuasion.

This revival of judicial review was not, however, a revival of an antigovernment, property-rights jurisprudence. Instead the rights asserted were those embodied in welfare state legislation *plus* the inchoate but rapidly developing right to participate—the latter forged in part from traditional notions of open judicial process and in part from the open government ideology and statutory victories of the politics of protest. Yet again, things did not work out very well. The notion of participation as a right subject to judicial enforcement turned out to be unmanageable, if not incoherent. Does everyone have this right? To participate how and with what effects? On what basis can a claim to participation be evaluated?

To the last question the courts have given two answers. Each reveals

---

2. *See, e.g.,* Corwin, *The "Higher Law" Background of American Constitutional Law,* 42 Harv. L. Rev. 149 (1928); McCloskey, *Economic Due Process and the Supreme Court: An Exhumation and Reburial,* 1962 Sup. Ct. Rev. 34.

3. *See* L. Tribe, American Constitutional Law 466–55 (1978).

4. The classic commentary based predominately on the jurisprudence of this period is L. Jaffe, Judicial Review of Administrative Action (1965).

5. *See* Stewart, *supra* note 1 at 1711–47.

the fragility of the conceptual underpinnings for participatory rights.[6] The first is that participation, whether in agency decision processes or in courts, is to be granted to persons who are the beneficiaries (or disbeneficiaries) of substantive statutory rights. But, as Justice Rehnquist enjoys asking,[7] how can the courts say that statutes creating substantive rights include rights to participation that are nowhere provided by the statute? To do so must be to redefine the substantive statutory right. For if the participatory right is a function of the substantive right, in Rehnquist's view the beneficiary should be required to "take the bitter [the absence of desired forms of participation] with the sweet [the substantive legislative benefit]."

The appropriate response to Rehnquist might be that the participatory right comes out of the due process clause of the Constitution. That, indeed, is the second answer to the question of how to ground and develop a general right of participation. But, alas, the due process clause is an answer in the form of a question: What process is "due"? The answer to that question leads back to the previous quandary: The due process clause protects claims to life, liberty, or property. In statutory claims, what is "due" is presumably a process appropriate to the type of "property" or "liberty" that the legislation provides. If so, then the process that is due should emerge by close attention to the statutory text. Where, then, could the Court be looking when it finds a process to be due that is different from the one provided by the statute?

The uncharitable answer that emerges from the due process cases of the late sixties and early seventies is that it is looking into a mirror. The process that is due is one that roughly conforms to, or at least borrows its decisional techniques from, judicial process. But why should this be so? Are agencies doing the same things as courts? Are they operating with similar legal powers, political demands, and fiscal resources? The answers are obvious—so obvious that the Supreme Court seems in full retreat from its landmark "give 'em more process" administrative-due-process cases.[8] Along the way, it has stamped out the peculiarly activist,

6. For a more extended treatment *see* Mashaw, *Administrative Due Process: The Quest for a Dignitary Theory*, 61 Boston Univ. L. Rev. 885 (1981), and authorities there cited.
7. Arnett v. Kennedy, 416 U.S. 134 (1974).
8. *See, e.g.*, Van Alstyne, *Cracks in "The New Property": Adjudicative Due Process in the Administrative State*, 62 Cornell L. Rev. 445 (1977).

participation-enhancing efforts of the District of Columbia Court of Appeals in an opinion that reads like a temper tantrum.[9]

Retreat from enforcing a vague right that requires judicial redesign of administrative processes in the image of the judiciary seems sensible.[10] Justice Black warned the court in *Goldberg v. Kelly*,[11] the welfare case that started the wholesale attack on administrative procedures, that the judiciary would be unable to control the dynamics of administrative adjustment to its procedural rulings. Indeed, his prediction that the costs of giving hearings to ineligible persons prior to terminating their benefits would be taken out of the hides of eligible welfare applicants (by increasing barriers to qualification) rapidly materialized. But the problems with due process review are more general. In *Goldberg* the Court also seems to have misunderstood what caused decisional errors[12] and vastly overestimated the capacity of welfare bureaucracies to run a hearing system.[13] The risks of judicial intervention may thus include both new dysfunctional consequences for the supposed winners and the ultimate irrelevance of the judicial remedies provided. Impertinence and irrelevance may combine as well as alternate.

I do not, of course, want to assert that judicial review of administrative procedure is always a botch. But the risks of irrelevance or dysfunction seem to be high. Nor do those risks decrease materially when the issue for review is one of substance rather than procedure. Perhaps the leading modern Supreme Court case defining the appropriate posture for the courts to take when they engage in substantive judicial review of administrative action, *Citizens to Preserve Overton Park, Inc. v. Volpe*,[14] is both an elegant essay on judicial restraint and an atrociously simpleminded interpretation of the statutes governing the federal highway program.[15]

The courts are not necessarily to blame. Substantive rights—to a

9. Vermont Yankee Nuclear Power Corp. v. Natural Resources Defense Council, Inc., 435 U.S. 519 (1978).

10. The words "*Goldberg v. Kelly*" plugged into a Lexis terminal in June 1981 produced citations to 1,900 reported cases.

11. 397 U.S. 254 (1970).

12. Cooper, *Goldberg's Forgotten Footnote*, 64 Minn. L. Rev. 1107 (1980).

13. *See* Mashaw, *The Management Side of Due Process*, 59 Cornell L. Rev. 772 (1974).

14. 401 U.S. 402 (1971).

15. *See* Mashaw, *The Legal Structure of Frustration*, 122 U. Pa. L. Rev. 1, 40–44 (1973).

healthful environment, to a reasonably safe car or work place, to low-cost housing or hospital care—are imbedded in statutes of awesome complexity, sometimes, but not always, drafted to reflect the subtle politics of making haste slowly in a pluralist and federal political system. Determining under these statutory texts whether administrative action represents an appropriate understanding of congressional intent and, if not, forcing protection of the putative beneficiary's rights has often turned out to be a much more difficult task than saying "stop" to administrators or "no standing" to plaintiffs—the remedial and evasive techniques respectively of the conservative courts of the twenties and their progressive brethren in the post–New Deal era. Indeed, the Supreme Court's attempts to find a secure footing—a basis for affirming or denying rights—in the deluge of statutes that has flooded the contemporary legal landscape make it an easy object of ridicule. Consider the following pair of cases.

In the first[16] a group of environmentalists sought an injunction against an almost completed water project of great expense and enormous economic consequence. The claim was that the dam would destroy the habitat of a rare perch, the snail darter, contrary to the Endangered Species Act's instructions to federal officials to avoid actions harmful to the habitats of rare flora and fauna. Did the environmentalists have a "right" to stop the dam? "No," said the defendant officials. Congress could not have meant to protect species of the mind-boggling insignificance of the snail darter—a fish that was discovered only after this water project was well under way. Besides, Congress repeatedly appropriated money for the project after it was well aware of the snail darter problem. The appropriations committees consistently expressed the view that the act did not protect newly discovered species from nearly completed projects. "Wrong," said the Court. The answer is "yes." The act is clear and contains no exception relevant to this case.

Three years later a class of mentally retarded persons sued to enforce the Developmentally Disabled Assistance and Bill of Rights Act.[17] Included in the "bill of rights" section of the act was a provision declaring that the developmentally disabled have a right to habilitation

---

16. TVA v. Hill, 437 U.S. 153 (1978).
17. Pennhurst State School and Hospital v. Halderman, 451 U.S. 1 (1981).

and to appropriate treatment in least-restrictive environments. The state and local institutional defendants argued that the so-called bill of rights in the federal statute was just a suggestion. They pointed to the undeniable facts that (1) the compliance would be very expensive and (2) Congress had not appropriated sufficient money to facilitate implementation. "Right," said the Court. When adopting legislation that imposes obligations on states and localities receiving federal funds, Congress must say explicitly not only that the beneficiaries have rights and the states have obligations, but also that the funds are "conditioned" on acceptance by the states of the new legal relationship. Snail darters—1; developmentally disabled persons—0.

Can it be that Congress and the Court regard three-inch perch as more important than the developmentally disabled? Do they think the former is deserving of legal protection from administrative depredation while the latter is not? Surely there is some other explanation. Indeed, I think there is. The snail darter case requires only that the Court say "stop"; the developmental disabilities case asked that administrators be directed to take affirmative action under statutory language that would then have to be given substantive content. In that latter process the Court sees the federal judiciary being dragged inexorably into further disputes, perhaps into continuous monitoring of administrative activity and ultimately into some broad structural injunction through which the courts would attempt to take over administration.

There are, of course, ways of translating many claims for affirmative protection into a negative, and therefore judicially more manageable, form. "Give me a healthful environment" can thus become "Do not proceed without attending to my legislatively validated demand for a healthful environment." Enforcing such a right might involve courts in no more than enjoining administrative action that fails to take *appropriate* account of the interests the Congress meant to further or protect. But even this reinterpretation of rights will not suffice to guarantee surefooted or effective judicial surveillance of administrative activity. For example, Ackerman and Hassler, reviewing in *Clean Coal/Dirty Air*, what seems to be a multibillion dollar congressional-EPA "mistake," describe judicial review in the following terms: "Not only did EPA readily evade the Court of Appeals' effort to prompt policy reconsideration, but the flow of litigation only directed attention away from the need for long-range planning. Nor was this distortion an unhappy accident. . . . [L]itigation obscures as much as it instructs."[18] And in a study of hearings and judicial review in the Social Security disability program my colleagues and I found that the tens of thousands of judicial review proceedings that have been held since the disability program's inception have either had no perceptible impact on its functioning or have made it worse.

Again, I do not want to protest too much. Martin Shapiro, for example, has described judicial review as a court-agency partnership in implementation, and that description has some plausibility. From the political scientist's perspective—an interest in how the system of political accommodation functions over time—administrative law is certainly not a disaster. The government, the economy, and the social order are still functioning with a relatively low level of physical violence. Yet this important perception does not alter the fact, as Shapiro says, "that courts typically let the agency do what it pleases."[19] Nor does it suggest that courts, whether patting the agency on the head or kicking it in the shins, have any very good idea what has gone on in the context offered to them for review or how their actions will affect the dynamics of litigation, congressional action, or bureaucratic functioning.

What, after all, should we expect when the Supreme Court notes, in a routine recitation of the facts in a 1980 case, that the rule it is reviewing is based on an administrative record containing 105,000 pages?[20] And a written record, even (or especially) of that length, cannot provide a sharp and true picture of the reality of administration. The D.C. Circuit Court of Appeals has recently provided candid testimonial evidence for this conclusion. In *Sierra Club v. Costle*,[21] reviewing the EPA decision Ackerman and Hassler[22] describe as a colossal boner, the court concludes:

Since the issues in this proceeding were joined in 1973 when the Navajo Indians first complained about sulfur dioxide fumes over their Southwest homes, we have had several lawsuits, almost four years of substantive and procedural

18. B. ACKERMAN & W. HASSLER, CLEAN COAL/DIRTY AIR 25 (1981).

19. M. SHAPIRO, THE SUPREME COURT AND ADMINISTRATIVE AGENCIES 265 (1968).

20. Industrial Union Dept., AFL-CIO v. American Petroleum Inst., 448 U.S. 607 (1980).

21. 657 F.2d 298 (D.C. Cir. 1981).

22. *Op. cit. supra* note 18.

maneuvering before the EPA, and now this extended court challenge. In the interim, Congress has amended the Clean Air Act once and may be ready to do so again. The standard we uphold has already been in effect for almost two years, and could be revised within another two years.

We reach our decision after interminable record searching (and considerable soul searching). We have read the record with as hard a look as mortal judges can probably give its thousands of pages. We have adopted a simple and straightforward standard of review, probed the agency's rationale, studied its references (and those of appellants), endeavored to understand them where they were intelligible (parts were simply impenetrable), and on close questions given the agency the benefit of the doubt out of deference for the terrible complexity of its job. We are not engineers, computer modelers, economists or statisticians, although many of the documents in this record require such expertise— and more.

Cases like this highlight the enormous responsibilities Congress has entrusted to the courts in proceedings of such length, complexity and disorder. Conflicting interests play fiercely for enormous stakes, advocates are prolific and agile, obfuscation runs high, common sense correspondingly low, the public intent is often obscured.

We cannot redo the agency's job; Congress has told us, at least in proceedings under this Act, that it will not brook reversal for small procedural errors; Vermont Yankee reinforces the admonition. So in the end we can only make our best effort to understand, to see if the result makes sense, and to assure that nothing unlawful or irrational has taken place. In this case, we have taken a long while to come to a short conclusion: the rule is reasonable.[23]

For good reason, being "judicious" is almost synonymous with exercising restraint. Why should anyone believe that particular issues raised in episodic litigation between parties having peculiar litigating interests should provide the judiciary with sufficient information for it to understand the administrative, political, social, economic, or scientific reality of a congressional-administrative program, much less provide an opportunity to take effective action to mold that reality in desirable forms?[24] That the courts generally do not hold such a belief is a testament to their wisdom. That they sometimes act as if they did is perhaps a result of our general tendency to exert unreasonable pressure

23. 657 F.2d at 410.

24. For an extended argument of this general form *see* D. HOROWITZ, THE COURTS AND SOCIAL POLICY (1977).

on all public institutions. If we demand persistently enough that the judges pull our chestnuts out of the fire, they will sometimes try.

If, then, by "administrative law" we mean that set of doctrines concerning the rights of citizens to hold administrators accountable in court, administrative law has a simple lesson: the citizen has a right to keep officials from straying beyond some large and loose requirements of clear statutory language, procedural regularity, and substantive rationality. Within those boundaries there lies a gigantic policy space, invisible to the legal order because devoid of justiciable rights. Moreover, as the administrative state has grown, as more "rights" have been generated and defined by a combination of legislative and administrative action, this externally oriented administrative law, that is, a law oriented toward justiciable rights enforceable against administrators in court, has become increasingly irrelevant to the realization of our collective ideals. Consider one final example: wage and price regulation as practiced in the Nixon and Carter administrations.

The Economic Stabilization Act of 1970 empowered President Nixon to "issue such orders and regulations as he may deem appropriate to stabilize prices, rents, wages, and salaries."[25] There was little more to the act than that. It went on merely to provide that the president could delegate his power to any agency or officer of the government; to establish penalties for violations of regulations issued under the act; and to empower the federal district courts to issue injunctions against violations. The statute provided for executive and, on redelegation of the powers, administrative governance pure and simple.

The president exercised the powers conferred by issuing an order freezing wages, rents, and prices as of a certain date and delegated his power to administer the act to a Cost of Living Council headed by the secretary of the treasury. Under the president's executive order, the council was given the power to adopt subsidiary rules and regulations and to grant waivers from and make interpretations of the meaning of the freeze order. A plaintiff union representing employees whose employer refused, because of the freeze, to pay bargained-for wage increases haled the recalcitrant employer and the secretary of the treasury into court.[26] The plaintiff had many complaints, but as the court

25. 84 Stat. 799 (1970).
26. Amalgamated Meat Cutters v. Connally, 337 F. Supp. 737 (1971).

recognized they came down to this: the Economic Stabilization Act institutes a form of administrative governance—free from legislative direction, public participation, and judicial control—that challenges directly the traditional conception of the rule of law.

The court was sympathetic but ultimately unmoved. The union, it suggested, had failed to appreciate the legal constraints within which the president and the council would operate. First, the Congress had exercised its basic lawmaking task by providing a lower boundary on the stabilized level of wages, prices, and rents (that existing on May 25, 1970), by prohibiting "gross inequity," and by conferring the authority only for short time periods, subject to congressional review prior to reauthorization. Second, the administrators would operate with the usual constraints of the Federal Administrative Procedure Act and subject to judicial review. That is, the council was subject to the conventional constraints of administrative law concerning public participation in rulemaking, hearings in contested cases, and judicial review of the legality of rules and orders.

All of this seems quite comforting—until one asks some simple questions, such as: Does the council have to make any rules elaborating its interpretation of the order and the grounds upon which waivers are available? If so, does it have to allow public participation? Are hearings required before waivers are denied or interpretations given? Is judicial review likely to have any substantial bite in this context? The answers are no, no, no, and no.[27]

Without getting into legal technicalities, the basic reason for these answers is to be found in our prior historical excursion. Administrative law, whether judicially created or statutorily imposed, contains a plethora of devices to preserve agency discretion thought essential to effective administration. If that law is not to be aptly characterized by Mr. Bumble's aphorism, it must in the wage and price control context permit expansive breathing space. The council had to respond to 50,000 complaints, 6,000 requests for waiver, and 750,000 requests for interpretation in its first ninety days. Most of this work must be done "informally," that is, outside whatever transparent procedures, open hearings, and judicial review proceedings usually satisfy us that the

27. For a somewhat more extended discussion *see* MASHAW AND MERRILL, INTRODUCTION TO THE AMERICAN PUBLIC LAW SYSTEM 207–12 (1975).

"rule of law" has been maintained. In its emphasis on informal process the Cost of Living Council was typical, not atypical, of administrative behavior.

## THE CHALLENGE OF LEGAL REALISM

We begin, therefore, by conceding the legal realists' insight. The legally required means of agency implementation, as developed by courts and legislatures, may sometimes inform but cannot control administration. The normative structures created by legislation and by judicial decisionmaking are often, if not usually, removed from the concrete experience of bureaucratic implementation. The law in action is, in Karl Llewellyn's famous line, developed by "people who have the doing in charge."[28]

The point was long ago enunciated in Thurman Arnold's trenchant observations on law in general. "'Law' is primarily a great reservoir of emotionally important social symbols. . . . The observer should constantly keep in mind that the function of law is not so much to guide society, as to comfort it."[29] And Arnold explained the court-centered nature of American administrative law, its tendency to equate legality either with the opportunity for judicial review or with the use of courtlike processes, in terms of the symbolic content of "court" and "bureau":

A court is a body of judges whose decisions are either: (a) right, (b) caused by the fault of someone else (usually the legislature), or (c) unfortunate but unavoidable accidents due to the circumstance that no human system can be perfect. A bureau is a body which, if it happens to make a wrong decision has no one to blame but itself, and if it happens to make a right decision, offers us no assurance that it will do so again.[30]

But what are we to do when symbolic legality wears thin? when the idea that bureaus are subject to review by courts and may be required to use courtlike procedure no longer consoles us? when not only Arnold but most of the observers of the rule of law on parade are shouting that the emperor has no clothes?

28. K. LLEWELLYN, THE BRAMBLE BUSH 3 (1960).
29. T. ARNOLD, THE SYMBOLS OF GOVERNMENT 34 (1935).
30. *Id.* at 205–06.

Murray Edelman summed up the chants of the crowd in the following terms:

> Administrative agencies are to be understood as economic and political instruments of the parties they regulate and benefit not of a reified "society," "general will," or "public interest." At the same time they perform this instrumental function, they perform an equally important expressive function for the polity as a whole: to create and sustain an impression that induces acquiescence in the public in the face of private tactics that might otherwise be expected to produce resentment, protest and resistance. The instrumental function . . . has been observed, demonstrated and documented by every careful observer of regulatory agencies. . . . The expressive function has received less attention from scholars, though the quiescence of masses in the face of demonstrable denial of what is promised them clearly calls for explanation.[31]

Edelman's explanation is reminiscent of Arnold's. Agencies allay public fears through the symbols of administrative law. The agency "inevitably manipulates and evokes the myths, rituals, and other symbols attached to the state in our culture."[32] But Edelman's critique is more troublesome. In 1935 Arnold was concerned with explaining why bureaus were vilified and therefore required both to take on the inefficient trappings of judicial due process and to appear subservient to the rule of law as embodied in a meddlesome and often inappropriate judicial review. Edelman, thirty years later, sees these symbols as camouflaging a seizure of state power by already successful private interests. Inefficient but comforting symbolism has become a fraud. The forms of legislation mask substantive injustice.

The emptiness of "public interest" and most other legislative formulae and the "discretionary" or "political" nature of administration have since the 1960s become the conventional wisdom of students of administration. And if administrative behavior is not guided by law, it is then a puzzle to be explained in terms of some hidden interest of the bureau or its public and private clientele. Popular explanations include economic theories of private acquisition of regulation or of bureau budget-maximizing (or stabilizing), as well as micropolitical theories of interest-group politics and of congressional-bureau organization.[33]

31. M. Edelman, The Symbolic Uses of Politics 56 (1964).
32. *Id.* at 57.
33. *See, e.g.*, G. Kolko, The Triumph of Conservatism (1963); A. Downs, Inside Bureaucracy (1967); W. Niskanen, Bureaucracy and Representative Government

Idealism seems to have passed through realism to cynicism without even a pause at skepticism.

Skeptics have, however, begun to emerge. In *The Politics of Regulation,* James Q. Wilson and his associates argue that regulatory activities and the politics that produce regulatory legislation are too varied to be explained satisfactorily by a parsimonious set of hypotheses.[34] Indeed, so varied and conflicting are the political, economic, professional, and institutional factors that affect each bureau's behavior that no single influence has decisive effects. Wilson's primary conclusion from a summary of nine studies of state and federal regulatory agencies highlights "the largely unsupervised nature of most regulatory activity. Whoever first wished to see regulation carried on by quasi-independent agencies and commissions has had his boldest dreams come true."[35]

The Wilson findings are to some degree consoling. Administration may operate within a set of legitimating constraints that are largely symbolic, but at least administration is not always a simple power grab. Further exploration of wage–price administration can produce a similar moral. On reading Robert Kagan's[36] excellent participant-observer study of the implementation of the Nixon freeze order, for example, one comes away with the sense that the council staff struggled valiantly to develop coherent and sensible policies and to do justice in individual cases within the constraints of those policies.

Moreover, in the next experiment with wage–price controls, the Carter "voluntary" wage–price control program, one discovers significant attention paid to clear policy statement and regularized procedures, notwithstanding the facts (1) that the program was an executive creation—Congress had given no instructions—and thus (2) that significant judicial review of implementing decisions was not to be expected, *except* to enforce the agency's own regulations and procedures.[37] By adopting detailed statement of policies and procedures, the

---

(1971); M. FIORINA, CONGRESS: KEYSTONE TO THE WASHINGTON ESTABLISHMENT (1978); G. ARNOLD, CONGRESS AND THE BUREAUCRACY (1979); Stigler, *The Theory of Economic Regulation,* 2 Bell J. of Econ. & Mgmt. Science 3 (1971); Peltzman, *Toward a More General Theory of Regulation,* 19 J. of Law & Econ. 211 (1976).

34. J. Q. WILSON, ED., THE POLITICS OF REGULATION 393 (1980).

35. *Id.* at 391.

36. R. KAGAN, REGULATORY JUSTICE (1978).

37. *Cf.* American Federation of Labor v. Kahn, 618 F.2d 784 (D.C. Cir. 1979).

agency was tying its own hands, presumably in the interest of open administration. Administrative law may be almost irrelevant to what happens inside the administrative black box, but it is not necessarily a cover for pure fraud. The bankruptcy of an external administrative law is not necessarily a sign of moral decay, of the depravity of public life in the administrative state.

Yet I prefer solvency. As we have observed, the problem with an externally oriented administrative law is not mere irrelevance. Arnold did not seek to demonstrate the symbolic quality of law merely to describe the wisdom of inefficacy. Symbols have effects, and from his perspective and the perspectives of many since[38] the court-centered symbols of the rule of law were getting in the way of meaningful action. And while Wilson's findings may convince us that Edelman's rather cynical view is not true generally, the latter's description has a ring of occasional truth. If conventional legal symbols are inappropriate to serve as the model for administrative behavior, then what can take their place? Where are the norms that guide administrative aspirations, if not administrative behavior?

The answers to Arnold's legal realist challenge cannot lie in either the cynicism of an Edelman (for that is defeat) or in Wilson's description of a dense complexity. The challenge is to admit the limitations of an externally oriented administrative law and yet to affirm a vision of administration that is subject to the normative evaluation and improvement that is the promise of legal discourse; to view the administrative process, like the judicial and legislative processes, as somehow in pursuit of justice and the general welfare; to see "administration," like "democracy" and "the rule of law," as a motivating ideal.

In part the disposition to construct such a vision is a pragmatic response to my personal inability to move firmly into the camp of the cynics. But even if the effort is in some sense a working out of individual psychic need, the exploration seems to have a broader utility. That society has collective needs, at least collective wants, seems inescapable.

---

38. *See e.g.,* Wright, *The Courts and the Rulemaking Process: The Limits of Judicial Review,* 59 Cornell L. Rev. 375 (1974). The question of how much administrative action has to look like court action could be proposed, uncharitably, as the single topic of administrative law—one that has somehow riveted the attention of the bench and bar for generations. *Cf.,* for a recent instance, Gellhorn and Robinson, *Rulemaking "Due Process": An Inconclusive Dialogue,* 48 U. Chi. L. Rev. 201 (1981).

And, since we lack the altruistic genetic programming of the social insect, these needs and wants can be satisfied only through a bureaucratized application of collective authority. We need somehow to come to terms with our constant demand for institutions—bureaucracies—that once created we then excoriate.

If a set of external controls called administrative law no longer comforts us as we seek to manage our love–hate relationship with bureaucracy, perhaps we can see more clearly what needs to be done by turning to look inside the bureau, while retaining a normative perspective. Might there not be an internal law of administration that guides the conduct of administrators? And might not that law be capable of generalization, critique, improvement; even of producing a sense of satisfaction, acceptance, and justice quite apart from its connection to external legal institutions? Might there be in bureaucratic operation not merely the pure play of ambition, self-interest, or inertia that confounds our collective ideals but also a striving for normative goodness—complex and compromised perhaps, but only sometimes absent?

The search for such a vision inside the bureaucracy is, indeed, reminiscent of the realist technique. The purpose of this quest, however, is not to describe power but to structure responsibility. For the task of improving the quality of administrative justice is one that must be carried forward primarily by administrators. The task is too complex for the nonexpert, too time and resource consuming for outside institutions with competing interests. Moreover, the task requires a positive commitment to maintaining and balancing the full range of values that impinge on the system's functioning. The twists and turns of political agendas, the episodic and random interests of courts and of outside commentators provide information on social perceptions and expectations and shed some light on the ultimate effects of bureaucratic routines. But the job of evaluating the significance of these external communications and, having thus evaluated them, responding with appropriate action can reside only with the bureaucracy itself.

The central position of the bureaucracy thus implies a correlative central responsibility for the quality of administrative justice. The bureau is not a mere receptacle for the perspective and preferences of other institutions, a vector sum of contending external forces that impinge on its functioning. It is a focus for political initiative combined with technical competence, for the assertion of values beyond the time horizon of most other political actors. An externally oriented administrative law may be adequate when defined in terms of constraints and abstract ideals; an internal perspective would be inadequate without a more instrumental vision of the particular system of administrative justice that is sought to be produced.

For the line administrator this should be obvious. He or she continually faces decisions for which external standards provide no binding, perhaps no relevant, guidelines. Administration goes on, not just in terms of technical rules and bureaucratic routines but within some structure of guiding norms or salient images of the appropriate means for wielding legal power. And, like the actors in the external legal order, the administrator confronts conflicting modes of conceptualizing the normative "goodness" of the administrative system that is to be constructed. What are the images of "good administration" that guide bureaucratic behavior, that permit evaluation and hierarchical control? How can this internal law be conceptualized in terms of its ideal types, and to what degree do these ideals conflict? What are the techniques by which administrative ideals are concretely realized, reinforced, and sanctioned? How are they connected to or influenced by the norms of the external law of administration? If one could answer these questions, at least a partial description of administrative law from an internal perspective would emerge.

## THE TASK AHEAD

The pages that follow make but a necessary beginning. My attempt, obviously, is to reorient discussion. I will concentrate on a particular administrative system—the adjudication of claims for social security disability benefits. Descriptively, I will explain the administrative mission; how the system is structured and managed; what the effects of structure and management are on the definition and redefinition of goals and on the output of implementing decisions. Instead of describing and analyzing the top of the pyramid of administrative decisionmaking, judicial review, or even administrative "hearings," I will be concerned primarily with the system for managing routine administrative action by low-level administrators. For it is here that 100 percent of bureaucratic implementation begins, and most of it ends.

Second, I will generate and elaborate some conceptions of administrative justice and evaluate my exemplary bureaucracy's performance against those conceptions. The technique for developing these conceptions, or "models," of justice is in part empirical and in part intuitive and analytic. By examining patterns of criticism of the performance of the disability decision process we will observe the types of claims for legitimation that are made on the system. These claims seem to imply distinctive visions of how disability decisionmaking *ought* to be organized, visions that the history and structure of the program support. Although the patterns of claims and the relevant statutory provisions project these visions as relatively unformed images, we can develop a clearer picture of the characteristics of each model of justice—what gives each its distinctive structure and justificatory appeal.

Third, we will be forced to recognize that the models of justice suggested by the structure and the critics of the program are competitive. Implementing decisions will at critical points exalt one vision while suppressing others. The administrative system must choose which model of justice to employ. I will explore the dominant approach—the model of bureaucratic rationality—in some theoretical and empirical detail. The elaboration of that model, of its strengths, weaknesses, and imperatives, within the context of the disability program will occupy many of the pages that follow.

Finally, I will attempt to come to a balanced view of system performance—to assess the quality of bureaucratic justice in the disability program. Such an assessment includes an appreciation not only of the degree to which the logic of a bureaucratically rational system has been concretely realized, but also the way the tensions between that model and competing ideals of justice have been managed. The definition of *bureaucratic justice* that emerges from the analysis is not wholly satisfactory. When one steps back from administrative implementation to ask what it is that we want from it, and forward into the empirical realities of a particular system, it becomes clear that structuring and controlling a system of administrative action that also can claim to provide "justice" is a very subtle enterprise.

## THE DISABILITY PROGRAM AS AN EXEMPLARY INQUIRY

There are always multiple reasons for studying what one chooses to study. Some reasons are personal: I had appraised other aspects of the disability program;[39] I knew something about it; I had contacts; and I

---

39. *See* Mashaw et al., Social Security Hearings and Appeals (1978).

knew the Social Security Administration (SSA) to be a remarkably open and cooperative bureaucracy. But there is a rationale beyond autobiography.

First, the disability system is a part of the apparatus of the modern welfare state that touches most Americans.[40] It is important and it is representative of our increasingly prevalent systems of mass justice. SSA operates the largest system of administrative adjudication in the Western world. It makes well over 3 million determinations per year on claims for benefits under the Old-Age, Survivors, Disability, and Health Insurance (OASDHI) programs. The portion of the Social Security system considered here, the disability program, is itself massive. Since 1974, initial claims for disability benefits (under both Title II [Disability Insurance] and Title XVI [Supplemental Security Income] of the Social Security Act) have averaged nearly 1,250,000 annually.

Moreover, a substantial number of these claims are decided more than once. In a typical year in the 1970s, for example, approximately 250,000 denials at the initial stage were appealed for a reconsideration decision. Denials at the reconsideration stage prompted about 150,000 requests for hearings before administrative law judges. Twenty-five thousand of these hearing cases went on to a final administrative appeal before the Appeals Council, and there were approximately 10,000 filings for judicial review of social security disability decisions in the federal district courts.

There are perhaps 5,600 state agency personnel (supported by 5,000 more) whose sole function is to adjudicate disability claims. Over 625 federal administrative law judges hear administrative appeals from state agency denials. This total of more than 6,000 adjudicators approaches the size of the combined judicial systems of the state and federal governments of the United States. And the claims that these officials adjudicate are not small. The average, present, discounted value of the stream of income from a successful disability application is over $30,000. Disability claims, on the average, thus have a value three times that required by statute for the pursuit of many civil actions in federal district courts. More than 4.3 million disabled workers and their

---

40. For a basic statutory history of the program up to 1974 *see* COMMITTEE ON WAYS AND MEANS, 95TH CONG., 1ST SESS., COMMITTEE STAFF REPORT ON THE DISABILITY INSURANCE PROGRAM 107–25 (1974).

dependents draw annual benefits, which in fiscal year 1982 totaled $21.2 billion. When the Medicaid and Medicare payments for which these beneficiaries are automatically eligible are included, the total figure is $32.4 billion. By any measure the system is massive.

Second, the levels of the decision process that decide most of the cases, the initial and reconsideration stages of the state agency process, are all but invisible in the literature. With what I sometimes call administrative law's sure instinct for the capillary, the debate about the SSA disability decision process has focused on ALJ hearings and judicial review, that is, on court and courtlike procedures. While administrative lawyers harangue each other concerning the fine points of the Supreme Court's or the D.C. Circuit's most recent procedural ruling, billions of dollars per year are being transferred, for good or ill, by an invisible army of bureaucratic adjudicators to whom court decisions may have absolutely no relevance.

Third, the system contains a series of political and economic stresses that, when combined with its massive size, seem certain to generate an interesting normative-managerial complexity. The basic purpose of the program is benevolent, yet it has always been a benevolence combined with caution. Disability insurance was proposed but not included in the original social security legislation. Attempts to enact such a program continued from 1935 to 1950 before the first legislative steps were taken. It was not until 1960 that a benefits program was produced approximating the one we have today.

Yet by 1967 the liberalizing trend of the fifties and early sixties had ended. Since that time the politics of social security, and particularly the disability program, has moved from retrenchment to occasional disaffection. As sticky structural unemployment, economic shocks, and an aging population have accelerated application rates while shrinking the proportion of the population paying FICA taxes, Congress has been forced into the politically unrewarding pastime of raising taxes and limiting benefits. The divided political consciousness, the "help the poor but punish the chiselers" mentality that has always been a part of the politics of public welfare programs, has begun to afflict the disability program. Indeed, the sacred cow status of the whole social security program has diminished in a Congress starved for fiscal protein.

Moreover, one should not assume from this sketchy history that "cautious benevolence" represents merely an adjectival-nominative

linkage of distinct programmatic periods. The story is not just benevolence in good times and caution in bad. The countervailing tendencies
are built into the program and are represented by the political history
and accreting statutory mandates of each period. The Congress has
continuously believed the program to be both essential to a basic system
of income security *and* an open invitation to drop out of the work force.
It has just as continuously attempted to mediate this tension by the
device Tom Wolfe called "Mau-Mauing the Flak-Catchers."[41] In oversight, budget, and legislative hearings, Congress has alternately berated
SSA for its unresponsiveness to claimants *and* for its laxity in letting
them on the rolls. Indeed, it has had the chutzpah to criticize administration while saddling SSA with a contracted-out state agency administrative system that is burdened with all the delicate federal–state relations issues that such systems necessarily entail.[42]

The disability program thus roots our general normative inquiry in an
appropriate factual context. For when we ask how administration
should respond to normative ambiguity and administrative complexity,
we can hardly define *should* without attending to *could*. Criticism and
the reformist instinct must be harnessed to an appreciation of reality.
We thus turn to the task of building normative models of administration in the context of the social security disability program—a context
characterized by cautious benevolence and repeated criticism.

41. T. WOLFE, RADICAL CHIC AND MAU-MAUING THE FLAK CATCHERS (1970).
42. *See, e.g.*, M. DERTHICK, THE INFLUENCE OF FEDERAL GRANTS (1970); Tomlinson and
Mashaw, *The Enforcement of Federal Standards in Grant-In-Aid Programs: Suggestions
for Beneficiary Involvement*, 58 Va. L. Rev. 600 (1972) (and authorities there cited).

# 2 · Justice Models for a Disability Program

## THE DEMAND FOR JUSTICE

There is a substantial critical literature on the administration of disability benefits under Titles II and XVI of the Social Security Act.[1] One strand of the commentary is concerned that the disability program fails to provide adequate service to claimants and beneficiaries.[2] This view at least implicitly characterizes the program's purposes as paternalistic and therapeutic, purposes that would seem to require a major role for health care, vocational, social service, and other professionals in program administration. The failure of the bureaucratic decision process to emphasize the role of professional judgment and to adopt a service orientation is seen as the program's major deficiency.

A second, more "legalistic" perspective is concerned primarily with the capacity of individual claimants to assert and defend their rights to disability benefits.[3] This literature is concerned with such problems as

1. 42 U.S.C. §§401–433, 1381–1383c (1976 & Supp. III 1979). The critical commentary is arranged here in terms of its principal preoccupations. I do not mean to suggest that the literature cited as exemplifying one critical perspective does not respond at all to the central concerns of the others.

2. *See, e.g.*, S. Nagi, Disability and Rehabilitation: Legal Clinical and Self Concept and Measurement (1970); Department of Health, Education, and Welfare, Office of the Inspector General, Final Report: Service Delivering Assessment of SSA Disability Programs (1978); Social Security Administration, Office of Administration, Report of the Special Study Group—Service to the Public (mimeo, 1971); Subcommittee on Social Security of the Committee on Ways and Means, Disability Adjudicative Structure 52–92, 95th Cong., 2d Sess. (1978).

3. *See, e.g.*, R. Dixon, Social Security Disability and Mass Justice (1973); G. Goldsborough et al., The Social Security Administration (mimeo, George Washington University National Law Center, 1973); Popkin, *Effect of Representation on a Claimant's*

the inadequacy of the notices of denial sent to rejected applicants; the need for representation of claimants in disability hearings; the lack of adversarial testing of the evidence provided by participants in the adjudicatory process; the substantial reversal rate of those cases that are heard orally by independent administrative law judges and on review in federal courts. In sum, the concern is with the failure of the disability decision process to provide the essential ingredients of judicial trials.

A third strand of the critical literature chides SSA for failing to manage the adjudication of claims in ways that produce predictable and consistent outcomes.[4] The concern is that the system may be out of control, and the suggestions for reform are essentially managerial: SSA should provide more complete and objective criteria for the exercise of adjudicatory discretion; greater control should be gained over the internal routines of the disability decision services in the states; the system of management oversight and statistical quality assurance should be strengthened. In short, the system is viewed in bureaucratic terms and criticized for its inadequate management controls.

This pattern of criticism is curious. First, why is the disability program's adjudicatory function viewed in such divergent ways? Is the disagreement about the program's purposes or about the appropriate means for achieving those purposes or both? Second, why does the criticism tend to fall into the described pattern? What unifies each perspective? Something specific to this program? Or some more general notions about administrative justice? Third, why, given the continuous and repetitive nature of the criticism—some of it from powerful political actors—has the program not been modified to eliminate the problems that one or all of the critics perceive?

---

*Success Rate*, 31 Ad. L. Rev. 449 (1979); Yourman, *Report on a Study of Social Security Beneficiary Hearings, Appeals and Judicial Review in Subcommittee on Social Security,* in Sub Comm. on Admin. of Soc. Sec. Laws House Ways and Means Committee, 95th Cong., 2d Sess., Recent Studies Relevant to the Disability Hearings and Appeals Crisis 125 (1975) (hereinafter cited as "Recent Studies").

4. *See, e.g.*, Subcommittee on Administration of Social Security Laws, Committee on Ways and Means, Committee Print, Administration of Social Security Disability Program, 86th Cong., 2d Sess. (1960); Report of the Comptroller General of the U.S., "The Social Security Administration Should Provide More Management and Leadership in Determining Who is Eligible for Disability Benefits" (1976); Report of the Comptroller General of the U.S., "A Plan for Improving the Disability Determination Process by Bringing it Under Complete Federal Management Should be Developed" (1978).

In reflecting on these curiosities I have come to some hypotheses that seem to have interesting implications, not just for the disability program but for the evaluation of administrative adjudication generally. First, these criticisms reflect distinct conceptual models of administrative justice. Second, each of the models is coherent and attractive. But, third, the models, while not mutually exclusive, are highly competitive: the internal logic of any one of them tends to drive the characteristics of the others from the field as it works itself out in concrete situations.

If these hypotheses are correct, then it may also follow that the best system of administrative adjudication may be the one most open to criticism. A compromise that seeks to preserve the values and to respond at once to the insights of all of these conceptions of justice will, from the perspective of each separate conception, appear incoherent and unjust. The best system of administrative adjudication that can be devised may fall tragically short of our inconsistent ideals.

But these speculations are premature. We must return to the beginning to build the models of justice to which I have alluded and to see what the claim of each is to provide the dominant conception of justice in the disability program. Only then can we begin to speculate about the historically contingent choices that we observe in that program and to set the stage for exploring the normative "goodness" of the model that seems to have won the competition for the heart of the disability program.

## THREE MODELS OF JUSTICE

Assume, therefore, a disability program: not just any program, but one having the general statutory features of the programs embodied in Titles II and XVI of the Social Security Act, that is, a program whose statutory standard for income support payments harnesses medical, personal, and vocational criteria to the task of determining whether an individual can work. In the language of the Social Security Act:

an individual shall be determined to be under a disability only if his physical or mental impairment or impairments are of such severity that he is not only unable to do his previous work but cannot, considering his age, education and work experience, engage in any other kind of substantial gainful work which exists in the national economy, regardless of whether such work exists in the immediate area in which he lives, or whether a specific job vacancy exists for him, or whether he would be hired if he applied for work. For purposes of the preceding sentence (with respect to any individual), "work which exists in the national economy" means work which exists in significant numbers either in the region where such individual lives or in several regions of the country.[5]

Qualification under that standard entitles the recipient both to income support and, after a waiting period, to medical benefits.[6] The eligibility determination also includes an analysis of the applicant's fitness for referral to a vocational rehabilitation program[7] and a judgment concerning the scheduling of a "continuing disability investigation" to redetermine eligibility at some future date.[8] The problematic nature of recovery is cushioned by trial work periods during which time a return to beneficiary status requires no waiting periods or reapplication.[9]

The statute also gives some guidance concerning the administrative structure for making disability determinations. Claims are to be processed by state agencies, preferably state vocational rehabilitation services.[10] Disappointed claimants are entitled to hearings before a federal administrative law judge[11] and, thereafter, to judicial review in federal district courts.[12]

How should SSA flesh out this substantive and procedural skeleton? What is administrative justice to mean in the disability program?

The *justice* of an administrative system, as I shall employ the term, means simply this: those qualities of a decision process that provide

5. 42 U.S.C. §423 (d) (2) (1976). *See also id.* §1382c (a) (3) (A) and (B) for the identical definition of disability under section XVI of the Social Security Act.

6. *See* Social Security Disability Amendments of 1980, Pub. L. No. 96–265, §303, 94 Stat. 441, 451-52 (1980) (amending 42 U.S.C. §423 [1976]). Sections 103 and 104 of the same act amend Medicare eligibility provisions; *see* 42 U.S.C. §426 (1976).

7. 42 U.S.C. §422 (a) (1976).

8. *See* Social Security Disability Amendments of 1980, Pub. L. No. 96–265, §311, 94 Stat. 411, 460 (1980), which amends 42 U.S.C. §421 (1976) and provides for disability reviews every three years except when disability is permanent, in which case the secretary is to conduct review as he determines to be "appropriate."

9. Social Security Disability Amendments of 1980, Pub. L. No. 96–265, §§301, 303, 94 Stat. 441, 449-53 (1980) (amending 42 U.S.C. §425 (1976)).

10. Social Security Disability Amendments of 1980, Pub. L. No. 92-265, §304, 94 Stat. 441, 453-57 (1980) (amending 42 U.S.C. §421 (1976)).

11. *See* V. ROSENBLUM, THE ADMINISTRATIVE LAW JUDGE IN THE ADMINISTRATIVE PROCESS, RECENT STUDIES 171 (1975); 42 U.S.C.A. §405 (b) (1980 Supp.).

12. *See* 42 U.S.C. §405 (g) (1976).

arguments for the acceptability of its decisions. I do not mean to suggest, of course, that all arguments—moral, legal, or political—are the same or that to be just a process must avoid all complaint or even all assertions of illegitimacy. I am here merely developing some distinct structures of justificatory argument. For present purposes we need not strongly distinguish among the possible sources of their claims to acceptability. Nor shall I attempt to demonstrate that everyone is powerfully attached to one or more of the arguments suggested. These justificatory structures, once identified, should appear to be ubiquitous in the legal structure of public institutions and in ordinary experience.

The three strands in the critical literature on the disability program suggest three types of justice arguments: (1) that decisions should be accurate and efficient concrete realizations of the legislative will; (2) that decisions should provide appropriate support or therapy from the perspective of relevant professional cultures; and (3) that decisions should be fairly arrived at when assessed in the light of traditional processes for determining individual entitlements. Elaboration of these arguments in the context of the disability program produces three distinct models of administrative justice; models that I shall denominate *bureaucratic rationality, professional treatment,* and *moral judgment.*

## Bureaucratic Rationality

Given the democratically (legislatively) approved task—to pay disability benefits to eligible persons—the administrative goal in the ideal conception of bureaucratic rationality is to develop, at the least possible cost, a system for distinguishing between true and false claims. Adjudicating should be both accurate (the legislatively specified goal) and cost-effective. This approach can be stated more broadly by introducing trade-offs between error, administrative, and other "process" costs such that the goal becomes "minimize the sum of error and other associated costs."

A system focused on correctness defines the questions presented to it by implementing decisions in essentially factual and technocratic terms. Individual adjudicators must be concerned about the facts in the real world that relate to the truth or falsity of the claimed disability. At a managerial level the question becomes technocratic: What is the least-cost methodology for collecting and combining those facts about claims that will reveal the proper decision? To illustrate by contrast, this model would exclude questions of value or preference as obviously irrelevant to the administrative task, and it would view reliance on nonreplicable, nonreviewable *judgment* or *intuition* as a singularly unattractive methodology for decision. The legislature should have previously decided the value questions; and decision on the basis of intuition would cause authority to devolve from the bureau to individuals, thereby preventing a supervisory determination of whether any adjudicative action taken corresponded to a true state of the world.

The general decisional technique, then, is information retrieval and processing. In Weber's words, "Bureaucratic administration means fundamentally domination through knowledge."[13] And, of course, this application of knowledge must in any large-scale program be structured through the usual bureaucratic routines: selection and training of personnel, detailed specification of administrative tasks, specialization and division of labor, coordination via rules and hierarchical lines of authority, and hierarchical review of the accuracy and efficiency of decisionmaking. In the disability program, for example, decisionmaking goes on not in one head but, initially, in the heads of thousands of state agency examiners.

From the perspective of bureaucratic rationality, administrative justice is accurate decisionmaking carried on through processes appropriately rationalized to take account of costs. The legitimating force of this conception flows both from its claim to correct implementation of otherwise legitimate social decisions and from its attempt to realize society's preestablished goals in some particular substantive domain while conserving social resources for the pursuit of other valuable ends. No program, after all, exhausts our conception of good government, much less of a good society or a good life.

### Professional Treatment

The goal of the professional is to serve the client. The service delivery goal or ideal is most obvious, perhaps, in the queen of the professions, medicine; but it is also a defining characteristic of law and the ministry and of newer professions such as social work. Although one might view medicine, for example, as principally oriented toward science and there-

---

13. 1 M. WEBER, ECONOMY AND SOCIETY 225 (G. Roth & C. Wittich eds. 1968).

fore knowledge, such a view is fundamentally mistaken. The scientific side of medicine, its disease and pathology constructs, are generated by an attempt to treat complaints relating to biological and psychological functioning, pain, or deformity.[14] Characterization and explanation are important to treatment but not necessary. The physician is committed to treatment even if the patient's complaints cannot be characterized or explained within current scientific modes of conceptualizing medical problems. The value to be served by the professional is the elimination of the health complaints presented to him or her by patients. Curing a patient by eliminating a physically identifiable pathology may be good science, but if the patient still feels sick it is not good medicine. The objective is to wield the science so that it produces good as defined by the patient. This entails interpersonal and diagnostic intuition—clinical intelligence—as well as scientific knowledge.

An administrative system for disability decisionmaking based on professional treatment would, therefore, be client-oriented. It would seek to provide those services—income support, medical care, vocational rehabilitation, and counseling—that the client needed to improve his well-being and perhaps regain self-sufficiency. Such services, of course, would be constrained by cost. The professional must at least tailor advice or treatment to his or her own resources: some clients must be rejected or given less in order that others, who are needier, may be helped more. But the constraints on professional service tend to be conceptualized by professionals in terms of competing service modalities for or among clients, not as trade-offs between professional services and other social values.

Like bureaucratic rationality, professional judgment requires the collection of information that may be manipulated in accordance with standardized procedures. But in the professional treatment model the incompleteness of facts, the singularity of individual contexts, and the ultimately intuitive nature of judgment are recognized, if not exalted.[15] Disability decisions would be viewed not as attempts to establish the truth or falsity of some state of the world, but rather as prognoses of the

14. *See, e.g.,* Engelhardt, *Doctoring the Disease, Treating the Complaint, Helping the Patient: Some of the Works of Hygeia and Panacea,* in KNOWING AND VALUING: THE SEARCH FOR COMMON ROOTS 225–49 (H. Engelhardt & D. Callahan eds. 1980).

15. *See generally* M. LARSON, THE RISE OF PROFESSIONALISM: A SOCIOLOGICAL ANALYSIS (1977).

likely effects of disease or trauma on functioning, and as efforts to support the client while pursuing therapeutic and vocational prospects.

The basic techniques of professional treatment are personal examination and counseling. There is some specialization of functions—delegation to other professions or subprofessionals—but the judgment of what is to be done is holistic. The professional combines the information of others with his or her own observations and experience to reach conclusions that are as much art as science. Moreover, judgment is always subject to revision as conditions change, as attempted therapy proves unsatisfactory or therapeutic successes emerge. The application of clinical judgment entails a relationship and may involve repeated instances of service-oriented decisionmaking.

An administrative system for providing professional treatment would thus have characteristics rather different from those of the system supporting bureaucratic rationality. The basic idea would be to apply the appropriate profession to the problem at hand. And since these allocation decisions, decisions about needs or ability to help, are themselves professional judgments, they would be made best by the relevant professionals in conjunction with claimants. The administrative structure need, for example, only funnel claimant-clients to multiprofessional centers where they would be examined and counseled. Administration would include the facilitation of these contacts, coordination of multiprofessional teams, and implementation of professional judgments concerning particular cases. Substantive and procedural rules, hierarchical controls, and efficiency considerations would all be subordinated to the norms of the professional culture. The organization would be more a lateral network than a hierarchical command structure.

The basis for the legitimacy of professional treatment is in one respect similar to that of bureaucratic decisionmaking: the professional is master of an arcane body of knowledge and supports his judgment by appeals to expertise. But whereas the bureaucrat displays his or her knowledge through instrumentally rational routines designed to render transparent the connection between concrete decisions and legislatively validated policy, the professional's art remains opaque to the layman. The mystery of professional judgment is, nevertheless, acceptable because of the service ideal of professionalism. The element of mystery and charisma in the office of physician, priest, or lawyer is combined with the trusteeship implicit in professional–client relations.[16] Justice lies in having the appropriate professional judgment applied to one's particular situation *in the context of a service relationship.*

## Moral Judgment

The traditional goal of the adjudicatory process is to resolve disputes about rights, about the allocation of benefits and burdens. The paradigm adjudicatory situations are those of civil and criminal trial. In the former, the contest generally concerns competing claims to property or the mutual responsibilities of the litigants. Property claims of "It has been in my family for generations" confront counterclaims of "I bought it from a dealer" or "I have made productive use of it"; "The smell of your turkey farm is driving me mad" confronts "I was here first." In the latter, accused murderers claim self-defense or diminished responsibility. The goal in individual adjudications is to decide who deserves what.

To some degree these traditional notions of justice in adjudicatory process imply merely getting the facts right in order to apply existing legal rules. So conceived, the goal of a moral judgment model of justice is the same as that of a bureaucratic rationality model—factually correct realization of previously validated legal norms.[17] If this conception exhausted the notion of adjudicatory fairness, moral judgment's competition with bureaucratic rationality would entail merely a technical dispute about the most efficient way to find facts. But there is more to the competition than that.

The moral judgment model views decisionmaking as value defining.[18] The turkey farmer's neighbor makes a valid appeal not to be burdened by "noisome" smells, *provided* his conduct in locating nearby is "reasonable" and he is not being "overly sensitive." The turkey farmer also has a valid claim to carry on a legitimate business, *provided* he does so in ways that will not unreasonably burden his neighbors. The question is not just who did what, but who is to be preferred, all things considered, when interests and the values to which they can be relevantly connected

---

16. *See* T. Parsons, The Social System 428–79 (1951).

17. *See e.g.,* Mashaw, *Administrative Due Process as Social Cost Accounting,* 9 Hofstra L. Rev. 1423 (1981); Posner, *An Economic Approach to Legal Procedure and Judicial Administration,* 2 J. Leg. Stud. 399 (1973).

18. *See* Thibaut & Walker, *A Theory of Procedure,* 66 Calif. L. Rev. 541 (1978).

conflict. Similarly, the criminal trial seeks to establish not just whether a harmful and proscribed act took place but also whether or to what extent the actor is culpable.

This entitlement-awarding goal of the moral judgment model gives an obvious and distinctive cast to the basic issue for adjudicatory resolution. The issue is the deservingness of some or all of the parties in the context of certain events, transactions, or relationships that give rise to a claim. This issue, in turn, seems to imply certain things about a just process of proof and decision. For example, fair disposition of charges of culpability or lack of desert requires that claims be specifically stated and that any affected party be given an opportunity to rebut or explain allegations. And in order for this contextualized exploration of individual deservingness to be meaningful the decisionmaker must be neutral—that is, not previously connected with the relevant parties or events in ways that would impair the exercise of independent judgment on the evidence and arguments presented.

Moreover, given the generally threatening nature of an inquiry into moral desert, parties should be able to exclude from the decisional context information not directly related to the entitlements issue that gives rise to the disputed claim. This power of exclusion may take the form of pleading rules, of notions of standing or proper parties, and, more importantly, may permit total exclusion of directive judgment where claims are abandoned or disputants come to some mutually satisfactory agreement concerning the relevant allocation.[19] The goal is limited: to resolve particular claims of entitlement in a way that fairly allocates certain benefits and burdens, not to allocate benefits and burdens in general in accordance with the relative deservingness of individuals or groups. The decider is to a degree passive. The parties control how much of their lives or relationships is put at issue and what factual and normative arguments are brought to bear on the resolution of the dispute.

While the traditional examples of entitlements-oriented individualized adjudication involve adversary process, this feature is not critical. Claims to publicly provided benefits via nonadversary hearing processes may also conform to the model. Indeed, the Supreme Court has come

---

19. *See generally*, Damaska, *Structure of Authority and Comparative Criminal Procedure*, 84 Yale. L.J. 480 (1975).

very close to saying that such processes must involve a traditional oral hearing where substantive standards are so open-textured that each decision both defines the nature of the entitlement and awards or denies it to a particular party.[20]

The goals of this most traditional model of justice may suggest additional decisional techniques and routines designed to preserve party equality and control, promote agreed allocations, and protect the authority of the decider. But these are details that need not detain us. The important point is that the "justice" of this model inheres in its promise of a full and equal opportunity to obtain one's entitlements. Its authority rests on the neutral development and application of common moral principles within the contexts giving rise to entitlement claims.

## Comparison

As we have described them, each justice model is composed of distinctive goals, specific approaches to framing the questions for administrative determination, basic techniques for resolving those questions, and subsidiary decision processes and routines that functionally describe the model. The distinctive features of the three models are outlined in the accompanying chart. These features are, of course, meant to indicate the central tendencies, not to suggest that features, and whole models, do not shade one into another at the margins.

### Features of the Three Justice Models

| Dimension/ Model | Legitimating Values | Primary Goal | Structure or Organization | Cognitive Technique |
|---|---|---|---|---|
| Bureaucratic Rationality | Accuracy & Efficiency | Program Implementation | Hierarchical | Information Processing |
| Professional Treatment | Service | Client Satisfaction | Interpersonal | Clinical Application of Knowledge |
| Moral Judgment | Fairness | Conflict Resolution | Independent | Contextual Interpretation |

20. *See* Califano v. Yamasaki, 442 U.S. 682 (1979).

A number of real-world administrative agencies seem to approximate one or another of the ideal types. A motor vehicle safety inspection bureau might exemplify the bureaucratically rational agency. The goal is to keep unsafe vehicles off the road. A "safe" vehicle can be defined in terms of a series of objective mechanical or physical characteristics. Each inspection decision matches these characteristics to some vehicle and approves or disapproves its continued operation. The bureau infrastructure chooses testing locations, trains personnel, maintains equipment, monitors inspector performance, and seeks to contain costs. The latter may be narrowly defined as direct administrative or budgetary cost or may include such items as motorists' time and inconvenience. The bureau may even seek to calibrate its efforts to match inspection costs and accident prevention gains at the margin.[21]

The professional treatment model finds examples in public hospitals and legal services agencies. The professional treatment features of these institutions are, of course, somewhat attenuated. But the dominance of the service ideal and the professional–client relational context are visible in the autonomy of the individual lawyer or doctor once the physician–patient or lawyer–client relationship has been established.[22] An administrative superstructure may determine the total resources available for treatment, counseling, or litigation, but the use of these resources is governed by a professional judgment that responds to a culture and training acquired quite independently from the agency and the agency's mission. The professional defines and legitimates the actions of the agency, rather than the other way round.[23] Medicare and Medicaid initially took this approach to its almost ideal form. The bureau was to raise money, pay the bills, and otherwise stay out of the way of the physician–patient relationship. Any monitoring or policing could be done by the professionals themselves. That medical care became the growth sector of the social welfare budget is not surprising.[24]

This is not to say that professionals who work in public institutional

21. *See* W. Crain, Vehicle Safety Inspection Systems: How Effective? (1980).

22. *See e.g.*, Bellow & Kettleson, *The Politics of Society in Legal Services Work*, 36 NLADA Briefcase 5 (1979).

23. M. Larson, *supra* note 15, at 190.

24. *See generally*, T. Marmor, The Politics of Medicare (1970); B. Stevens and R. Stevens, Welfare Medicine in America: A Case Study of Medicaid (1974).

settings are not molded by that context. The content of the service ideal, in particular the willingness to consider interests beyond the treatment or counseling of a particular client, will have somewhat different emphasis in public institutions and private professional practice and will vary from institution to institution. But the core of the professional model remains. When action comes to be justified, sound professional judgment is an adequate explanation. And the adequacy of bureaucratic organization will be evaluated in terms of its tendency to permit fulfillment of the professional's role in relation to client or patient needs, provided the professional culture is sufficiently robust. If not, the professional treatment model will be transformed. Public welfare agencies were once also examples of administration via professional treatment. But the profession's conceptual and political base was too fragile to withstand the attacks of welfare rights activists. Social welfare programs have thus been increasingly fragmented functionally and bureaucratized organizationally as they have coped with assertions of justice claims in an essentially adversary mode.

Agencies whose organization responds to the moral judgment model are the familiar terrain of the traditional federal administrative law practice. The National Labor Relations Board, the Federal Trade Commission, the Federal Communications Commission all spring readily to mind. Each administers a vague statute and elaborates, via contested cases, the operational content of concepts such as *fairness* or *the public interest*. Indeed, affected interests have struggled mightily to retain the forms of adversary process as one or another of these independent regulatory commissions has experimented, in the interest of expediency, with a more nearly "legislative" technique for policy development and with more "bureaucratized" techniques for implementation.[25]

Yet as the struggle over the required modes of action in the "alphabet" agencies suggests, the paradigm examples of our models contain internal tensions that reflect alternative justice perspectives. My intuition is that this is generally the case. It may be possible to give a historical and ideological account of American law that would reveal a constant ebb and flow of private-entitlements, public-managerial and

25. *See, e.g.*, National Petroleum Refiners Ass'n. v. FTC, 482 F.2d 672 (D.C. Cir. 1973), *cert. denied*, 415 U.S. 952 (1974); United States v. Stoner Broadcasting Co., 351 U.S. 192 (1956); and FPC v. Texaco, 377 U.S. 33 (1964).

professional-therapeutic ideals harnessed to the underlying social interests that give shape, over time, to our legal institutions. For now it is
enough to suggest that examples of this stress abound in the jurisprudence of administrative law.[26] And, as we shall see, competition among
the models of justice that we have just elaborated also describes the
dynamics of development in the disability program.

## CHOOSING A MODEL FOR DISABILITY DECISIONMAKING

Chosing among justice models for the disability program is not a simple
matter. Each has attractive features by comparison with the others and
also responds to some aspect(s) of the statutory mandate. Consider the
initial arguments for each.

First, for bureaucratic rationality: as we noted in chapter 1, a disability program was proposed in the original planning that led to the Social
Security Act of 1935, but no such program was even haltingly begun
until 1950, and it did not become a full-fledged early-retirement benefits scheme until 1960. Congressional consideration consistently reveals a single dominant reason for reluctance to rationalize the Social
Security scheme by adding disability benefits: moral hazard. The disability program could easily turn into a residual unemployment program.
Intense applicant pressure to expand the beneficiary class is to be
expected in cyclical economic downturns. The program thus requires
very tight administration to maintain its integrity.

The experience of private disability insurance in the 1920s suggested
that adversarial adjudication was not such a system. Several insurers
were bankrupted by judicial expansion of their policies' conception of
the covered risk; and all private carriers abandoned the field when
judicial construction, in the face of rising unemployment, made disability actuarially unpredictable. Nor did farming out disability determinations to the medical profession seem an attractive way to structure a
controllable decision process. A rational hierarchical structure might
easily be viewed as the only reasonable prospect for containing either
program or administrative costs.

But the virtues of bureaucratic process can be portrayed in more

26. See Mashaw, Conflict and Compromise Among Models of Administrative Justice,
1981 Duke L.J. 401, 421–31.

positive terms than by simple contrast to the potential profligacy of its competitors. The disability program is a legislative statement of a complicated new social goal—cautious benevolence. That goal is likely to be realized only through some organization tailored specifically to the legislative purpose, not through organizations burdened by the historic perspectives of service-oriented professions or the dominant legal culture. Only bureaucratic rationality promises implementation of "the program" rather than the pursuit of some other set of values.

But the professional model is not so easily dismissed. The legislative goal may embrace professional values and seek to funnel resources to their realization. The statutory definition of disability obviously demands professional input. The disease or trauma must be medically determinable—a standard that seems to contemplate a delegation of authority to the medical profession to establish the basic condition underlying eligibility. Moreover, to the extent that medical professionalism might prove inadequate to the task of assessing vocational capacity, the Congress required some delegation of decisional authority to state vocational rehabilitation services, presumably staffed by professional therapists and counselors. Indeed, there is evidence that the Congress relied heavily on the professional rehabilitation perspective of these state agencies to constrain the awarding of benefits for permanent or long-term disablement.[27] Rehabilitation specialists could be expected to emphasize rehabilitative potential, training, and transferability of skills. They would use benefits to supplement and support their rehabilitative ideals.

As a strategic matter, reliance on professional judgment also had much to recommend it. Bipolar (disabled/not disabled) decisions could be expected to create enormous stress within the system unless connected to some other set of service-oriented activities that would ameliorate the all or nothing nature of the game. And those other activities or programs were generally operated by various types of service professionals. The adjudicatory process should therefore be structured to emphasize the routing of claimants to appropriate treatment. And this can be done only via some variant of the professional treatment model.

---

27. Committee on Ways and Means, Staff Report on the Disability Insurance Program 111–12 (1974). *See also* M. Derthick, Policy-making for Social Security 303 (1979).

The establishment of a new nationwide benefits program with decisionmaking at or near the claimant's residence and operating under a rather vague all-things-considered eligibility criterion would in any event face significant problems of bureaucratic control. Unless one imagines that an underlying professional culture or ethic will tend to harmonize decisional perspectives, it might seem reasonable to assume that the state agencies would pursue local interests, institutional interests, or the varied interests of the adjudicative staff, rather than congressional purposes. Real bureaucracies do not conform to the ideal type,[28] and their predicted deviance from the norm of efficient program implementation may exceed that of professionals.

Finally, deep skepticism concerning the efficacy of either bureaucratic rationality or professional treatment may provide the strongest argument for viewing administration as, at base, a mechanism for awarding benefits on the basis of ordinary moral judgment. On this view, bureaucrats or professionals will often either persuade claimants of their ineligibility or be persuaded of their eligibility. Thus, those forms of administration, like compromise in civil and criminal litigation, may keep the level of formal legal dispute at a tolerable level. But given the complexity of the factors to be considered and the critical interests at stake in these decisions, the question in the end is a value conflict about the distribution of resources. The question is not just what the claimant's skills, impairments, experience, and so forth are, but whether persons with that particular set of characteristics *ought* to have access to public support. Resolving that question in an acceptable way requires the opportunity for an individualized hearing and for the customary appeal outside the bureau to a court of general jurisdiction. It is these traditional legal forms of administration, the argument might add, that Congress has most elaborately provided in the Social Security Act.

---

28. Administrative deviance from legislative purposes has spawned a vast literature in a variety of disciplines. *See, e.g.*, G. ARNOLD, CONGRESS AND THE BUREAUCRACY (1979) (political economy); P. BLAU, THE DYNAMICS OF BUREAUCRACY (rev. ed. 1963) (sociology); A. DOWNS, INSIDE BUREAUCRACY (1975) (political economy); W. NISKANEN, BUREAUCRACY AND REPRESENTATIVE GOVERNMENT (1971) (economics); H. SIMON, ADMINISTRATIVE BEHAVIOR (3d ed. 1976) (organization theory); THE POLITICS OF REGULATION (J. Wilson ed. 1980) (political science); March, *Bounded Rationality, Ambiguity and the Engineering of Choice*, 10 Bell J. Econ. 587 (1979) (organization theory); Stigler, *The Theory of Economic Regulation*, 2 Bell J. Econ. 3 (1971) (economics).

But the evenhanded conceptual treatment of competitive justice models in the preceding paragraphs should not mislead. Bureaucratic rationality was predictably to be the dominant modality; professional treatment and moral judgment play supporting roles. Social Security payments were already being made on Old-Age and Survivors Insurance (OASI) claims, and the preexisting structure—a bureaucratically routinized claims-determinations-plus-payments conception—was reasonably well-suited to the disability program. Disability insurance, soon to be followed by health insurance, attempted to rationalize a social security scheme that relied primarily on cash benefits to ameliorate health-related economic dislocations: retirement and death. SSA had a strong sense of mission in administering the OASI programs, and that mission—the accurate, speedy, and inexpensive disposition of claims—was no less important in the new disability program. Responsible discharge of that mission, of course, included preserving the fund for future beneficiaries. And, as we have noted, this responsibility seemed to imply a controllable and therefore an essentially hierarchical decisional structure.

Moreover, as a contingent historical matter, organizing the basic administration of the program around a model of professional treatment, or hearings structured to explore individual desert, had even more decisive drawbacks than our conceptual exploration has suggested. A delegation of broad decisional authority to medical professionals had two plausible variants, both of which were politically unattractive. The first variation, as we have noted, abandoned budgetary control. If SSA were to take the physicians' judgments that their patients were disabled, it would necessarily forego control over the level of generosity of the program. And given either a sympathetic physician-patient relationship or a physician preference for conservative therapeutic advice ("You really shouldn't be working") or both, the program could mushroom. The alternative, creation of SSA-run treatment and diagnostic centers, ran headlong into a political impasse. Forswearing that brand of administration (socialized medicine) had been the price of the American Medical Association's benign neglect of the program during its legislative formulation.[29]

There was also the obvious problem that medicine's professional concerns, diagnosis and treatment of disease or trauma, did not exhaust

29. *See* M. DERTHICK, *supra* note 27, at 295–314.

the factors to be considered in disability decisionmaking. Impairments had to be translated into residual functional capacities that could then be related to the demands of various occupations. This was a job for some kind of vocational rehabilitation specialist or job counselor. And while these sorts of professionals existed in state agencies, theirs was not nearly so unified a set of professional skills, scientific methodologies, or cultural norms as was the medical profession's. Outside some matrix of bureaucratic standards, routines, and structures, the vocational professionals' decisional behavior might be both unpredictable and inconsistent. Simple delegation to professionals did not seem a responsible strategy.

Hence, when the statute delegated the initial disability determination process to state rehabilitation agencies—an obvious and significant concession to the treatment-oriented professional model of administration—the concession was limited. It was a delegation by contract to another bureaucracy. Both the contract and the existing hierarchical structures could be used to mold professional judgment in appropriate forms.

A compelling case for a broad delegation to professionals could have been made only if the disability program were part of a broader range of SSA-administered, health-related social services. But SSA was not, as the Veterans Administration more nearly is,[30] or some state social services were,[31] a full-service social welfare administration. As of 1959, the date of enactment of the disability benefits program, SSA had no medical care component. And when Medicare and Medicaid were adopted, they emerged as fee-for-service programs rather than as a publicly operated health care system. Vocational rehabilitation was historically a state function; sheltered work environments were provided largely by private nonprofit organizations; and jobs programs were scattered about in other departments. The fragmented structure of social welfare virtually foreclosed a vision of a professionally administered, service-oriented approach to the vocational problems of persons with impaired health and limited capacities.

Nor was individualized adjudication by independent hearing officers a politically appropriate model for Social Security disability determina-

---

30. *See, e.g.,* S. Levitan & K. Cleary, Old Wars Remain Unfinished: The Veterans Benefits System (1973).

31. P. Nonet, Administrative Justice 1969.

tions. The administration was not merely a neutral decider of disability claims. It had a positive program of income security to administer. And, like any goal-oriented enterprise, it was viewed as responsible for active pursuit of information sufficient to perform its decisional task. In the words of a judge chastising a different administrative agency for its investigative passivity, SSA was not "an umpire blandly calling balls and strikes."[32]

SSA thus had a responsibility for implementation that required it to be investigatorily active. That responsibility did not necessarily exclude a traditional model of adjudication, but the dynamics of such a scheme would be awkward. SSA could retain control over factual development, for example, by adopting the basic approach of the IRS. SSA investigators could decide either to honor claims or to refer claimants to a hearing. At the hearing the SSA investigator would, of course, present the case for denial. But this would mean that disability adjudication would occur in an essentially adversary mode. Such a posture seems peculiar for a social welfare agency. SSA could hardly view itself as an adversary charged with defeating the claims of the sick, the maimed, and the developmentally retarded. Nor does a commitment to maintaining judgment in a broad, moral, and ultimately subjective form seem consistent with responsible management of a massive national benefits program.

Yet the retirement and survivors programs had made concessions to the traditional moral judgment model in the form of nonadversary hearings and judicial review. The disability program could not be structured otherwise and maintain the insurance-entitlement conception of Social Security benefits. The bureaucratic rationality–moral judgment compromise was thus struck, in part, in the form of a temporal separation—bureaucracy first, followed by individualized hearings for the dissatisfied. The positive bureaucratic function has, however, influenced the hearing process.[33] The hearing officer operates in an investigatory mode, seeking out evidence, conducting an oral hearing, and ultimately deciding the case.

This synthesis of divergent models of justice has obtained the blessings of the external legal order. The program has been defended success-

32. Scenic Hudson Preservation Conference v. FPC, 354 F.2d 608, 620 (2d Cir. 1965).
33. *See* J. MASHAW ET AL., SOCIAL SECURITY HEARINGS AND APPEALS (1978).

fully against demands for pretermination oral hearings by the invocation of the critical involvement of medical judgments in the decision process.[34] Attempts to judicialize the hearing process by moving to adversary presentation have been resisted successfully by appeal to the positive purposes of the program and to the demands of administrative efficiency.[35] Indeed, the synthesis has sometimes been reinforced by the evidentiary demands of reviewing courts,[36] which have required additional professional involvement by vocational experts in the hearing process.

But the legitimation of synthesis or compromise does not necessarily signal the attainment of a happy blending of justice models. Indeed, the combination of ingredients has proved quite volatile as each model has sought to remain coherent by responding to its own internal imperatives. Bureaucratic rationality's demands for accuracy and efficiency, implying as they do objectification of norms and a fact-seeking orientation, will be undermined by professional insistence on the artistry or ethics of a treatment modality[37] or by the highly textured search for moral deservingness inherent in traditional adjudication. Similarly, the just-allocation dimension of moral judgment is lost in a system of objective rules and facts determined by experts.[38] The traditional forms of adjudication then become not merely excess baggage for bureaucratic rationality but useless constraints on its efficiency. Likewise, professional judgment constrained by objective criteria and harnessed to the efficiency imperatives of programmatic rationality ceases to be professional judgment.[39] The story of disability administration is thus, in many respects, a story of systemic stress in which the supporting roles provided for professional treatment and moral judgment may be reinterpreted to cast the judges, doctors, and vocational experts in the role of subversives.

34. Mathews v. Eldridge, 424 U.S. 319 (1976).
35. Richardson v. Wright, 405 U.S. 208 (1972).
36. See MASHAW, supra note 33, at 74.
37. See, e.g., Welch, Professional Standards Review Organizations—Problems and Prospects, 289 New Eng. J. of Med. 291 (1973); Willett, PSRO Today: A Lawyer's Assessment, 292 New Eng. J. of Med. 340 (1975).
38. Cf. Thibaut & Walker, supra note 18.
39. D. Stone, Professionals and Social Science (unpublished paper, Duke University School of Public Policy (Mar. 1976)).

## SYSTEMIC STRESS: PROFESSIONALS AS SUBVERSIVES

### Judges and the Hearing Process

The tale of stress and woe resulting from the provision of a de novo hearing for disappointed disability applicants is too long to recount in its recondite detail.[40] Suffice it to say that the historic position of the administrative law judges (ALJs) has been that their function is to provide justice by methods as similar as possible to those of a traditional judicial trial, mediated by the social welfare goals of the system. In particular, the judges are clear that they are to be independent of SSA and to provide handcrafted justice of the conventional trial type. Some strongly believe that their only adjudicatory guides should be the all-things-considered statutory definition of disability and the evolving judicial notions of due process and substantial evidence.

SSA management takes a different view. From its perspective it is not at all clear that Congress intended SSA hearing officers to have "independence" in the Administrative Procedure Act's (APA) sense. Even conceding that independence, the managerial definition of its attributes is quite different. SSA management views itself as under an obligation to structure ALJ discretion by regulation and to monitor and sanction their behavior in order to assure that the output of ALJ hearings in fact implements the goals of the disability program.

Management is concerned, in short, about the error-proneness and inefficiency of ALJ hearings. Congress has exerted intense pressure on SSA to reduce claim-processing time,[41] and the major area of delay is the hearing process. Moreover, the ALJs are, as a group, much more lenient in granting claims than are state disability examiners. Claimants who request de novo state agency reconsideration of initial denials obtain an award in about 15 percent of the appealed causes. Those who then go to a de novo ALJ hearing obtain an award in *over 50 percent* of their

---

40. *See* Rosenblum, *supra* note 11. *See also* Subcommittee on Social Security, Committee on Ways and Means, Social Security Administrative Law Judges: Survey and Issue Paper, 96th Cong., 1st Sess. (1979).

41. *See, e.g.,* House Ways and Means Committee, Subcommittee on Social Security Appeals, 94th Cong., 1st Sess. (1975). Legislative interest in the delay issue ultimately produced section 308 of the Social Security Amendments of 1980, Pub. L. No. 96–265, § 308, 94 Stat. 441, 458 (1980), which requires the SSA to establish timeliness standards. Some reviewing courts have imposed their own standards. *See, e.g.,* White v. Mathews, 559 F.2d 852 (2d Cir. 1977).

appeals.[42] There are many possible explanations for this phenomenon, but it poses a rather clear threat to the underlying bureaucratic process. Since requesting and obtaining a hearing is virtually costless, what is to prevent ultimate shift of control of the program to the ALJs via a nearly 100 percent appeal rate?

At one point this systemic stress provoked SSA management to respond in an almost schizophrenic fashion. On the one hand, SSA proposed[43] (but subsequently withdrew)[44] regulations that would have provided representation for the government in ALJ hearings. Underlying that proposal was an abandonment of the historic nonadversary posture of SSA administration in a desperate gamble to deal with ALJ profligacy by evening up the odds.

At the same time that it was proposing to facilitate the formal triumph of adversary trial, SSA was engaged in a series of activities designed to bring ALJ hearings under greater managerial control and to orient them toward the accuracy and efficiency goals of rational bureaucratic implementation. First, SSA has made an attempt to make the disability standard more objective and its application more routine. Judgment under these new regulations may involve merely classifying claimants under four quasi-objective criteria and reading the ultimate conclusion off the regulatory charts. Second, the ALJ corps has been subjected to hierarchical review in a management rather than an appellate mode.

Judge Kaufman, describing the ALJs' claims in a class action suit against SSA, gives the judge's-eye view of these efforts:

The first practice challenged in the complaint is the Bureau's "Regional Office Peer Review Program." According to Nash, various officials of the Bureau of Hearings and Appeals review the work of ALJs outside the normal appellate process. In conjunction with this ongoing review, the appellees or their staffs give plaintiff and all other ALJs detailed, purportedly mandatory instructions concerning the proper length of hearings and opinions, the amount of evidence required in specific cases, and the proper use of expert witnesses. Through the

42. The actual figures for the Title II DI program in fiscal year 1979 are 17.3 percent and 56.7 percent, respectively. Social Security Administration, ANNUAL REPORT FOR FISCAL YEAR 1979 4 (1980).

43. *See* Notice of Proposed Rulemaking, "Experiments to Improve the Hearing Process by Having SSA Represented at the Hearing," 45 Fed. Reg. 2345 (Jan. 11, 1980).

44. See Notice of Withdrawal as of July 14, 1980, of NPRM, 45 Fed. Reg. 4716 (1980).

Peer Review Program, the Bureau has allegedly arrogated to itself the power to control the conduct of hearings vested in ALJs by the Administrative Procedure Act, 5 USC §556.

Nash also avers that an arbitrary monthly production quota has been established for him and all his colleagues. Unless an ALJ renders a specified number of decisions per month, the agency, appellant claims, threatens to file incompetence charges against him with the Civil Service Commission. . . .

An additional threat to the ALJs' statutory independence is allegedly posed by the so-called "Quality Assurance Program," which attempts to control the number of decisions denying Social Security Benefits. The agency has "let it be known" that the average 50% "reversal rate" of prior denials of benefits reversed for all ALJs is an "acceptable" one. Appellant further claims in his amended complaint that the reversal rates of all ALJs are monitored, and those who deviate from the mean are counseled and admonished to bring their rates in line with the national average. This attempt to influence the ALJs' decision making process, it is urged, violates 5 USC §556 and the Fifth Amendment to the Constitution.

Nash's fourth claim centers upon plans that call for the national implementation (in whole or in part) of an "Employee Pool System." . . . Under this program, many of the ALJs' judicial responsibilities—including the writing of decisions—are vested in clerical and managerial personnel. The use of such "mass production" techniques, it is charged, violates the APA.[45]

From what I know of the quality assurance program of the Office of Hearings and Appeals (OHA), this complaint is overdrawn.[46] The production "quota" is a target, and only large deviations from it produce even an inquiry from OHA. There is to my knowledge no attempt to assign everyone a 50 percent reversal rate, but the quality assurance data plus special validation studies demonstrate that the most error-prone judges are those whose reversal rate deviates most from the mean. Deviance is, therefore, used as a basis for inquiry and counseling. And the "pool system" might be more positively characterized as an attempt to increase production by providing ALJs with increased professional and paraprofessional staff.

Yet however one characterizes the attempts to manage the ALJ corps, the basic point remains: the hearing process fits uneasily into the bureaucratic scheme. If the ALJ hearing is to be closely controlled by

45. Nash v. Califano, 613 F.2d 10, 12-13 (2d Cir. 1980).

46. *See* Chassman & Ralston, *Social Security Disability Hearings: A Case Study in Quality Assurance and Due Process*, 65 Cornell L. Rev. 803 (1980).

substantive rules, procedural routines, and management oversight, then surely the ALJs are correct to wonder why a formal hearing and a neutral judge, the trappings provided by the APA,[47] are appropriate. A hearing to apply objective criteria subject to management supervision has little of the legitimating symbolism of the proverbial day in court. On the other hand, if the logic of decisional neutrality and individual moral desert is to dominate the hearing stage, how is SSA to maintain control of the program? An increasingly objective and stringent approach at the state agency level would only fuel the escalating appeal rate and exacerbate the discontinuity between the two levels of decision. If SSA is to control the program it must control the hearing stage of the decision process.

### Doctors and Vocational Experts

Protecting bureaucratic rationality from displacement by the professional treatment model does not appear nearly so difficult as fending off the progressive logic of individualized adjudication. The jurisdictional challenge of the treating physician can in one sense easily be met. By regulation,[48] disability examiners are instructed to ignore conclusions of treating physicians concerning a claimant-patient's capacity to work. The reports of treating physicians are carefully analyzed for their clinical findings, of course, but not for their professional judgment concerning the therapeutic desirability of continued work. The programmatic profligacy of conservative medical advice is thus avoided.

This defensive strategy, however, reveals a deeper problem. As we shall discuss in greater detail below, medical judgments are required with respect to certain critical elements of disability decisionmaking. Eliminating physician judgment creates gaps in the chain of data required for instrumentally rational decisionmaking. Bureaucratic power will then be seen to rest not on knowledge but on values specified (or at least generated) by the bureaucratic process itself.

The delegation of power to state vocational rehabilitation professionals produces similar stress and a response that ultimately deprofessionalizes judgment—that is, removes it from the therapeutic context. One might imagine, for example, that a vocational rehabilitation coun-

47. 5 U.S.C. §§551-559 (1976).
48. 20 C.F.R. §404.1527 (1981).

selor would view claimants as falling roughly into three categories: (1) those not sufficiently disabled to require rehabilitation service or, a fortiori, income support; (2) those requiring services to regain self-sufficiency, but who are not permanently disabled; and (3) those who are too impaired to justify rehabilitation efforts and who should be afforded early retirement supported by disability benefits. SSA's concern is that the third category will be overpopulated if examiners view claimants from the perspective of rehabilitation.

That this should be the case is understandable given the institutional context of state rehabilitation services. Those services are scarce, and the agency's measure of success is job placement. Rehabilitation professionals will, like treating physicians, be conservative in their estimates of a claimant's work potential. For resources will have been wasted if the claimant is provided services but cannot ultimately be placed. Where there is doubt about the effectiveness of rehabilitation, the safer course is to provide a disability pension. This tendency is reinforced by the structure of state and federal funding. Rehabilitation services come partially from state-funded programs, to which the rehabilitation professional is attached. The disability pension comes entirely from federal dollars through a program having no explicit budget constraint.

Obviously, then, if SSA is to retain control of the definition of disability, and thereby the fiscal integrity of the program, it must avoid decisionmaking in the predictable mode of the state rehabilitation counselor. The story of how this has been accomplished is in a sense the administrative history of the disability system—its contract, regulatory, and supervisory activity, a subject that will occupy much of our subsequent discussion. Suffice it to say that the current state agency process is so nearly federal and so divorced from the line activity of state rehabilitation services that a visit to a state Disability Determination Service and observation of the disability examiner at work give hardly a clue to the historic association of disability adjudication and vocational rehabilitation.

Our story up to this point might be summarized as follows: in the beginning three models of justice were structured into the disability program. The theoretical inconsistencies among these models of justice have been reflected in historical conflict. Over time the internal imperatives of bureaucratic rationality have triumphed by pushing professional judgment into a controllable hierarchical or evidentiary role and by making significant progress toward "bureaucratizing" the hearing process to eliminate much of its "moral judgment" flavor. The story of administrative justice in the disability program, thus summarized, raises two questions: first, how is this apparent triumph to be explained? What are the programmatic, structural, and political factors that can account for bureaucratic rationality's success? Second, and more important, is that success a good thing? If not, what should be done to produce a different synthesis or mix of the program's justice models?

In the pages that follow we shall examine these questions from a particular perspective. The discussion is concerned preeminently with what I call the logic of the model—with the means by which a bureaucratic structure attempts to solve certain issues that result from the problematic nature of its aspiration to rationality. For it seems that it is the drive to solve those problems that produces, paradoxically, both the imperative to overwhelm competitive models of justice and the opportunities for their positive contributions. We begin therefore with a more detailed elaboration of the normative aspirations of bureaucratic rationality and with a specification of the conditions under which these aspirations might be achievable. And as we compare those conditions with the realities of the disability program, we shall see that perfect justice in the rational bureaucratic mode is impossible.

# PART II · BUREAUCRATIC RATIONALITY: SEARCHING FOR THE GOOD WITHIN THE CONSTRAINTS OF THE POSSIBLE

# 3 · On Living with the Impossibility of Rational Administration

The model of bureaucratic rationality employs an instrumentalist definition of rationality. It presumes that a judgment or decision, if rational, takes into account the values that are at stake in the decision and the ways in which a decision one way or another will contribute to the realization of those values. Truly effective decisionmaking in this mode obviously requires at least three things: an understanding of the values or goals that are to be pursued; knowledge of the relevant facts; and an accurate prediction of the connection between a particular decision, given the factual context, and the accomplishment of one or more of the decisionmaker's goals.

Applying this basic view of rationality, one can then say that disability adjudicators behave rationally to the extent that they have (1) internalized an appropriate definition of disability, (2) collected information sufficient to allow a determination of whether a particular claimant meets that definition; and (3) understood the way in which a particular decision to grant or to deny disability benefits furthers the statutory goal of income support for the disabled population. If we assume an appropriate understanding of the goals and access to the relevant facts, the third element is not problematic. A correct classification of the claimant as disabled or not furthers the statutory goals; an incorrect classification retards their achievement. From this perspective the basic goal of disability administration is correctness.

It follows that at the more general level of system rationality the SSA adjudicatory system will be rational to the extent that it promotes correct decisionmaking by individual adjudicators. That is, the administrative system will be rational to the extent that it promotes an appropriate understanding of the goals of income support for the disabled

49

population and the collection of relevant and adequate evidence for the decision of individual cases. Many of the criticisms of SSA administration by prior observers fall into one of these two categories: either that SSA has failed to provide an adequate understanding of the goals or purposes of the disability system through elaboration and communication of the definition of disability, or that it has failed to develop and monitor the utilization of techniques that would provide appropriate and relevant information for decisionmaking.

A focus on administrative rationality in this instrumental sense is certainly warranted. The notion that the function of administrators is to apply legislative policy to shifting or multiple factual situations that cannot be fully known or efficiently assimilated at the legislative stage is deeply embedded in our traditional view of the American constitutional system. As we have noted, much of the set of quasi-constitutional legal doctrines commonly called administrative law has to do with judicial oversight of administrative rationality. Litigants are invited by this body of law to put to courts the question whether the administrators have properly understood legislative policy, whether they have accurately found the facts, and whether they have explained how, on those facts, a particular decision contributes to the realization of legislatively specified goals. The invitation is accepted each year by thousands of disappointed applicants for disability benefits.

Serious evaluation of administrative performance requires more, however, than measurement of outcomes against the ideal of instrumental rationality. Consideration must be given to the limits of instrumental rationality in the context of a particular administrative program. Those limits are of at least three types. First, there are certain necessary conditions for the successful application of an instrumentalist method to a set of decisional tasks. To the degree that these conditions are not met, individual (much less bureaucratic) decisionmaking cannot fully conform to the ideal type. Second, organizational (as distinguished from individual) decisions present special difficulties for, and therefore limitations on, rational decisionmaking. Bureaus are not organisms, and ensuring rational behavior by all those individuals who might act for the bureau is a task for which management science has not produced tidy formulae. Third, rationality, as we have here defined it (the effective pursuit of some set of programmatic goals), does not exhaust our ambitions for a good life or a good government. Rational administration of disability benefits (or of any other program) comes at a cost—the opportunity costs of pursuing other social goals. Pursuit of rational administration in any program is limited by competition with these other goals.

Of course, the notion that instrumental rationality in its pure form is unachievable is not headline news. The proponents and elaborators of the idea of "bounded rationality" now have a Nobel laureate[1] in their ranks, and exploration of the difficulties of implementation has become a special field of policy studies.[2] Indeed, the idea that legislative statements of policy routinely overpromise when gauged by administrative performance seems to have been *the* political idea of the 1970s, as politicians competed with each other in their zeal to teach us to think small.

But the general idea that reason is bounded and implementation difficult, however true, even profound, does not tell us *how* limited or *how* difficult. To moderate our expectations appropriately we need to know more about how these general problems affect the disability program. I will reserve direct consideration of the third limitation on rational administration to the discussion of efficiency in the next chapter. For now I will consider only the first two. To restate: we are here concerned with the ways in which the Disability Insurance (DI) program, as legislatively formulated, and the political, bureaucratic, and social context of its operation, limit administrative pursuit of instrumental rationality. In discussing these limitations, I will provide the predicate for a set of realistic expectations about SSA performance viewed as a system of rational administration and, simultaneously, introduce many of the issues of program administration that will be explored in detail in chapters 5, 6, and 7.

1. The reference is, of course, to Herbert Simon. The discussion that follows owes much to the work of Simon, James March, Ed Lindblom, their colleagues, students, and disciples. *See generally*, E. LINDBLOM & D. BRAYBROOKE, A STRATEGY OF DECISION (1963); C. Lindblom, *The Science of Muddling Through*, 19 Pub. Admin. Rev. 79 (1959); J. G. MARCH AND H. A. SIMON, ORGANIZATIONS (1958); R. CYERT AND J. G. MARCH, A BEHAVIORAL THEORY OF THE FIRM (1963); H. SIMON, MODELS OF MAN (1957); H. SIMON, ADMINISTRATIVE BEHAVIOR (3d ed. 1976); March, *Bounded Rationality, Ambiguity and the Engineering of Choice* 10 Bell J. Econ. 587 (1978).

2. *See* J. L. PRESSMAN & A. WILDAVSKY, IMPLEMENTATION (2d ed. 1979)

## AMBIGUITY, INCOHERENCE, AND UNCERTAINTY

SSA's pursuit of instrumental rationality is impaired both by the ambiguity and incoherence of the goals of the disability benefits program and by the uncertainties that infect the factual contexts presented to its adjudicators for authoritative resolution. These problems would affect the rationality of the decision process even if decisions were made by one or a small number of adjudicators and therefore posed no special problems of organizational engineering or bureaucratic control.

### Does Anyone Know What this Program is About?

A pure model of instrumental rationality must presume that the values or reference goals for decisionmaking are absolute (that is, that the choice of one goal over another is not morally distressing), relevant, stable, consistent, precise, and exogenous (that is, not in part a function of the choices that the decisionmaker himself makes). The absence of any one of these conditions will impair a decisionmaker's capacity to act in an instrumentally rational fashion. None of these conditions fully obtains in the disability (or indeed in any) program.

*Absoluteness and Consistency* The congressional choice with respect to who is to be supported by the disability program is apparently absolute. Persons are disabled if *unable* to work by reason of their *medical condition* at any job in the *national* economy. But on closer examination the underlying incoherence of the disability standard reveals the legislature's distress at its choice. A basic policy question for the legislature, for example, was whether the disability program should support (a) persons who have medical problems and who cannot find work on that account or (b) only persons who have medical problems and on that account are neither substantially gainfully employed nor indeed able to work. The Congress explicitly chose the latter definition of disability. A worker who has a health problem but who has the stamina, dexterity, and mental acuity to do some job in the national economy is not disabled, even though it is clear that employers have access to a labor pool of healthy workers that they will uniformly prefer to hire.

This definition of disability is rather peculiar, but peculiar for a clear reason. Congress has attempted to separate disability from unemployment. The latter risk has its own separately structured insurance program. Because the good sense of attempting such a separation is not intuitively obvious, and because the unemployment insurance scheme is administered by different personnel, SSA should anticipate that it will not be easy for its adjudicators to grasp the appropriate concept of disability. Rational administration would employ every reasonable means to insure that the legislative value choice is clarified and brought forcefully to bear in individual cases.

Yet as SSA pursues this administrative task it must surely wonder what rigid adherence to the statutory definition might mean. The statutory standard suggests that the answer to both the question, "Would the claimant ever be hired?" and the question "Is the claimant disabled?" should be, "No." It presumes that ability to do a job has some meaning divorced from its operative economic context. But can it really be sensible to say that although a person is, because of medical impairments, too far back in the labor queue ever to be employed, yet that same person is not disabled because of these same medical impairments? Words like *unemployed, unemployable,* and *disabled* may convey different senses of an individual's *relative* position in the labor queue. But obviously each relative position merges into the next; there is no clear dividing line between the categories.

Does Congress then really mean it? Apparently not—at least sometimes. The recognition that disability cannot be sharply distinguished from unemployability and the Congress's regret at having to make a categorical choice was expressed in the first disability oversight hearings before the Harrison subcommittee in 1960. The committee declared that SSA should avoid turning disability into unemployment but that it should be "realistic" about it.[3] In short, SSA should implement the congressional choice without, somehow, forgetting its poignancy.

The poignant choice problems posed by the dichotomized continuum are, of course, familiar. But this feature of the SSA program is, nevertheless, particularly striking. Not only must claimants be classified as disabled or not disabled, but payment amounts are not related to the degree of disability or, in the Title II program, to need. Benefits are statutorily prescribed to equal retirement or survivors' benefits: disabil-

---

3. Subcommittee on the Administration of the Social Security Laws, Committee on Ways and Means, 86th Cong. 2d Sess. Administration of Social Security Disability Program—(Comm. Print 1960).

ity is simply a socially approved form of early retirement. And, of course, a decision that a claimant is not disabled carries with it by implication the stigma of socially unexcused economic failure. The availability of rating schedules, familiar in workmen's compensation or veterans' programs, would not eliminate these difficult issues of classification. But the opportunities that graded benefits sometimes provide for compromise and adjustment would certainly relieve some of the stress that the disability determination now entails.

The lack of absoluteness in the congressional choice of this binary classification scheme is further revealed by the inconsistency of the criteria that SSA is instructed to employ in making the classifications. The statute requires that disability be assessed while putting aside the likelihood of the claimant's being hired. Yet it also makes the claimant's age independently significant. Why should this be the case? It is possible, of course, that age is a proxy for some other criterion that is directly related to functional capacity. For example, it might be thought to be a proxy for "adaptability" to new work environments. But no general relationship between age and adaptability has ever been established. A different explanation for the statutory inclusion of age as a criterion of disability seems plausible. The Congress was establishing income support for the disabled, not for the aged. Yet it could not fully escape its desire to provide in some way for persons who were too young for retirement under the retirement insurance program, but for whom age was a major, perhaps determinative, factor in the competition for jobs.[4]

The statutory requirement that SSA consider the claimant's education and work experience has a similar explanation. A person with the physical and mental capacity to learn new tasks can, after all, be trained to do them. His or her current knowledge and skill is not determinative. If the disability program is designed to deal with long-term or permanent functional incapacity, why is current skill level important? Additional education and skill training can be acquired. A more salient criterion would have been aptitude.

---

4. Indeed, the statutory history of the disability program might be viewed as simply a liberalization of the retirement program. Congress began by using disability as an excuse for not making retirement insurance contributions, and when it first made the taxes negative (began to pay benefits) it limited payments to persons over fifty. See COMMITTEE ON WAYS AND MEANS, COMMITTEE STAFF REPORT ON THE DISABILITY INSURANCE PROGRAM 110–15 (Comm. Print 1974).

The answer, again, seems to be legislative regret. The poorly educated are surely a source of social concern. Because we often suspect that poor design in our public educational institutions, racism, or culturally induced notions of sex roles have lasting effects on individuals, we often also feel some sense of social responsibility for an individual's lack of productive skills. The rapid advance of technology, from which most of us benefit, may increase our concern for those seemingly displaced by change. Moreover, we know that the necessary investment in training or retraining can often not be financed either privately (by employer training programs or loans in private capital markets) or publicly (by manpower programs, vocational rehabilitation, loan subsidies, and the like). As a collective expression of our regret for these failures—or at simple economic realities: human capital investment, like investment in physical capital, is not always worthwhile—vocational criteria are grafted onto a program that is ostensibly designed to exclude consideration of the general unemployment problems of marginal workers in a competitive market for skills.

There is in these remarks no necessary criticism of the legislative mandate. Social policy as legislatively crafted into programmatic directives should not be expected to emerge as a set of fully coherent approaches to unitary goals. Nor should we expect administration of legislative programs to ignore the interplay and competition between dominant purposes forcefully expressed and subsidiary purposes regretfully omitted or somewhat incoherently included. Yet, because dominant purposes are not absolute and subsidiary purposes compete, it will always be possible to find that from the perspective of one or another goal the administrator's actions are instrumentally irrational.

*Precision* The goal specified by the Social Security Act—to provide benefits to disabled persons—is not very precise. There is no external referent, that is, a clear case of disability, with which particular claimants can be compared. Indeed, it may not even be possible to know very much after the fact about the tendency of the system to differentiate appropriately between the able and the disabled. That persons declared to be disabled in general fail to return to work or to a level of functioning that would permit substantial gainful employment is in some sense a test of the correctness of disability determinations. But since the decision to grant benefits confirms the claimants' perceptions and provides an alternative source of income, the award itself is likely to have substantial impact on future behavior. An affirmative decision is in some sense a self-fulfilling prophesy.

Alternatively, that a denied claimant, through truly heroic effort, returns to work does not necessarily mean that he or she was meant to be excluded from benefits. To the contrary, Congress may well have believed that persons suffering *that* degree of pain or difficulty when working should be excused from the work force. For surely Congress did not intend that disability be so construed that persons should be considered able to do work that means certain death or terrible anguish. Yet death is always more or less certain and anguish merges almost imperceptibly into discomfort. To put the point more generally, the line that Congress drew through the ability–disability continuum when establishing its eligibility standard cannot be precisely located. This imprecision obviously limits the degree to which one can say with confidence that any particular decision is or is not a correct application of the statute.

*Relevance* Given the general constitutional presumption of legislative supremacy, one might have hoped that the relevance of statutory goals to SSA decisionmaking would be nonproblematic. In some sense it is. If the question is merely whether the secretary of HEW should follow the directions of the legislature, as against his or her own preferences, the answer is obvious. But most questions are not nearly so straightforward. The question for the administrator is often a question of which source of legislative intent is the relevant source from which to divine the statute's meaning.

For example, consider the recurrent problem of determining the appropriate administrative response to judicial review of disability determinations. Legislative supremacy in policy determination is no less well established than judicial supremacy in the interpretation of the legislature's expressions. Surely SSA must defer to judicial judgments. But how much deference should it pay?

At a minimum SSA must follow the orders of courts in particular cases. Any other course would be contemptuous in the narrow legal sense of that term. But what of the courts' interpretations of statutory policy? Suppose, for example, that a court interprets the Social Security Act to demand expeditious claims processing and further holds that expedition means rendering a decision within x days of the filing of a claim? Or that the benevolent purposes of the act can be accomplished only by establishing a legal presumption that inability to do one's former work entitles a claimant to benefits absent proof by SSA that he or she can perform other jobs in the national economy? Or suppose the interpretation of the disability standard by many reviewing courts over a substantial period of time, by the pattern of remands and reversals as much as by the technical grounds for judicial disapproval, reveals a common belief that SSA's interpretation of disability excludes from the class of eligible persons many whom the courts would find disabled?

These suppositions are, of course, not merely hypothetical. They describe events[5] or patterns[6] in the judicial review of SSA disability decisions. Assuming that SSA believes that these judicial interpretations are inappropriate, how should it respond? One defensible response might be that the administration will comply only with direct orders of lower federal courts and with the general interpretations provided by the Supreme Court. SSA after all has a national responsibility, while federal courts have only a limited geographic jurisdiction. In some situations, an attempt to generalize the policy prescriptions of one district or circuit court will lead to conflict with the views of another court or many other courts. Some judicial interpretations will have to be ignored or limited to compliance in a particular district or circuit.

Note that this position implies that in general the statute is the relevant guide but that sometimes and in some places a particular judicial interpretation provides the relevant criterion for decisionmaking. But what can it mean to say that the statute is the guide? That statement translates into "SSA's interpretation of the statute is the guide." From whence comes that interpretation? It emerges, obviously, out of SSA's experience in administering the program and in relating to the Congress and to the courts as overseers of its activities. Which is to say, there are at least two relevant, nonjudicial sources of interpretive guidance: the Congress and SSA itself. The value matrix within which SSA operates is thus defined by the interaction of the various institutions that have the statute in their charge and whose interpretations of it may conflict. The statute is clearly relevant, but which statute: the one

5. *See* White v. Mathews 559 F.2d 852 (2d Cir. 1977) (time constraints); Kerner v. Flemming, 283 F.2d 916 (2d Cir. 1960) (burden of proof).

6. The pattern of disagreement by federal district courts is remarkably strong. Over the period 1970–75 the courts reversed or remanded 46 percent of the disability cases decided. Mashaw et al., Social Security Hearings and Appeals 129 (1978).

perceived by SSA; by the House Subcommittee on Social Security; or by the federal courts?

These possibilities for institutional conflict concerning potentially relevant goals suggest that two other conditions for the application of instrumental rationality also will not hold: goals will not be stable, nor will they be exogenous to the process of administration.

*Stability* The foregoing discussion of the relevance of statutorily specified value might be titled "Variations on a Theme from Eighth-Grade Civics," with the genius of the American system of checks and balances as the melody. The only change in the conventional model—and it is one that this essay insists upon—is that Bureaucracy has been admitted to the pantheon of institutional heroes. But whatever genius there is in the American constitutional system, it is not the ability to produce a stable equilibrium. One cannot predict a priori whose perception of the goals of the DI program—the courts', the administrators', or the legislators'—will be ascendent; or, more realistically, what mix of those views will best describe the policies in fact being employed. The constitutional presuppositions of democratic pluralism seem to be that this state of affairs is to be applauded. Institutions *should* check and balance each other. It is the process of governance, not the achievement of static equilibrium, that is important.

The prior discussion in fact understates the pervasive instability of the DI value matrix. For instability results not just from competition among the branches of government, but also from competition within the branches over the direction of policy. The Congress, for example, communicates with SSA concerning the goals of DI management in a number of ways. It enacts statutes as a primary, formal mode of communication; but it also communicates through appropriations hearings, oversight hearings, discussions of proposed legislative changes, and in 100,000 individual contacts per year as each Congressman engages in casework. These different voices will make it difficult to find a stable and ordered set of congressional values or goals at any one time. In its casework incarnation the Congress seems concerned primarily with the expeditious payment of claimants; in others it is concerned primarily with actuarial projections which suggest that increases in DI payments threaten to bankrupt the Social Security system. As one state agency official wrote to Congressman Burke, then chairman of the Subcommittee on Social Security, "frequently members of Congress who may express concern at the financial picture of the Social Security Trust Fund, will nevertheless exert their influence to request review and favorable consideration of a constituent's claim because he is a deserving individual."[7] An administrative response that seeks to further the goal of generosity or timeliness will appear irrational when viewed from the perspective of a concurrent congressional concern with fiscal restraint. And, of course, communications in the same form will change over time. As we noted in chapter 1, the statutory history of the program reveals constant reordering of the congressional balance between caution and benevolence.

The 1980 amendments to the Social Security Act are a good example.[8] That legislation emphasizes caution. The fiscal and administrative (or management) concerns of the 1970s are evident in: (1) the limitation placed on total family benefits under the Title II program and the reduction of payment levels for younger workers; (2) the secretary's heightened control over state agencies, including a requirement that by FY 1982 at least 65 percent of all state agency awards be reviewed by SSA prior to implementation; and (3) the new requirement that states review all awards at least every three years, unless a determination is made at the outset that the disability is "permanent."

Yet there is still concern with the beneficent purposes of the program. For example, the two-year waiting period for Medicare benefits is eliminated for beneficiaries requalifying for benefits after a lapse of no more than five years. Earnings in sheltered workshops and extraordinary work expenses due to a severe disability are required to be disregarded for purposes of determining "substantial gainful activity," and SSI benefits are continued for persons enrolled in approved vocational rehabilitation programs. Transitional payments for persons terminated after a trial work period are also extended. To a substantial degree, of course, these liberalizing provisions were proposed as a means for encouraging reentry into the work force, thereby reducing program costs. But, as with work incentive provisions in welfare legislation generally, it is difficult to know whether the secondary effects of

7. Subcommittee on Social Security, House Ways and Means Committee, 94th Cong., 2d Sess., Disability Insurance—Issue Paper 37 (1976) (hereinafter cited as "Issue Paper").

8. Social Security Disability Amendments of 1980, Pub. L. No. 96–265, 94 Stat. 441 (1980).

caseload reduction or the primary effects of increased benefits should be considered to dominate a complex set of legislative purposes. The balance remains unstable.

*Exogenous Goals*  Finally, it seems clear that the values or goals that are pursued by the disability program will be, in substantial part, a function of how SSA administers the program. At one level this is obvious. Under the statute, SSA has the authority to promulgate regulations that define certain critical terms. The level at which SSA pegs the dollar amount that defines substantial gainful activity, for example, will qualify or disqualify thousands of potential beneficiaries and will have an important bearing on the degree to which the program supports the goal of maintaining work incentives.

But there are subtler ways in which administration will shape the values of the system. The use or nonuse of personnel who have peculiar professional perspectives, for example, physicians or vocational experts, at critical stages in the decision process will determine whether the values instinct in those professional capacities will help shape the output of the system. The detail with which SSA requires that certain medical or vocational characteristics of claimants be explored or documented and the degree of discretion accorded decisionmakers in evaluating the meaning of the evidence will determine in some substantial degree whether the program is directed at the support of persons suffering from a single major medical problem or more broadly at a population whose total life circumstances, including medical difficulties, make them unsuitable for substantial work. Indeed, as I will explore in more detail in later chapters, these decisions have a pervasive and ultimately decisive impact on the character of the disability program.

Goals are thus developed in part by looking back at the effects of decisions or decision structures and asking whether what is happening satisfies our present expectations. In some sense one could not know what the values or purposes of the program were—or, more clearly, what their priorities were—except by running the program and seeing what turned up. The basic idea of instrumental rationality—first goals, then implementing action—may be reversed in the real world of administration.[9]

---

9. *See generally*, V. Pressman & A. Wildavsky, *supra* note 2.

That values or priorities emerge in the process of implementing the program does not mean, I hasten to add, that the program cannot be criticized. The managerial task is to recognize emerging values or disvalues and to act to reinforce acceptable behavior while deterring the unacceptable. Moreover, it seems sensible to expect that over time this learning by doing will be fed back into the system. More meaningful elaboration of the norms that govern decisional behavior and better systems for communicating those norms and monitoring their implementation should result. In short, one can certainly be critical of a system that fails to use hindsight to improve its administration.

The difficulties inherent in specifying appropriate goals for the SSA's system of benefits adjudication thus do not imply that those goals are, or must remain, wholly unintelligible or indeterminate. It is possible to choose administrative strategies that tend both to make goals more determinate and explicit and to put value choice in a context that permits institutional dialogue and political accountability. I will have occasion to discuss these techniques in later pages and to evaluate SSA's performance in those terms. The attempt to identify the program's value matrix does, however, suggest skepticism with respect to critical evaluations of SSA performance that implicitly or explicitly specify a single set of relevant, absolute, consistent, stable, precise, and exogenous goals for the disability program and fault SSA for its failure to implement them.

### The Frustrating Search for a Fact

To the extent that values or goals are obscure it is of course difficult to know what facts are relevant to decisionmaking. But apart from that difficulty, and assuming that one understands what facts need to be established to justify an award of DI benefits, there nevertheless remains a substantial degree of evidentiary uncertainty in the disability decision. Indeed, there are several different kinds of factual uncertainty that afflict the disability determination process. At a minimum the following problems are sometimes present: fragmentary evidence; subjective evidence; predictive extrapolation; and, finally, "facts" that are inherently unknowable.

*Fragmentary Evidence* There are often gaps in the record affecting a claimant's medical or vocational history. Indeed, existing medical records are often unavailable. That statement may seem peculiar, but five minutes spent with any disability examiner will reveal that the bane of his or her professional life is the inability to get existing medical records from doctors or hospitals within a reasonable period of time. Many claimants are sent out for consultative examinations (CEs) at SSA expense for no reason other than their relative speed. Contemporary medical examinations or vocational skills tests bearing on the same issues can clearly fill some gaps. But given the expense and sometimes the delay involved in obtaining CEs, many records must remain fragmentary. Moreover, contemporary evidence is not always a perfect substitute for the missing records. For example, when an examiner needs to know what a claimant's condition was at some critical date in the past because his Title II coverage has expired, then contemporary evidence of disability can hardly be determinative.

*Subjective Evidence* The problem of subjective evidence is also reasonably straightforward. Medical diagnostic evidence consists not just of technological or scientific artifacts, like EKG charts or chemical analysis of bodily fluids, but also of medical evaluations and interpretations of these data. In addition, much clinical evidence consists merely of visual, verbal, or manual examination. Interpretation or evaluation of all these medical indicators involves the judgment of medical professionals and is influenced by a host of subjective factors that are difficult to bring to light or to evaluate.

The critical evidence in a disability case—evidence concerning the claimant's functional capacity (that is, not what he's got, but how well he can function with what he's got)—is often also highly colored by subjective factors. To the extent that there is any direct evidence on this issue the information usually comes from the claimant himself, from friends or relatives who have an interest in supporting his claim, or from a treating physician who says that the claimant "shouldn't work." In other cases, it is supplied by an SSA staff physician and is based on an evaluation of the medical evidence of record or, less frequently, on a CE. But in either case this so-called evidence is merely a judgment; and, in the second, it is a judgment made by a doctor who has never seen the patient.

*Predictive Extrapolation* The problem of predictive extrapolation is quite simply the problem of predicting the future on the basis of the past. The disability standard asks whether a claimant has impairments that will permanently or for at least twelve months prevent his or her participation in substantial gainful activity in the national economy. Obviously the question of the duration of the impairment depends not only on how persons normally respond to a particular disease or trauma but also on how this particular person has responded to his or her disease or trauma and what the prognosis is for improvement or deterioration based on that prior history. Yet medical prognosis is a notoriously uncertain business for physicians. More important, in many cases the disability determination is a determination concerning whether a claimant can perform jobs that he or she has never before performed. That is, it is a prediction about how the claimant's prior vocational and medical history will condition his or her response to some new job environment. In answer to the question, "Can X do Y job?" one can easily imagine responsible predictions of the form "probably so" or "probably not." The disability system requires that the question be answered "yes" or "no."

*The Permanently Obscure* Finally there are facts about the disability decision that one is tempted to classify as inherently unknowable. The ability to function depends substantially on such abstractions as motivation, tolerance for pain, and energy levels. These are not testable characteristics of persons in the way that blood type is, yet they may be highly relevant to the question of a claimant's functional capacity. On the same facts one might reach contradictory conclusions: that a claimant suffered intolerable pain from his or her medical condition or that he or she was a malingerer; that his or her condition so sapped the claimant's energy levels that sustained performance in a job was impossible or that, in psychiatric jargon, the claimant was obtaining secondary gains from his or her status as a patient. In many cases the real effects of a medical abnormality on the claimant's functioning may remain forever mysterious.

Facts are, of course, not always fragmentary, subjective, or unknowable. Prediction of future behavior on the basis of past facts is not always a shot in the dark. The point remains, however, that any suggestion that disability adjudicators should be better informed about the facts of individual cases in order to be able to make more rational decisions about them must be examined in some detail. An attempt to get better information is not always worthwhile. If the complaint is that evidence is fragmentary, then the basic policy question is, "Will an attempt to fill the gaps be cost-effective?" If the problem is subjectivity, the critical issues may revolve around the degree to which subjective evidence should be considered relevant or the acceptable ways in which it may be verified. If the concern is with predictive extrapolation, the focus of inquiry should probably be on the methodology of extrapolation and the capacity of professional deciders or witnesses to make such predictive judgments. With respect to the "mysterious" elements of disability adjudication, a call for better information is simply beside the point. In this situation a finding that a particular state of the world exists must rest on a presumption, that is, on some decision rule about what to do under uncertainty. Such a decision rule must in turn be based on a preference or value. One's assessment of the adequacy of system performance will then turn upon one's opinion of whether SSA has chosen the correct value, not whether it has found the correct fact.

## INCOMPETENCE, SUBVERSION, AND ARBITRARINESS

In fact, the prior discussion understates the difficulties of rational administration. For it speaks only of rationality, not of administration. System design further complicates the pursuit of instrumental rationality. We shall approach these issues as variations on three general themes: (1) limits on organizational capacity; (2) competition between program goals and organizational goals; and (3) competition between program goals and the personal values of adjudicators.

### The Limits of Organizational Competence

Value ambiguity and factual uncertainty would plague a hypothetical human decisionmaker who was attempting to sort out what goals had been set for her by the legislative program in her charge and what the true situation was with respect to persons who came before her claiming disability benefits. Moreover, our hypothetical individual might also have limited understanding or faulty perception. Indeed, we expect real individuals, and by analogy most hypothetical ones, to have limitations that impair their ability to make rational decisions. Following Herbert Simon and others, we might better describe decisionmaking as a process of limited, or bounded, rationality. Individuals "satisfice" rather than "optimize."

Optimizing behavior is the epitome of instrumental rationality. The optimizing decisionmaker attempts to take account of all relevant values and all relevant facts, plus the costs of decisionmaking, in order to maximize the total net benefit from every decision. The satisficing decisionmaker, on the other hand, makes individual decisions based on some subset of the relevant values and facts. His effort is to reach a satisfactory decision, even though some other decision based on better information and more cogent reflection on a fuller range of values might be more beneficial, even after taking account of the costs of a more comprehensive decisional methodology. In some sense these two models of decisionmaking might be viewed as normative and positive models. The optimizing model is the ideal; the satisficing model more aptly describes the behavior of actual human beings.

An attempt to evaluate the real-world behavior of organizations must take account of both models. For while organizations have some strengths relative to individuals, such as quantitative decisionmaking capacity and opportunities for specialization, they are not omnicompetent. Given the fact that maximization is generally unattainable, the critic of institutions should thus be concerned with the reasonableness of structures for decisionmaking that modify the pursuit of the ideal. Put in other terms, the question is whether the organization has made sensible judgments about how to deal with the bounds on its competence.

A series of general limits on rational organizational behavior in the optimizing mode suggest themselves. The first is cognitive competence. Neither individuals nor organizations can faultlessly collect and process all the information that is relevant to decisions they must make. Thus, when considering a number of organizational issues (such as whether individual adjudicators should be forced to get more information about claims, whether SSA executive-level managers should collect more information about how claims are in fact being decided, or whether SSA should give more instructions to its first-line decisional personnel), one must consider the capacities of individual decisionmakers and of the organization to process and utilize the additional information. What level of information is the right level will always be debatable. State agency decisionmakers, for example, complain that they receive both too little and too much information from Baltimore and from their SSA regional offices. Not surprisingly, SSA's quality assurance (QA) program collects less information than one would like to have about the determinants of disability decisions, while at the same time tending to overwhelm the administration's ability to analyze the data that the system generates.

Second, there are communication problems in any organization. Without making any attempt to elaborate the many failings of language, I think it is useful to mention a crucial problem for administration of SSA's far-flung adjudicatory system: the difficulty of communicating one message without also communicating other messages that are both unintended and undesired. For example, when SSA communicates via its medical listings, that certain specified medical conditions are per se disabling, it also seems to communicate a negative pregnant: conditions that do not satisfy the medical listings are presumptively nondisabling. Despite SSA's many attempts to stamp out this notion, it persists.

One moral we may draw from this experience is that attempts to reduce erroneous judgment by providing objective criteria will, because of communication difficulty, induce a certain level of error of a different type. In addition, attempts to rectify specific problems, such as excessive delay in claims processing, may cause decisionmakers to focus on that one purpose or value to the exclusion of others, such as full development of the evidence. Delay may be replaced by error.

The communications problem in organizations is sometimes described as organizational slack. Information filters through organizations. Each retransmission through the hierarchy dilutes the message, and some filters are more powerful or selective than others. Hence as information moves up or down bureaucratic ladders it will lose force, and its meaning may change. But this is not a necessary consequence. Sometimes messages seem to have passed through a series of increasingly powerful amplifiers. What began as a reflective "What about X?" becomes first, "Do X," and then, "X is imperative!" One cannot evaluate organizational rationality solely on the basis of messages sent. The question is, "What meaning and effect will they have when they reach their destination?" At a managerial level, the question is how to design a communications system that puts filters and amplifiers of the right types in the right places.

In addition, some messages are very difficult to communicate. Obviously SSA would like to be able to instruct its disability examiners (through rules, training programs or what have you) to exercise good judgment. It would like someone to persuade the whole corps of examiners to emulate the best examiner—that person who makes the fewest errors, processes the most cases, and wastes the least money on unproductive development. To some degree good judgment about development or decisionmaking can be described, located, studied, and discussed. The whole system can be informed of the methods that seem to be performing best.

Yet some substantial amount of the "experience" of the system will not yield up its secrets to study or permit their transmission through straightforward cognitive techniques. Some of it resides in what one might call the feel or craft of decisionmakers. This sort of clinical intelligence is difficult to retrieve across individuals or across time and to communicate explicitly. It involves things like the sense of what works and what doesn't when ferreting out information, what evidence is reliable and what is not—things that are an implicit part of the culture of the system but are not to be found in manuals or regulations. To the extent that this information emerges at the explicit cognitive level at all, it makes up the conventional wisdom of the bureaucracy.

There are obviously limits to the ability of a bureaucracy to utilize this type of information or intelligence. The conventional wisdom at SSA that treating-physician reports that a claimant is "disabled" should be taken with the proverbial grain of salt can be communicated by regulation. The sense of when that grain adds sufficient flavor to pass the disability program's taste test cannot. Indeed, it seems in some sense metaphorical to suggest that the organization, as distinguished from the individual members of the organization, possesses this so-called clinical intelligence. For this reason when the bureaucracy attempts to rely on such intelligence, usually characterized as "expertise" or "experience," either to justify some explicit policy or to justify its failure to adopt one, we become suspicious that the administrators are merely asserting a preference and papering over a lack of knowledge. Our ideology of administrative accountability for instrumentally rational action teaches us to discount facts that cannot be proved and wisdom that cannot be communicated to outsiders.

Yet surely the systematic suppression of reliance on clinical intelligence is not warranted. We would view as wildly irrational any person (or organization) who, when making decisions, ignored all beliefs that he or she could not prove. When evaluating administrative rationality, we must give some credence to the administrators' feel for the system they administer. How much? is a question of more than routine difficulty.[10]

The transmission of clinical intelligence, the experience or wisdom of the gifted adjudicator, is especially troublesome for SSA. That sort of information is both generated and communicated in most organizations through personal contacts, often across formal organizational lines. But because disability examiners are locked into state bureaucracies, the usual means for creating these important lateral contacts— common training programs, rotation, special working groups—are unavailable. The absence of effective lateral contact networks puts an enormous, perhaps impossible, burden on the hierarchial supervisory structure.[11]

## The Subversiveness of Organizations

The preceding discussion treats SSA as having no goals of its own. Under conditions of limited capacity it strives to discern the ambiguous goals of the Social Security program and to implement those goals in the context of uncertain facts. From this perspective, much administrative action that is on its face wrongheaded can be explained as a valiant attempt to cope with inherent difficulties. Yet surely this Panglossian view of administration is unrealistic. Organizations and the bureaucrats who inhabit them have their own goals, desires, motivations. Action that seemingly contradicts statutory purposes may be taken not only because those purposes are vague and their application uncertain, but also because it is in the interests either of the organization or of particular decisionmakers to behave in that fashion.

First, the organization's interests. The notion of the organization having goals or interests is, of course, somewhat metaphorical. Those interests are difficult to distinguish from the professional interests of top management or perhaps the long-term interests of the bureau's employees generally. Yet there is a technical literature that treats of the bureau's utility function,[12] and it is habitual at a commonsense level to

10. *See* Glazer, *Should Judges Administer Social Services?* 50 The Public Interest 64 (1978).

11. *See generally*, J. GALBRAITH, DESIGNING COMPLEX ORGANIZATIONS (1973).

12. *See, e.g.*, W. NISKANEN, BUREAUCRACY AND REPRESENTATIVE GOVERNMENT (1971).

view organizations, if not as having goals of their own, at least as behaving *as if* they did.[13] Moreover, to the degree that bureaucratic goals have reality they may conflict with the achievement of the legislature's programmatic purposes.

A number of plausible goals might be posited for any organization: to preserve itself; to increase its status and wealth and, through their attachment to the organization, the status and/or wealth of its managers and employers. And, of course, these high-order goals may be translated into a series of lower-level, bureaucratic imperatives: stay out of political trouble; protect the bureau's reputation; develop and market programs or administrative activities that increase the budget; demand more highly qualified (higher status) staff; or identify the bureau with the positions of important political actors. The critical question is to what degree the pursuit of organizational goals undermines the pursuit of program goals.

Such undermining might easily occur in the administration of the disability program. For example, organizational aims might explain why SSA has never strongly advocated federalization of the state agency process and why it has been extremely cautious in developing precise regulatory criteria for disability decisionmaking. Federalization would bring into SSA an army of low-level administrators—the state adjudicatory staff—that would add nothing to its prestige and much to its housekeeping chores. Moreover, continued postfederalization difficulties with consistency, error rates, delays, and the like (which could certainly be expected) would no longer be explicable, at least in part, in terms of the difficulties of administration when confronted with divided authority and the politics of federalism.

Similarly, the attempt to resolve the ambiguities and inconsistencies of the disability program's goals through regulatory precision may impose enormous political costs on the agency. Conflict over goals will become explicit as regulatory rationalization exalts one policy basis for the disability benefits program over others. SSA will be unable to present itself as all things to all interests, and those in the Congress and the affected populations who perceive threats to their interests will strike back. It might be difficult for the agency to emerge from the

13. The classic treatment is A. Downs, Inside Bureaucracy (1957).

political battles that would ensue with its prestige enhanced or, indeed, intact.[14]

The consideration of these hypothetical bureaucratic motives for two of SSA's historic administrative postures certainly cautions against ready acceptance of that posture as programmatically, as distinguished from bureaucratically, rational. Yet, as always, the situation is murky. To some degree bureaucratic and programmatic goals coincide. Surely regulatory precision may oversimplify standards and cause the pursuit of the social goals of the disability program, in their full and sometimes baffling complexity, to be lost. And engaging in political battles as a matter of daily routine may both impair the integrity of the regulatory effort and demoralize administration of the program in all its dimensions.

Waging political battles also takes resources away from the pursuit of other goals. Such battles should not be undertaken unless prospects for success are reasonably good and the policy benefits outweigh the political and resource costs. As one looks at the federalization issue, the net programmatic gains do not strongly support the suggestion that SSA should lead a fight for federalization. For one thing, federalization of the state agency personnel would cause a substantial one-time increase in the number of federal employees and would increase the size of the SSA work force by over 10 percent. Increasing the size of the federal bureaucracy has never been a politically popular move.

There is also state politics to be considered. State employees, particularly those high in the administrative hierarchy, know and understand the politics of their state government and are threatened by a shift to a political arena that is less familiar. They can thus be expected to wage some political campaign to maintain the status quo. And, of course, the simple shift from a state to a federal agency would cause problems for other state officials by interfering with existing patronage arrangements. One should not forget that state civil service is not a simple meritocracy; and that it matters to someone *who* decides procurement questions—ranging from leases to computers to ballpoint pens.

Finally, there is a sense in which the medical community distrusts direct federal relationships that might bypass existing structures orga-

14. For a parallel story concerning the National Labor Relations Board *see* Bernstein, *The NLRB's Adjudication-Rulemaking Dilemma Under the Administrative Procedure Act*, 79 Yale L.J. 571 (1970).

nized along state lines. Every federal involvement is still seen by many in the medical community as an incremental step toward "socialized medicine." These concerns about the medical community's reactions are, of course, quite vague and elusive, but they may nevertheless be realistic. It may be *programmatically* rational for SSA to choose to define agency valor in relation to the federalization issue by its "better part" (that is, discretion), which ironically, and in another sense, is what many believe maximizes bureaucratic utility anyway.

Other examples of the problematics of organizationally rational behavior abound. SSA has several hundred employees whose sole job is to respond to congressional inquiries about cases. In addition, the agency notifies inquiring congressmen of an award before it notifies the claimant. How does this activity promote any of the goals of the disability program? One would have to answer that the relationship is, at best, mysterious. Congressional inquiries almost never provide any information about claims, and response to them is pure cost. Indeed, there is some evidence that a congressional inquiry slows down the processing of a claim. And the practice of giving congressmen first crack at notifying successful claimants certainly does nothing for SSA's reputation for impartiality. As one would expect, congressmen and congressional staffs claim that they have been effective in their intervention with SSA, which is to say that they have somehow managed to secure favored treatment for their constituents.

Why does SSA persist in the practice of responding to congressional inquiries? The obvious answer is that it believes it politically wise to do so. Congressional inquiries in some ways interfere with the rational functioning of the program. But because many congressmen view such casework as the single most important activity in support of their incumbency, the interference that might be expected were SSA to attempt to stop the practice might be infinitely more threatening to program effectiveness.

## The Zero-Sum Bureaucratic Game

A standard beginning to instructional sessions on the use of simple computers is the arresting statement, "The machine is stupid; it won't give you back anything that you haven't put into it." In short, you can tell the machine what to think about and how to think about it and it will carry out your instructions precisely. Put in that way, the limitations of the computer brain are also its virtues. It is fully controllable. It will not interject a different value set or skewed factual perceptions between its controller and the desired outputs.

With people, on the other hand, there is no strict relationship between input and output. Or, perhaps more precisely, one cannot be certain what the relationship will be between any particular input and a decisional output. There is no way to account for the preexisting "inputs" of either facts or logic and, hence, for their effects on the eventual decisions that are made. If we believed that disability decisions should be wholly controllable by careful manipulation of the logical and factual input into decisionmaking, we would use computers rather than human beings to make disability decisions. In part, we do not use machines because we doubt our ability to anticipate all the values, logical techniques, and factual requirements that together will determine the outcome of particular disability claims. A person, unlike a machine, can respond to enormous ranges of variation in the way that information is presented or organized and can reorder decision processes or priority rules when the circumstances require it. Moreover, many of these judgments are of a qualitative sort that resists sensitive translation into the binary language of electrical circuitry.

Our preference for human rather than machine forms of thinking in disability adjudication does not, however, imply that we do not wish to control the range of creativity or discretion that is exercised in any particular case. For without appropriate controls the adjudicatory system can make no progress toward mimicking the politically and legally preferred model of administrative action—instrumental rationality. We want discretion to be constrained by programmatically specified values and a perception of true states of the world.

In exercising control over human adjudicators, the administrators at SSA (or any adjudicatory system) must contend with two types of human rationality that may skew decisionmaking about disability claims in inappropriate directions, that is, directions that depart from official policy.

One type of rationality might be called *contextual rationality*. Human decisionmakers appear in context; they have personal intellectual and emotional histories and they operate in an environment that is richer in behavioral signals than the hundreds of pages of instructions in the Disability Insurance State Manual (DISM). The decisionmaker's history and personal involvement, of course, are to some degree defined by professional association with the Social Security system. The task is to screen out inappropriate contextual influences.

Without belaboring the point, we can mention three critical problems of contextual rationality that impinge on the Social Security structure. The first is how to control decisionmakers who exercise their discretionary judgment within the context of their own personal value set. One of the commonest definitions of an arbitrary adjudicatory system is one in which the person who decides a particular controversy is more important than the merits of the case. In order to avoid arbitrariness SSA must somehow constrain the personal values of its deciders by the institutional values of the system. We have already noted, for example, the enormous difficulty SSA is experiencing with its administrative law judges, who have a statutory guarantee of independence. As one state agency employee put it to the Congress, "The system encourages them to be Robin Hoods and give away the king's deer."[15] That anonymous commentator failed to mention, of course, that state agency personnel aren't exactly making gifts out of their own forest either. Indeed, they are paid by the baron (with the king's money) to give the king's deer to the baron's vassals. Which brings us to the second contextual problem: state agency decisionmakers operate in an organizational context that includes much more than their agency's contractual attachment to the federal Social Security system. SSA must somehow attempt to control for the inappropriate effects of local and state politics and bureaucratic structure.

Third, the Social Security system obviously makes use of existing professions, particularly the medical profession. It must therefore contend with divergences between the aims of a treatment-oriented medical culture and the disability program's adjudicatory culture—a culture constructed around discrete decisions concerning claims of entitlement. Each of these contextual interfaces, the personal, the political, and the professional, can present quite perplexing problems for the design and operation of the DI adjudicatory process.

A second form of intrusive human rationality might be termed *game rationality*. People have personal preferences and values which they seek to maximize in relation to those of the other actors in their

15. Issue Paper, *supra* note 7, at 35.

environment. When the satisfaction of their preferences conflicts with the satisfaction of the preferences of others, they will (altruism aside) attempt to maximize their own utilities. This is a zero-sum game in which there are winners and losers, and one of the losers may be the program.

The management of the adjudicatory system must thus contend with the games bureaucrats play. SSA adjudicatory personnel, like everyone else, will sometimes wish to avoid work, to avoid stress, and to avoid threatening supervision. Arguably the SSA appellate review mechanism permits employees to exercise all these preferences at once. If the disability adjudicator grants a claim there is no appellate supervision; less work, therefore, need be devoted to justification and documentation of the original decision; and the adjudicator avoids the psychological stress of denying an often poignant plea for help.

If these sorts of motivations to grant claims are in fact operative, then SSA should have a very serious interest in devising techniques outside the appellate review structure to counterbalance the tendency of individual adjudicators to make themselves better off at the expense of payroll taxpayers. From this perspective, Congress's recent directive that SSA review a high proportion of state agency awards might be viewed as an attempt to balance an inherent systemic skew toward granting claims.

## SHOULD WE DECLARE BUREAUCRATIC RATIONALITY "PERMANENTLY DISABLED"?

A disability administrator faced with these problems—value indeterminancy, factual ambiguity, and organizational stress—might respond in many ways (suicide perhaps). One is to reassert the ideal of bureaucratic rationality by ignoring system dissonance. Clear choices can be made among competing program goals. Statutory vagueness can be replaced by regulatory precision. The complexities and uncertainties of factual contexts can be transformed by rules of relevance, presumptions in case of doubt, and objective proxies for the unknown or unknowable. Organizational slack can be reduced both by clear rules and by intensive oversight reinforced by objective performance standards. The system can be made controllable within the limits of some residual intractability of the human materials. But should it be? Would such a pattern of implementation realize the ideal of bureaucratic rationality by implementing the Social Security disability program? Or would it substantially transform it in the act of implementation and thereby ensure failure in its own terms? The answer is, of course, obvious. The techniques of rationalization suggested necessarily entail value choices (goal selection and systematic skewing of factual error), and the bureaucratic rationality model, because purely instrumental, provides no basis for making such choices. Attempting to make the program conform to the ideal type may simply redefine it in ways that we often associate with "bureaucracy" in its pejorative sense: a sense that connotes rigidity, narrowness, and perhaps the ultimate stupidity—forgetting what you were trying to accomplish. Bureaucratic rationality may not be permanently disabled, but it has determinable impairments. These weaknesses provide entry points for alternative conceptions of administrative justice— conceptions that in turn produce a compromised and sometimes uncontrollable system.

At the time of the adoption of the original OASI program it was proposed that decisionmaking on claims be undertaken by rotating boards of local, volunteer decisionmakers. The proposal was to set up something that looked rather like a cross between a civil jury and a draft board, institutions that clearly emphasize intuitive judgment and uncontrolled discretion. The proposal was ultimately discarded, but it reflects the sense of the designers of the initial retirement and survivors system that the question of access to publicly funded support was, even at the level of the individual case, in some sense a moral judgment about who *ought* to be supported at public expense.

The addition of the disability program to the Social Security scheme underscores that recognition. It is a part of the explicit political underpinning for the program that decisions in disability cases are individual. The question is not whether an average person with some set of relevant characteristics would be disabled, but whether *this* person, considering virtually all his or her life circumstances bearing on employment, is disabled. Such judgments will certainly never be fully controllable through skillful systems engineering.

To put the matter another way, there is some desire that adjudicative personnel exercise not only a relatively controllable systematic rationality but also a relatively uncontrollable intuitive rationality. By intuitive rationality I mean an exercise of judgment that is not explained, or perhaps explainable, through a reasoned connection of value premises and factual findings. These sorts of intuitive judgments are particularly common in personal relationships—choosing a friend or a lover or making decisions about familial well-being—but they are also fairly widespread in political and legal systems. The collective judgment of a legislature, for example, is rarely explained (nor do we expect it to be) in a detail that we think even remotely descriptive of the considerations that informed collective judgment. The decisions of juries are another familiar example from our legal system. Jury-style intuitive judgments are also highly likely in contexts other than formal trials where the choice between competing values is so distressing that it must be submerged or camouflaged in some way—situations that Calabresi and Bobbit have characterized as "Tragic Choices."

Indeed, quite often the allocation of decisionmaking to an intuitive decider signals the importance of value choice in the process of decisionmaking. We understand and expect that the decision will itself create or recognize values or preferences. This aspect of disability adjudication was previously identified as a major argument for structuring the process in accordance with traditional notions of adversary adjudication. But, allocations of power to intuitive decisionmaking bodies or decisionmakers also occur in situations in which the decision is recognized as involving some combination of science with "art" or "experience": situations that we have previously characterized as involving a professional judgment that cannot necessarily be fully explained through some linear logic that links previously specified goals with current factual findings.

This tension between systematic and intuitive rationality lies at the base of some of the perennial conundrums of disability administration. Critics have continuously complained, for example, that SSA has failed to specify adequately its policy through regulations that would control individual decisionmaking in DI cases. This is obviously a demand for systematic rationality. But it should be clear that any attempt to systematize decisionmaking through regulation necessarily involves both the construction of general categories and the specification of the effect of finding that a case fits into one or more of those categories. If that regulatory effort is effective, the individual decider will not be able to "do justice," all things considered.

It is also often said that it makes no sense to have a system in which different law is applied at the state agency level than at the hearing level, where the case is put before ALJs. State Disability Determination Service (DDS) personnel historically have been bound by much more detailed instructions in the DISM than those applicable to ALJs in subsequent hearings. This difference in the law to be applied is compounded by differences in the decisionmaking process. The ALJ sees and talks with the claimant, whereas state agency personnel rarely have personal contact and act almost exclusively on the basis of documentary evidence. What this suggests, of course, is that the ALJ, operating with less detailed instructions and a personalized process of decision, is expected to exercise a more intuitive judgment about the claim than are agency personnel. The multilevel decisional structure is thus in some sense inconsistent; it opts for systematic rationality at one level and intuitive rationality at the next. It fails to carry through the logic of bureaucratic rationality.

Yet, if one is at all skeptical about the possibility of operationalizing the instrumental rationality paradigm, this apparently inconsistent structure is not necessarily inappropriate. Some mixture of justice models and decisional techniques may be necessary to deal with the predictable failures of the systems engineers to fully rationalize bureaucratic implementation. Assuming for the moment that the appeal structure is a good mechanism for sorting out those claims that require individualized or intuitive attention, the question, then, is whether the qualifications for ALJs as compared to those for DDS personnel make the judges superior intuitive decisionmakers. That issue would depend in turn on how much of what type of intuition was desired and what types of personnel were thought to possess it. Reforms might include making ALJs more systematic, allowing disability examiners more intuitive discretion, using some combination of these techniques, changing the "sorting" mechanism, or using entirely different deciders.

## AN EMERGING CRITICAL STANCE

How should we summarize the evaluative posture implicit in the foregoing account of the problematics of bureaucratic rationality? First, this preliminary analysis suggests that an evaluation of the SSA adjudicatory process should recognize the necessity for administrative choices between, or for combinations of, alternative models of rationality— systematic versus intuitive rationality; satisficing versus optimizing;

creativity versus control. The discussion of instrumental rationality has re-created in slightly different terms a number of the tensions between the bureaucratic rationality, professional judgment, and moral entitlements models of justice that were encountered in chapter 2. Second, there are special organizational problems to be confronted. The limits on organizational competence, plus rational motivational forces operating on personnel and on the administrative organization as a whole, may divert attention from the pursuit of program goals. Finally, we noted in connection with some exemplary policy issues—federalization, policy clarification, and congressional inquiries—the political dimension of SSA decisionmaking. These epistemological, organizational, and political difficulties counsel modesty, at the very least, when evaluating SSA's attempts to operate in a bureaucratically rational mode. Life in a bureaucracy is very complicated.

The realization that the ideal of instrumentally rational administration cannot be achieved does not justify a resigned cynicism, however, only a more balanced idealism. Our normative questions need only take account of a complex and compromised reality. In the pages that follow they will, therefore, take something like the following forms: Have reasonable choices been made, given the complex, compromised, and evolving goals of the program and the difficulties that beset factfinding? How well does the system encourage its members to resist the temptation to put the pursuit of personal or institutional preferences before implementation of the program? As the agency looks back on its actions and makes use of its experience, does it develop both more coherent policy and more effective administrative processes? Does SSA accept a primary responsibility for the development of a unique form of bureaucratic justice? Or does it merely reflect the shifting political forces that cluster around the disability program? That the quality of administration can be appraised only in such terms implies that the issues are issues of judgment and balance, but it clearly does not imply that administration cannot be better or worse. Before appraising the SSA disability program in more detail, however, we must address one final, complicating dimension of administrative decisionmaking—the question of costs.

# 4 · How Much Are Good Decisions Worth?

The discussion of rationality in chapter 3 was untroubled by questions of cost. But obviously, in the absence of innovation, one gets more accurate decision processes only at an increased price. Adjudicative errors are themselves costly, but we are not prepared to pay literally any price to avoid them. How much should we be willing to pay to decide disability claims correctly? And in what coin are those costs measured? Indeed, what does it mean to talk about administrative efficiency in the context of a program whose decisional outputs cannot be known to be correct or incorrect? Can one sensibly ask how much we want to pay for a product that cannot be identified? In addition, are there not other dimensions of quality decisionmaking that should be taken into account when decision processes are designed? What about timelines, uniformity, and a sense of fair treatment? Might not delay, inconsistency, and a sense of injustice be costly effects of a decision process that seeks accuracy? And, if so, shouldn't the design of the system seek to minimize these costs as well?

But one question at at time. Let me begin by talking generally about the problem of assessing the efficiency of an administrative system that implements policy by accurately adjudicating claims for benefits. We can in that way creep up on the question of how much direct administrative expense is justifiably incurred to correctly decide a disability claim. That rather straightforward question—one that Congress and SSA must face annually—is hard enough. I will then introduce the problematics of accuracy and the range of nonmonetizable costs that might emerge as incidental effects of a particular form of accuracy-seeking adjudicatory process.[1]

---

1. This chapter draws extensively from prior publications that explore the same issues in different contexts and, occasionally, in more technical detail. *See*, MASHAW ET AL.,

## THE JUSTICE MARKET

In civil litigation, private investment in accurate fact-finding and appropriate application of legal rules can be viewed as being mediated by a price system not unlike the one that operates in other markets. The smooth functioning of the litigation market is, thus, the goal of an efficiency-oriented public policy.[2] In a commercial contract dispute, for example, the provision of a highly formal dispute resolution process—judicial trial—may be a satisfactory public policy. Parties may invest in the use of that process in discrete parts (threats, pleadings, motions, discovery), meanwhile retaining the option to compromise or to go to arbitration or mediation at any stage. Moreover, the investment in the various components of formal trial process can be calibrated in terms of the predicted value to the party of that particular component. In short, expenditure on the dispute resolution process relates fairly directly to the willingness of individual combatants to pay process costs. And willingness to pay reflects judgments concerning the economic value to be obtained from some particular payment. Litigants will not spend more than a claim (or a related set of claims) is worth to get it decided.

To be sure, the judicially supervised litigation process is often decried as cumbersome and expensive. But that may not be very different from complaints that automobiles are too expensive. Both court litigation and autos are available when nothing else will do. If disputants or travelers want to allocate scarce resources to other things, they choose less expensive alternatives. And ultimately the amounts of litigation and automobiles that are produced reflect these individual market choices. This is not to say that markets for litigation (or motor cars) are perfect. Only that they produce a broadly acceptable measure of how much society is willing to pay to resolve certain types of disputes. To the extent that deviations from market results are desired, the process can then be modified by subsidies to, or constraints on, particular choices.

---

SOCIAL SECURITY HEARINGS AND APPEALS (1978); *Administrative Due Process as Social Cost Accouting*, 9 Hofstra L. Rev. 1423 (1981); *Administrative Due Process: The Quest for a Dignitary Theory*, 61 Boston Univ. L. Rev. 885 (1981); *How Much of What Quality: A Comment on Conscientious Procedural Design*, 65 Cornell L. Rev. 823 (1980); and *The Supreme Court's Due Process Calculus for Administrative Adjudication in Mathews v. Eldridge: Three Factors in Search of a Theory of Value*, 44 U. Chi. L. Rev. 28 (1976).

2. *See generally*, Posner, *An Economic Approach to Legal Procedure and Judicial Administration*, 2 J. Leg. Stud. 399 (1973).

However imperfect, even this base of market process and individual investment decisions is largely unavailable for, indeed inappropriate to, the determination of an acceptable level of expenditure for DI decision-making. To ask how much a disabled person is willing to pay to get the government to fork over on a valid claim is not only crass, it is obviously misplaced: it substitutes social insecurity for Social Security. The program after all presumes that general social welfare is enhanced by public support of the disabled. In such a program the other party to disputes, the government, is interested in seeing valid claims paid, not in maintaining the largest possible balance in the trust fund. Nor should the government's decisions to make investments in processes that might avoid payments on invalid claims be self-interested or market-oriented decisions. They also should be decisions directed at maximizing general welfare and thus, indirectly, the welfare of the claimants who are the government's technical adversaries.

At some point, or with respect to certain types of process, the administrative or legislative decision may be to allocate resources to the resolution of disability claims, at least in part, in accordance with willingness to pay. But the starting point is a collective judgment concerning the costs and benefits of alternative structures and processes for administrative determination of eligibility—not a free market for litigation. The basic rationale for the program is distributive justice, not allocational efficiency.

## THE COSTS OF ERROR

How then should we begin to estimate the appropriate level of government expenditure on the DI decision process? One possibility is by asking, "How much is a disability claim worth?" The answer is on the average about 30,000 current dollars.[3] Is it then worth $30,000 per claim not to make an error? If so, enormous increases in SSA's budget for DI administration would seem warranted. These $30,000 claims are being decided, on the average, for less than $500 per claim.[4] At the

---

3. *See* General Accounting Office, Report on Controls Over Medical Examinations Necessary for Better Determinations of Disability by the Social Security Administration, H.R.D. 79–119 (Oct. 9, 1979).

4. The total administrative expense allocable to the disability program for 1978 was $327,000,000. H.R. Rep. No. 100, 96th Cong., 1st Sess. 19 (1979). During this same period, the program processed 1,300,000 cases. Dividing the cost by the number of cases

current cost/benefit ratio (1:60), a change in the decision process that increased accuracy by 1 percent would justify a 60 percent increase in administrative expense. If this is the proper approach to determining the appropriate level of administrative expense in the DI program, there is a lot of room for high-cost improvements in the decision process (assuming, of course, that improvements can be identified).

But this suggested approach is troublesome. We do not observe Congress or SSA eagerly throwing large pots of money at the DI decision process. The persons who are the most knowledgeable about the system do not seem to perceive large gains resulting from modest increases in the accuracy of system performance. The rationale for this perception may be attributable to the recognition, at the budgetary level, of a basic reality of disability adjudication. Functional ability or disability is a continuum; only the decisions are bipolar. And, on reflection, a decision classifying a decathlon gold medalist as disabled or a patient in a quasi-vegetative state as not disabled seems somehow a bigger, more costly error than the potentially erroneous assignment of the perennial marginal case (say a fifty-five-year-old, semiskilled white male with high blood pressure and chronic lower back syndrome) to either category. We need somehow to develop an approach that recognizes the differential costs of error (or benefits of accuracy).

Such an approach is possible, although certainly not without serious difficulties. Presumably, DI claims can be placed on two related scales that reflect the social benefits and social costs of disability decisions. First, the value of giving an individual disability benefits is greatest with respect to individuals who are severely handicapped and for whom work, were it possible at all, would add to the pain and frustration that accompany severe physical or emotional illnesses. The social value of making payments to these claimants is obviously great. Such payments respond to the core humanitarian instincts of the social insurance program. This social value of making disability payments declines as individuals suffer less severe handicaps, which impose lesser costs on work effort. In the limit, no social value at all would be assigned to

---

gives an average case processing cost of about $300. In fact, since the administrative costs of the program include expenditures for items other than the processing of claims, this figure is somewhat high. However, this analysis assumes a more conservative $500 average case processing cost.

disability payments to an individual with no physical or emotional illness.

The second scale on which claims can be placed is that of social cost. These costs include lost productivity when people leave the work force to receive disability payments, as well as the demoralization that taxpayers experience when forced to contribute to the support of others. Presumably, claimants would occupy roughly the same place on the two scales. Those who are most deserving, that is, those with respect to whom we derive the most satisfaction from paying benefits, are also those from whom society loses least when they leave the work force. And their support at public expense imposes very small psychic costs on taxpayers.

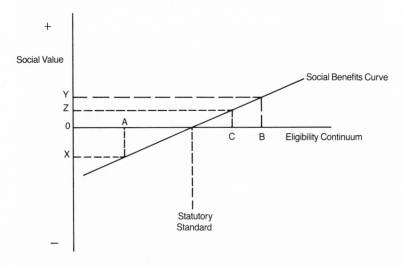

The accompanying figure is a graphic depiction of these combined scales.[5] The net social benefit curve rises from left to right as we consider persons who have more and more severe conditions. The intersection of the social benefits curve with the horizontal axis is taken

5. Note that both the horizontal and vertical axes employ a cardinal, but undisclosed ordering. One way to imagine the construction of the horizontal axis is a perfect plebiscite in which voters assign "deservingness" numbers on a scale of 1–100 to well-defined clusters of relevant personal characteristics. The task of administration is then to assign individual claimants to the correct characteristics-cluster and to determine whether the

to be the statutory definition of disability. To the right of the intersection the value of making the payment exceeds the social costs; the disability program defines individuals falling in this segment of the graph as disabled in order to capture these net benefits. To the left of the intersection social costs exceed social benefits and the individual is classified as not disabled in order to avoid these net social costs.

The implications of this analysis for the problem of appropriate administrative costs are rather straightforward. If a claimant "really" at position A is found by SSA to be at position B, there is a net social loss (OX). The same is true for the reverse type of error (OY). And obviously the forgone benefits in the latter case are less than those associated with a similar error concerning a claimant "really" at position C (OZ). Presumably the more costly the potential error, the more we are willing to pay to avoid it.

Although this analysis responds in a not unrealistic way to the political judgments that seem to underlie transfer programs like DI, it does so at a significant cost in operational content. Indeed, we have lapsed into the rather metaphoric language of social utility—a commodity that not only has no dollar prices attached to it, but which also assumes that individual preferences can be aggregated in some unspecified way. This approach also requires that we be able to (1) identify errors, (2) determine their relative magnitudes, and (3) assess their respective social values. These are tall orders indeed. Moreover, once we have done this the social value of accuracy will emerge in a different currency ("utils," "ergs," or whatever) from that of administrative costs ($).

Yet the analysis is not without important implications for the management of the DI system of adjudication. First, it suggests that the question of the *relative* costs of erroneous denials (false negatives) and erroneous grants (false positives) must be explicitly addressed. Any attempt to eliminate either type of error will induce errors of the opposite type. Hence, a move in the direction of eliminating false negatives—for example, by relaxing standards of proof with respect to some criterion of eligibility—will induce some additional number of

---

cluster falls below or above the score that has been determined to be necessary for eligibility. The vertical scale is constructed in the same way, this time asking voters to indicate the intensity of their joy or unhappiness at the prospect of a public transfer of a specified size being made to a person occupying determinate places on the horizontal scale.

false positives. The converse is equally true. In order for such a change to be justified, therefore, one would have to believe (direct administrative and other costs aside) that the total value of false negatives prevented (the number of errors prevented times their respective social value) would exceed the total value of the false positives induced.

This computation is not a simple matter, but it is not impossible to make some headway when considering it. One might ask, for example, whether the system is one that has a strong preference for one type of error as against the other. (The criminal justice system, for example, strongly prefers false negatives, whereas the process of medical diagnosis is structured to reflect a primary concern with avoiding that type of error.) My reading of the history of the disability program, analysis of its procedural and evidentiary rules, and observations of its operations reveal no strong reasons to believe that either type of error should be viewed as systematically more costly than the other. Caution and benevolence have, so far as I can tell, equal status. For that reason, the social welfare function graphed in the figure is equidistant from the horizontal axis on each side of the eligibility standard. This conclusion makes the cost/benefit calculation for any proposed action more difficult. A strong skew in the values would permit many rough judgments that are otherwise unavailable. Nevertheless, the *absence* of a skew has important policy implications: it counsels against succumbing to one or the other of the strong and competing political demands for generosity and for stringency.

This notion of the relative costs of various types of errors has another interesting implication. Structures, processes, or decision rules that tend to eliminate either type of error near the poles of the eligibility continuum are presumptively attractive. They should be adopted unless there is some reason to believe that equal and opposite effects will occur or that a very large number of errors will be induced in marginal cases. Although these sorts of estimates are sometimes difficult to make with confidence, certain types of error-saving devices, for example, some objective and easily applied standards of disability or nondisability, hold out the prospect for relatively nonproblematic gains.

## MARGINAL CASES, INCONSISTENCY, AND THE PROBLEMATICS OF ERROR IDENTIFICATION

The notion that marginal cases have low error costs may be to some degree undermined by the problem of inconsistency. Summing the costs of individual marginal errors may understate the true costs of error in marginal cases. There should be added to that cost, it might be argued, a more general demoralization cost that reflects our disappointment or anxiety when confronted with the inability of the system to make accurate determinations. That such costs exist is evident from the enormous concern with inconsistency expressed in prior studies of the DI system[6] and, indeed, with respect to adjudicatory systems generally. If these costs are associated with what we have previously termed *marginal cases*, then the costs of error in those cases may yet be quite large.

But there is a flaw in the argument. Demoralization costs do not arise from observing the error-proneness of the process. Demoralization results rather from the ease with which errors may be assigned to decisions by observers, or participants, who would have decided the case differently. Whether errors in fact occurred cannot be known definitively. This logical flaw does not, however, undermine the notion that we should be concerned about consistency. Indeed, it suggests an opportunity for nonproblematic gains. For if there were some device for eliminating the appearance of inconsistency with respect to cases that cannot be known to be accurately decided anyway, then demoralization costs resulting from inconsistency might be eliminated with no observed increase in error costs.

Unfortunately, the available techniques for producing consistency in decisions concerning close cases may require that we incur other types of costs. These techniques seem either to impair rationality or to infringe on other values or both. One might imagine, for example, the development of relatively objective standards for deciding even close cases in the DI system. (Indeed, as I shall discuss in more detail subsequently, SSA has recently adopted such standards.) Claimants could be assigned to categories with respect to age (18–44, 45–60, 61 and above, for example), residual functional capacity (for example, sedentary, light, medium, or heavy work as defined by the *Dictionary of Occupational Titles*), education (for example, illiterate, primary grades completed, high school completed), and work experience (for example,

6. *See, e.g.*, R. Dixon, Social Security Disability and Mass Justice 51–92 (1973); Comptroller General of the United States General Accounting Office, A Plan for Improving the Disability Determination Process by Bringing it Under Complete Federal Management Should be Developed (1978).

unskilled, semiskilled, skilled, again as defined by the *Dictionary of Occupational Titles*). These categories could then be combined in a grid such that each set of four categorical positions yielded a determinate conclusion—disabled or not disabled.

The use of such a device might enormously increase the consistency of determinations. But its value cannot be assessed without considering the obvious costs of such a system from other perspectives. For one thing, such a system will be viewed by some, perhaps many, as making irrational overgeneralizations. The grid is a form of stereotyping that inevitably makes large differences in outcomes (grant or denial) turn on insignificant differences in the relevant facts (being forty-five rather than forty-four, for example, or having a ninth- rather than an eighth-grade education). In addition, the symbolism of such a set of categories contradicts the notion of individualized determination. To the extent that such an ideal informs judgment concerning the acceptability of the decision process, the grid approach has substantial costs.

A similar difficulty attends utilization of another major device for limiting inconsistent results. Statistical information reveals a substantial disparity in the grant and denial rates of individual deciders and state agencies.[7] These disparities could be eliminated or sharply constrained by a quota system. State agencies or individual disability examiners could be given a grant rate (say 35 percent ± 5 percent) for each time period (say a month). Awards would then be made on a comparative or relative basis and award rate disparities would virtually disappear.

Such systems are widely used to reduce grading disparities in educational institutions. Yet a quota system also seems inconsistent with the basic goals of the DI program. The promise of Social Security is insurance against certain potential or inevitable hazards. And, while we may suspect that all DI adjudicators decide cases in terms of some implicit "curve" describing the relative deservingness of claimants, a process that made this idea explicit would be seen to conflict with the statutory policy of individual entitlement. It would introduce a symbolic competition among participants for benefits. Such a competition

7. In 1974 the staff of the Subcommittee on Social Security reported that state agency denial rates varied between 34 and 60 percent; ALJ denial rates ranged from 30 to 90 percent. Committee Staff Report in the Disability Insurance Program, Committee on Ways and Means, 43rd Cong., 2nd Sess., 5, n, 3 (1974).

may be appropriate in other adjudicatory contexts, FCC licensing, for example, or the award of government contracts, but it is hardly appropriate to the Social Security program.

To summarize, concern with the costs of inconsistency to some degree confuses the policy implications of an analysis of the costs and benefits of avoiding erroneous determinations. A focus on consistency suggests the potential costliness of "errors" in marginal decisions whereas a focus on the relative costs of error suggested that marginal decisions were unimportant. And while perceptions of inconsistency seem, on reflection, to be independent of the existence of errors, attempts to constrain inconsistency inevitably entail the costs of abandoning symbolically important program goals. Estimating the costs and benefits of devices for controlling inconsistency seems even more problematic than computing the net social welfare gains (or losses) from policies aimed at reducing error.

## THE ELUSIVE VALUE OF "PROCESS VALUES"

The nonerror costs of perceived inconsistency are but one type of decision-process cost that may have no direct relationship to the capacity of the system to produce accurate results. The regulatory grid or matrix solution to inconsistency, for example, might eliminate perceptions of inequality but would raise other issues concerning the individualization of the decision process. Indeed, we might generate a host of intuitively plausible process concerns that are not captured simply by the pursuit of accurate adjudication. If a decision process strives to be efficient, it must attend to these potential process externalities, to the values and disvalues that may be generated by the form of its pursuit of correctness. And where accuracy is impossible, or at least not demonstrable, the net social value of decisionmaking may turn critically on an assessment of "process value"[8] costs and benefits.

We cannot here attempt to fully elaborate what these process values might be. To some degree they are captured by features of the adversary

8. The term is Robert Summers's: *See* Summers, *Evaluating and Improving Legal Processes—A Plea for Process Values*, 60 Cornell L. Rev. 1 (1974). For other literature in a similar vein *see* Michelman, *Formal and Associational Aims in Procedural Due Process*, in DUE PROCESS, NOMOS XVIII, at 126 (J. Pennock RV. Chapman eds. 1977); Saphire, *Specifying Due Process Values: Toward A More Responsive Approach to Procedural Protection*, 127 U. Pa. L. Rev. 111 (1978).

process paradigm—party control and participation, individualization, strict equality of access, restraints on invasions of privacy, and transparency (notice of all opposing claims and facts, the giving of reasons)—a paradigm that supports the basic liberal values of individuality, autonomy, and self-respect. Rejection of the adversary adjudication paradigm necessarily entails nonsupport of some of these values, but they nevertheless retain vitality in a system pursuing bureaucratic rationality. Indeed, their association with adversary process is not indisputable.

## Equality

Strict equality of access to the decisionmaker in adversary systems, for example, assures equality only in a formal sense. A number of contextual factors may contribute to material or substantial inequality in the position of adversaries. The simplest difficulty involves the situation of adversaries who have different material resources with which to wage a courtroom or administrative battle. And it is not always the poor who are at a disadvantage in this respect. The availability of free legal resources to very low income persons may permit them to spend considerably more than a claim is really worth, thereby disadvantaging an adversary who is paying his or her own legal expenses.

Adversary procedure may also impose sharply different costs on the two parties to litigation. The ability of both sides to question any witness, for example, may so increase the cost of loss of privacy for one side (for example, rape victims) or so increase the risk of loss of reputation (for example, doctors involved in medical malpractice suits) that the adversary process becomes not an equal contest but a device for leveraging the position of one of the parties. Finally, the dynamics of adversary process may advantage certain sorts of claims in relation to opposing claims. Oral examination and cross-examination of witnesses, for example, is a much better device for developing the weaknesses, gaps, ambiguities, or uncertainties surrounding a proposed decision than it is for portraying the general scientific or commonsense notions that would support it. Adversary process accentuates the negative. Given these difficulties of furthering equality through adversary presentation, one should certainly be suspicious of general conclusions that urge adversariness as a preferred approach to equality as a process value.

More importantly for present purposes, equality has some quite sensible implications for nonadversary process. For example, if one assumes an essentially investigatory bureaucratic process in which the decisionmaker also has full responsibility for the development of the evidence, one would nevertheless believe that the different persons involved in different cases should have equal effort devoted to the collection of evidence and consideration of the outcome of their respective cases. Thus critics have been concerned upon discovering that there are substantial differences in the medical resources (decisional and developmental) devoted to cases in different state agencies or within state agencies, depending upon the decisionmaker involved. Although this inequality may be imperceptible to claimants in particular cases, as viewed by an outside observer it is certainly a blemish on the procedural fairness of the system as a whole. If the disparity were revealed to claimants whose claims received relatively modest effort, they would certainly feel that they had been treated unfairly—as being worth less than someone whose claim had been vigorously prosecuted.

Moreover, there is always the danger that investigatory decisionmakers will tailor their investigation of claims to fit stereotypes such as race, sex, age, or type of impairment. The stereotype will serve as a presumption for or against an award, and effort will be skewed toward supporting that prejudgment of the claim. Controlling for this type of inequality in development is quite difficult. One might specify rigorously the bits of evidence to be collected in each claim, and to that degree treat all cases alike. But claims require more or different development depending upon what is revealed by each bit of evidence procured. Development decisions must be made incrementally and in the context of a particular claim. Thus the formal equality of uniform development would almost certainly induce radical substantive inequality in the development of different cases.

### Transparency

Obviously the transparency of a decision process—its openness and comprehensibility—will make a worthwhile contribution to the sense of self-respect of any participant in it. The hallmark of decision processes that we describe as Kafkaesque is the participants' ignorance. An important decision concerning their lives seems to hang in the balance, yet they have no idea what is relevant to the decision, who will make it, or, in the extreme case, what precisely the decision is about.[9] Kafkaesque procedures take away the participants' ability to engage in rational planning about their situation or to make informed choices among alternatives. The participant begins to see himself as an object, susceptible to infinite manipulation by "the system." In order to be spared this sense of alienation, participants must have adequate notice of the issues to be decided and of the evidence that is relevant to those issues, and information about how the decision process itself works. Moreover, there must be some guarantee, usually by articulation of the basis for the decision, that the issues, evidence, and process were in fact meaningful to the outcome.

Such values can easily be ignored in a decision process like that found in the Social Security system. Because the program has beneficent purposes and an investigatory decision process that accepts responsibility for both development and decision of claims, it is tempting to regard an informed claimant as quite unimportant to the result in a case. Indeed, given the nonadversary structure and the subjectivity of much of the evidence, transparency might be viewed as an open invitation to abuse by the well-informed malingerer. But to treat process transparency as unimportant or dangerous is to forget that informing claimants serves important process values, whatever the system's judgment may be of the accuracy-enhancing value of using the claimant as a source of relevant insight and information about his or her claim.

### Privacy

Disability claims raise many issues that claimants may wish to keep as private as possible. Psychological disorders or diseases of the bowels and urinary tract, for example, often engender an intense feeling of shame or humiliation when the claimant is required to discuss them. Similarly, the claimant's lack of education, inarticulateness, or unsuccessful work history may be subjects of acute sensitivity. Such claimants might well prefer a relatively impersonal decision process—one in which decisions are made by a remote bureaucracy on the basis of documentary evidence. Having a personal, face-to-face conversation

---

9. *See, e.g.,* F. Kafka, *The Trial* (3d ed. 1956). Kafka gained many of his impressions of administrative processes as a bureaucrat in an agency dispensing disability benefits. M. Brod, *Franz Kafka,* 79–84 (1970).

with even a sympathetic disability adjudicator or administrative law judge may be painful. Privacy concerns may partly explain applicants' decisions not to appeal, and if so, might well deter applications at the initial stages were those stages personalized, as many studies have recommended. Personal treatment is not necessarily an unmitigated benefit.

Additional privacy issues are raised by the disability adjudication process. In many cases, the critical evidence concerning the claimant's residual functional capacity is either missing or circumstantially unreliable. Yet the development of reliable and complete evidence would be enormously intrusive. Secret surveillance of the claimant's daily activities or some stressful or deceptive form of testing that could not be undermined by the claimant's motivation to understate his ability might be the only means of developing such evidence. The use of consultative medical examinations, in which the claimant is sent to a doctor of Social Security's choosing, is certainly less intrusive than surveillance or coercive functional testing. Yet even this process requires that claimants be examined by unfamiliar physicians who play no therapeutic or supportive role that might otherwise mitigate loss of privacy. The usual value of open procedures (that is, procedures open to the public as a guarantee against arbitrariness in a closed authority structure) is, from the perspective of the privacy issue, also problematic. Indeed, Social Security proceedings, because of the confidentiality of the information provided by claimants, are not open proceedings without the claimant's consent.

### Humaneness

Humane treatment in a decision process is as important as it is ambiguous. An adjudicatory system that is unconcerned with the humaneness of its process would rightly be regarded as obtuse and indecent. Yet whether one has been treated humanely in any encounter with other people or institutions seems to depend almost wholly on one's personal preferences. Should the Social Security system, for example, choose a process of decision that emphasizes the claimant's dependency and need? In some sense it is inhumane to focus attention on a claimant's impairment by employing a paternalistic decision process that treats his or her contribution to the decision as unimportant. Yet it seems similarly inhumane to treat handicapped persons as if they were unimpaired. A decision process that relied on claimants to function as unimpaired persons would ignore important aspects of their personality. And, obviously, people with similar medical difficulties may have differing preferences concerning treatment as an equal, self-reliant, rights-bearing citizen or as a client or patient who is dependent on the system's aid in processing his or her claim.

The complexity and sensitivity of dealing with another person as "a human being" may make the engineering of a truly humane decision process virtually impossible. Nonproblematic general policies such as the use of surnames and a general attitude of pleasantness and helpfulness should certainly by adopted, but the system will not thereby avoid the contrary perceptions that it is cold and uncaring and intrusive and meddlesome.

### Appropriate Symbolism

The notion that a decision process should be attentive to symbolism might be regarded as giving undue importance to the obviously vague and potentially trivial. Yet surely this overstates the case against a concern with the symbolic. Even if we were convinced that all of the cases going beyond the initial level of decision in the disability process were as appropriately granted as denied, we would nevertheless balk at a randomized decision process, such as the flipping of a coin. Although we may not be able to do much better than coin tossing—or to know that we are doing better—in our attempts to discriminate between the not-quite-disabled and the barely disabled, we would be offended by coin tossing as a decision process. Although neutral and randomized, such a decision process would be an affront to our sense that each case should be decided on its own merits, as well as to our notion of the seriousness of the decision that must be made in disability cases.

The notion of appropriate seriousness, nevertheless, has no very determinate consequences for the structure of the disability decision process. It may tell us that coin tossing is out but it can hardly tell us where to stop on the spectrum from whimsy to high seriousness, as one moves from tossing coins to public referenda or to de novo hearings before the Supreme Court.

The symbolism of the decisional system also affects our willingness to treat decisions as final and legitimate. For certain sorts of decisions, for example, we are prepared to give finality and legitimacy to professional judgment. We may want to get more than one professional opinion; but if they coincide we are satisfied that an appropriate expertise has been applied to the problem. In other situations we prefer a social judgment and give, for example, finality and legitimacy to decisions of a jury composed of a small, randomized sample of our fellow citizens. Elsewhere we may want the symbolism of the court—nonexpert but neutral and detached in the way a jury might not be. In all these cases our choice is influenced by complex relationships among the symbolism of the decider, the type of decision to be made, and the ways in which judge or jury or professional processes of decisionmaking support other process values or preferred forms of rationality.

An investigatory system must also somehow deal with the problem of implicit adversariness. The disability decision process is explicitly non-adversary; no one ever directly represents only the interests of the government (or of FICA taxpayers) in protecting the trust fund. Moreover, by policy and practice disability adjudicators at every level, including ALJs, accept a responsibility for developing the necessary evidence for decision of a claim. Yet it is equally true that the system presumes some responsibility on the part of the claimant to pursue his or her own claim and to provide the evidentiary basis for decision. Moreover, it is certainly the perception of claimants who are denied benefits at the initial level that they are in a contest with a government bureaucracy that disagrees with their position.

In this contest there is no opportunity to negotiate a middle ground or alternative arrangement that would suit the interests and understanding of both parties. The game is zero-sum. Either the claimant gets payments and the government is out the money or the government keeps the money and the claimant gets nothing. In this context, it is quite easy for claimants to believe that investigative decisionmakers, employed by the government, are in fact in the business of upholding the government's prior position. And, if that were their goal, the claimant is then in an obviously unequal position, both in terms of expertise about the system and in terms of access to the decisionmaker.

Thus, even though SSA has rightly rejected construction of a process wholly in terms of professional or adversary models of justice, that rejection has costs. Those costs might nevertheless be somewhat ameliorated by the way the bureaucratic process is structured. SSA can, as we shall examine in more detail in chapter 10, seek to enhance the role of the medical profession and rely on the finality and legitimacy accorded medical judgments generally. Emphasizing the moral content of the disability decision and invoking the legitimating symbolism of quasi-judicial judgment after quasi-adversary process is also possible, although I believe it to be ill-advised. Mixing professional, moral, and bureaucratic judgment would, of course, make it difficult to maintain the legitimizing power of the symbols. But there is no reason to believe that there are no choices to be made—that all mixes or all pure models have equivalent symbolic costs and benefits.

## Participation

One of the most important, yet most elusive, process values is participation. In one way or another one constantly confronts the claim that the dignity and self-respect of the individual can be protected only through processes of government, and particularly processes of adjudication, in which there is adequate participation by affected interests. The basis for this connection between participation and self-respect is explained in various ways. It has become traditional in the due-process jurisprudence to make the connection only in circumstances in which the individual is attempting to defend some previously recognized "right."[10] Yet others would assert that participation is equally important in proceedings whose function it is to develop the content of rights, rather than merely to enforce rights previously specified. The latter claim, a persuasive one, is that our self-respect is called into question not only when our rights are dealt with in proceedings to which we are not admitted, but also when we are excluded from a process of social decisionmaking in which we might contribute to the elaboration or definition of the set of rights that we all hold.[11]

The latter point is pressed further by the argument that the true relationship between participation and self-respect is that participation increases self-respect to the degree that participation gives the participant *control* over the process of decisionmaking. Loss of control, it is argued, is particularly damaging to self-respect in those circumstances in which rights are amorphous and decisionmaking depends impor-

10. *See, e.g.*, Van Alstyne, *Cracks in "The New Property"; Adjudicative Due Process in the Administrative State*, 62 Cornell L. Rev. 445 (1977).

11. *See, e.g.*, Michelman, *op. cit. supra* note 8.

tantly on contextualizing the apparently relevant events or norms. It is in these situations that we are particularly conscious of the need to explain and justify our actions and in which the loss of the opportunity to do so denies our self-worth.[12]

Thus the spectrum of arguments seems to generate contradictory prescriptions. From one perspective (the "rights" perspective), the more clearly defined and less discretionary the contested right appears, the more concerned with individual participation the processes of decision should be. From the other view (the contextualization view), processes should be structured to permit intensive individual participation to the extent that rights are amorphous or discretion is paramount in the allocation of rewards or sanctions.

My own sense is that both are correct. Nevertheless, this does not answer the question of what type of participation in fact supports the value of dignity or self-respect. The principal proponents of the contextualization school argue strongly for adversary process as the form that maximizes the control of the participants. Yet that school admits that adversary process loses appeal to the extent that rights are well-defined and that adversariness may in fact contribute to an increased sense of powerlessness in situations in which disparity in the resources of the adversaries yields strikingly disparate power over the process.[13] If, as seems to be the case, these situations dominate disability adjudication, then the clear preference for adversary process vanishes. What type of process, then, will support perceptions of meaningful participation and therefore self-respect and self-worth?

Similar conundrums surround narrower choices in the procedural system. For example, does oral presentation of evidence and argument enhance meaningful participation more than written presentation? And how is this question affected by opportunities to participate either in person or by a representative?

## Conclusion

The preceding discussion makes painfully clear the difficulty of achieving a consensus process for administrative adjudication that gives

---

12. *See,* J. THIBAUT & L. WALKER, PROCEDURAL JUSTICE (1975); Walker, Lind & Thibaut, *The Relation Between Procedural and Distributive Justice,* 65 Va. L. Rev. 1401 (1979).

13. Thibaut & Walker, *A Theory of Procedure,* 66 Calif. L. Rev. 541 (1978).

appropriate weight to the multiple values and divergent interpretations that inform a conclusion that a decision process is or is not "fair." Indeed, a satisfactory collective solution seems impossible. The demand for dignity is ultimately a demand for a process that recognizes the uniqueness of individual perceptions and preferences. Such a demand can never be satisfied by a uniform process. Summing utilities across persons to reveal that a process maximizes general welfare, should that be possible, would provide only a pale substitute justification. A concern with dignitary interests thus invites contempt. The individualist focus presses relentlessly toward granting each claimant the opportunity to design his or her own procedure—an administrative nightmare and programmatic disaster.

Similarly, analysis of the costs of perceived unfairness is so subjective that contemplation of the amount or distribution of these costs leads to evaluative conundrums. The only way to be appropriately attentive to these costs—and therefore to the overall efficiency of the system—may be (1) to follow whatever basic fairness rules the general legal system makes applicable to bureaucratic routine[14] and (2) to permit individual process choices whenever those choices have no clearly detrimental impact on decisional accuracy.

## THE COSTS OF DELAY

The question of the costs of delay responds in some degree to the analysis of error costs presented above. Error costs are, after all, borne over some relevant time period. Any delay in deciding that a claim is valid or that an existing beneficiary has recovered can be viewed as an incurring of the costs of a false negative or a false positive over a certain period of time. Moreover, it is not unreasonable to expect that the relative costs of these errors should be viewed in much the same way as decisional errors: delay that affects the tails of the disability spectrum is more costly than delay that affects the marginal cases. This fact results from a social recognition of the presumably higher discount rate for future dollars of the seriously impaired and of the greater demoralization costs associated with support of the obviously robust. Delay costs

---

14. I have attempted elsewhere to derive some procedural values from the American liberal democratic tradition. Mashaw, *Administrative Due Process: The Quest for a Dignitary Theory*, 61 Boston Univ. L. Rev. 885 (1981).

might also be considered as a form of compound interest—each additional unit of delay in a case is more costly than the ones preceding it—which is partially compensated for by an ultimate decision that provides retroactive benefits or demands repayment.

There are aspects of the delay problem that will not, however, respond to the error-cost analysis. Properly denied claimants and properly continued beneficiaries must still wait for a determination. Those psychic costs of uncertainty may be modest or severe, but there seems no good way to determine abstractly by whom they are borne. The severely disabled may incur higher psychic costs from delay than the less critically impaired; but then again they may not. Too much depends on other aspects of a claimant's economic and psychological situation.

Thus, techniques designed to speed up the decision process, such as giving priority to easy cases at the severe-impairment tail of the disability continuum (known as "creaming"), will not necessarily speed the processing of claims that have high psychic costs of delay. If these latter costs are viewed as being randomly distributed, creaming will not, however, exacerbate the problem of delay costs unless it results in an increase in average processing time—which hardly seems inevitable.

## DIRECT ADMINISTRATIVE COSTS

Administrative costs are the least problematic costs encountered in an adjudicatory system. They are measurable and they can be expressed relatively unambiguously in money terms. Nevertheless, they can cause some serious problems because they can so easily be shifted or traded off against other costs that are neither measurable nor monetizable.

Shifting might occur, for example, between levels of the decision process, between administrative and program costs, between governmental and private administrative costs, and between administrative and social costs. To give an example of each: (1) lower levels of the decisional structure may impose greater costs at higher levels by increasing dissatisfaction and hence appeal rates or by poor development of evidence, which thus requires a greater expenditure of administrative effort to reach a decision in each case appealed; (2) shifts from process costs to program costs may occur if there is some systematic process cost advantage, such as the avoidance of the costs of full documentation or of a reasoned decision, attached to granting rather than denying claims; (3) shifts of costs to private parties occur when those parties are induced to substitute their effort, or those of their representatives, for the efforts of the agency in obtaining, organizing, and presenting evidence; (4) administrative costs may be reduced (presuming no change in technology) by shifting greater costs on to society through a reduction of the quality of the decision process (accuracy, fairness, or speed).

These shifts may be efficient or inefficient, depending upon the magnitudes involved. Their interesting and unifying feature, however, is a capacity to avoid appraisal. In each case the persons or bureaus that control the shifts will not reflect the shifted costs in their personal or institutional budgets. And, in the third and fourth examples outlined above, the shifted administrative costs will not appear anywhere in the public expenditure budget.

The fourth shift, involving trade-offs between concrete administrative costs and other less tangible costs, is perhaps the most troubling. Increased delay costs to claimants obviously are to some extent the flip side of administrative cost savings. But the former is a mushy, psychic cost that is hard to evaluate, much less balance against the more immediately comprehensible dollar savings from, for example, a hiring freeze. When we ask how much we are willing to pay for increased accuracy, consistency, fairness, or speed, we usually mean how many dollars of additional administrative costs are we willing to bear to achieve those results. But, because we have great difficulty monetizing and measuring improvements (cost reductions) in these dimensions of system quality, a crisp answer to that question is seldom possible. Indeed, the How much is it worth? question is so difficult that there is a constant danger either that it will be ignored or that when it is addressed, false absolutes ("due process," "accuracy," "efficiency," "fairness") will be substituted for critical analysis.

It seems clear that administrative efficiency and process fairness are not incompatible concepts. Conscientious attention to the former entails a concern with the latter. It also seems evident that, however difficult it may be to estimate the cost resulting from various aspects of a procedural system, bureau demands for increased budgets to support direct administrative costs can reflect more than the natural acquisitive activity of budget-maximizing bureaucrats. Indeed, the Congress's instinct to sharply constrain administrative costs, as it faces up to the relatively uncontrollable growth of SSA program costs, may be quite mistaken.

Finally, although "cost computation" may seem a euphemism for "hunch," given the ambiguity, complexity, and indeterminacy of some of the process value we have discussed, we can make some headway through analysis. We are not limited to bandying process buzzwords about. We and the Social Security Administration can confront, albeit with some humility, the task of determining whether bureaucratic action supports a plausible conception of administrative efficiency—all things considered.

# PART III · MANAGING THE SYSTEM: AN APPRAISAL OF SSA'S PERFORMANCE

# 5 · Developing and Communicating Administrative Policy

A person evaluating the adequacy of the disability decision process must take seriously the basic goals of bureaucratic administration— rationality and efficiency. Yet one's judgment must be tempered by the exquisite indeterminacy of estimating the degree to which they are achieved and by the inevitable competition among differing perspectives on each goal. Such an evaluation asks how the decision structure, as a whole, fosters or retards the realization of multiple values—values that, given our broad definition of efficiency, might be restated as involving rationality, efficiency, *and* process fairness. Changes that unambiguously increase the system's capacity to realize one or more of these values without sacrificing others are obviously desirable. Beyond these easy cases (should any exist), evaluative analysis can only weigh as carefully as possible the trade-offs among goals that are inherent in current processes or in proposals for reform.

This methodology, if such it can be called, is both awkward and complex. It is awkward because it attempts to find a middle ground between the indeterminacy of abstract theoretical analysis and the determinacy of concrete policy judgment. Such a methodology will satisfy neither the theoretician, who may quite plausibly believe that the problem of appropriate policy is fascinating but forever mysterious, nor the systems manager, who believes, equally plausibly, that what has in fact occurred was inevitable, given a complete understanding of the forces at work at any particular place or time in the system's history. The methodology is complex because it ultimately demands consideration of every value and value conflict thought to be involved in every process feature, existing or proposed. And it is, once again, awkward because this potential complexity must be reduced by intuitive judg-

ments of relevance and importance that cannot be persuasively explained. Responsible policy analysis involves its own difficult trade-offs
between simpleminded calls for action and sophisticated paralysis.

As an initial simplifying move, we shall view SSA as being involved in
three related tasks with respect to the DI decision process: (1) formulating, interpreting, and communicating substantive policy; (2) designing
decision processes that support both systemic rationality and important
dignitary values; and (3) exercising continuous management supervision and control over the implementation of the system's ideals.

## THE REGULATORY IMPERATIVE

We might begin by imagining a system in which disability decisionmakers are given the statute and told to decide cases, aided perhaps only
by the presumption that claimants having earnings of some specified
amount are engaged in substantial gainful activity (SGA) and are,
therefore, not disabled. Under such a system the question of accuracy
would be largely meaningless. One might disagree with the adjudicator's decision, but there would be no objective basis (other than the
SGA limit) for saying that any particular decision was erroneous. Error
assignment could be premised only upon some notion of the superiority
of supervisory judgment, based in turn, perhaps, on the greater experience of supervisory personnel. (Indeed, because there might also be no
way to know whether greater experience had any relationship to good
judgment, there might be no strong reason to view supervisory judgments as being more correct than initial judgments.) Effective supervision could be exercised only with respect to the one clear rule—Don't
pay claimants engaged in SGA—and perhaps at the boundaries of
discretion, such as not making payments to a claimant who has no
medical problems whatsoever.

This imaginary system gives virtually free rein to intuitive rationality.
As I noted in chapter 4, there is much to be said for this type of
rationality in some contexts, but it has major negative effects on the
manageability, the transparency, and the assignment of political responsibility in the system. These effects disqualify intuitive rationality
from serving as the principal model of appropriate adjudicatory behavior in the current DI program. In part because of fiscal concerns,
Congress demands a system that is manageable. Echoing its traditional
interest in "evening the odds" between its clients and the "bureau-

cracy," the bar, speaking for claimants, demands a system with transparent standards. DI adjudicators, shrinking from a wholly discretionary system in which each grant or denial would be their direct and total responsibility, join the Congress and the bar in demanding guidance that will place responsibility for policy at higher levels in the bureaucracy. These pressures from within and without the system tend to force the development of adjudicatory standards that will require decisionmaking to be systematic, manageable, and reviewable—that will begin to make the system conform to the model of bureaucratic rationality.

Moreover, adjudicatory standards for the DI program must be regulatory in character. The development of a common law for DI adjudication is impractical, in part because of the current appellate structure in SSA. The only opportunity for enunciating a unified set of precedents in the administrative structure is at the Appeals Council (AC) level. But AC review as currently constituted has a multitude of weaknesses as a vehicle for the establishment of adjudicatory policy. First, the AC decides 40,000 cases per year. As a set of precedents this number of decisions would produce immediate cognitive overload at lower levels of decisionmaking. Second, the AC's jurisprudence cannot remain unified because it, in turn, is subjected to the review of every federal district in the country. Third, the cases, as they come to the AC are poor vehicles for arriving at binding precedent. The issues are often blurred by the production of new evidence, and the potential government side of any policy dispute is not explicitly represented. And fourth, the AC is not the principal policy arm of the secretary or the commissioner with respect to the DI program. An attempt by the AC to give content to the program would both overstep its policy role and to some degree compromise the Office of Hearings and Appeals' position as quasi-external reviewer of disputed claims.

To be sure, all of these so-called weaknesses can be eliminated. The file can be closed, adversariness introduced, Article III court review eliminated, precedents selectively published, and the AC (or a "disability court") recognized as the major source of SSA policy. But all of these changes have costs. Happily, we need not consider each cost/benefit calculation for these major changes in the SSA decisional structure because one necessary change—selective publication—suggests that a precedent system in the DI program would of necessity take on certain characteristics of rulemaking activity. In choosing precedents for publication, administrators would have to make decisions concerning the importance and stability of the policies announced by the cases—that is, concerning the degree to which a policy is worth stating and the likelihood that it is well considered. These publication choices will thus represent the point at which the real policy decisions for the system are made. The enunciation of precedents will thus take on more the character of rulemaking than of deciding cases.

In addition, when one asks whether these essentially regulatory decisions should be tied to the vagaries of appellate review, the obvious answer emerges. Surely a more responsive and complete set of adjudicatory policies can be developed if the policy machinery is capable of acting without waiting for the right case to come along. Hence, some pure rulemaking activity would be desirable even if much adjudicatory policy were formulated through the mixed rulemaking medium of selective publication of case precedents.

To summarize: (1) the DI program faces irresistible demands for exhibition of systemic rationality; (2) systemic rationality requires specification of adjudicatory criteria; (3) adjudicatory standards cannot emerge as precedent or common law in the present decisional structure; (4) restructuring the decisional structure to produce effective precedent involves a selectivity that is the essence of rulemaking; (5) Q.E.D. In one way or another SSA must make rules to guide adjudication.

## HOW MUCH "RULISHNESS" IS ENOUGH?

The practical inevitability of SSA's engaging in regulatory activity does not, of course, make an overwhelming case for its desirability. Nor does it tell us much about the amount or nature of productive rulemaking. Yet the demands of the Congress, claimants' representatives, and low-level decisionmakers for clearer specification of standards have much to commend them from a normative perspective.

A clear or relatively clear rule tends to make DI adjudication more acceptable. A standard as vague as the statutory disability standard communicates little that is meaningful to persons who believe themselves unable to work because of illness or injury. It therefore has little chance either of informing the eligible how to prosecute a claim or of persuading the ineligible that their disappointment is not arbitrarily imposed. In a system that relies on rationality as a basis for legitimating its decisions, the importance of clear rules is obvious.

Moreover, the attempt to articulate standards may reduce the conceptual uncertainties that plague the quest for rationality in the DI program. If the problem is that Congress has failed to provide an external referent, a regulatory standard that says, "A case with characteristics $X_1 + X_2 + X_3$ is an appropriate case for an award (or denial)," puts to the Congress whether it had (or has) that referent in mind. If the problem is the incoherence of the criteria, a standard that says implicitly, "This is the best we can do in considering age as an independent factor in determining disability," puts to the Congress whether it prefers to accept this particular approach to compromising the disparate goals of the program or to give further instructions. In short, standards contribute to a policy dialogue that can tend, over time, toward a politically legitimated specificity or, alternatively, toward clearer instructions that the body politic prefers less instrumental rationality and/or candor in the resolution of entitlement disputes in the disability program. (And, presumably, more of something else, for example, individualized or intuitive judgment.)

The conventional wisdom that legislative oversight is sporadic and ineffectual may make the foregoing appear somewhat naive; but the conventional wisdom misdescribes the relationship of the Congress and SSA. Studies of the administration of the DI program by congressional committee staffs and the General Accounting Office are almost continuously under way. Oversight and budget hearings often explore SSA's efforts to remedy previously discovered problems surrounding the adjudication of claims. There is frequent discussion in and between Congress and SSA of legislative proposals that would affect both the procedure and the substance of the program. These legislative activities leave very clear footprints in the jungle of administrative policymaking. A real dialogue is clearly possible, and rulemaking initiatives further that dialogue.

While admitting these general advantages for rulemaking, we nevertheless know that "rule boundedness" is not an unmixed blessing. Objectification of standards, the use of presumptions, the routinization of evidentiary development, all tend to overgeneralize, to pigeonhole, to leave gaps. Rulemaking necessarily constrains sensitive exercise of individualized discretion. This characteristic of clear decision rules, like vagueness, can introduce errors or skew them systematically and inappropriately in one direction. What, if anything, can be said about good and bad, productive and counterproductive adjudicatory criteria?

A glance back at the figure on p. 83 may suggest at least a preliminary strategy. Misclassification of claims at the tails of the eligibility continuum has high social costs. These types of errors should be constrained, if possible, as a matter of high priority. Moreover, one would suspect that substantial progress can be made toward the objectification of standards for classifying the seriously disabled at one end of the spectrum and the only modestly disadvantaged at the other. Relatively objective medical definitions of severe and slight impairments, for example, are potentially available substitutes for the general disability definition. Although some error costs from overgeneralization will necessarily attend objectification, a medical consensus standard that persons having heart disease of a certain measurable severity cannot work seems unlikely to generate large numbers of false positives. And even these can be somewhat constrained by the SGA test.

The next step in a sensible regulatory strategy is much more difficult to define. As one moves toward the middle of the eligibility continuum the rewards from "correct" adjudication decrease, as does the likelihood that one dimension of the claimant's case, for example, medical impairment, would be determinative of functional capacity. Multiple criteria must be considered—medical condition, age, education, work experience—and no obvious calculus permits summing the results of these considerations. Attempts to control decisionmaking in this domain are, thus, both less imperative and less likely to be effective from the standpoint of reducing costly errors. It is difficult to formulate vocational regulations that constrain sufficiently to "systematize" rationality while leaving "appropriate" escape hatches for intuitive, discretionary judgment. The error costs from overgeneralization may here outweigh the gains from error avoidance. The adjudicator's feel for this type of case may often be better than any rule. Yet, if the DI program is to avoid other costs—particularly the costs of perceived inequality of outcomes—it cannot ignore the development of adjudicatory standards regarding vocational cases.

Viewed from the abstract perspective of sensible strategy, SSA's substantive regulatory activity has been quite exemplary. It has used medical impairment criteria to decide cases involving severe disabilities almost from the inception of the program, and those criteria have appeared as formal regulations since 1968. These medical criteria (the medical listings) are formulated and revised through a complex process that involves wide consultation with SSA's many consulting physicians and with the medical community generally. Criteria for vocational assessment, on the other hand, have developed very slowly. Various directives have incrementally become part of the Disability Insurance State Manual (DISM) and only recently have found their way into a relatively comprehensive regulatory form. Indeed, it is fair to say that SSA has been willing to objectify the more problematic vocational factors only under strong legislative pressure to make the program more manageable and to purge it of inconsistency.

The efficacy of SSA's regulatory effort cannot be assessed, however, solely on the basis of its general approach. A close look at the regulations themselves is required, and inquiry reveals that the general strategy of objectification of standards has been only partially completed.

## Medical Criteria

Since 1958 SSA has published and updated medical criteria—the so-called medical listings—that, if satisfied (and absent SGA), establish disability without consideration of vocational factors such as age, education, and prior work experience. These criteria define a severely disabled population and confine administrative discretion with respect to it. The medical criteria contain objective standards ("fixation of . . . spine at 30° or more from neutral position"), slightly judgmental elements ("abnormal apophyseal articulations as shown by X-ray"), and highly discretionary criteria ("appropriate sensory or motor loss"). Moreover, the regulations permit a finding on a medical basis alone that the claimant's medical condition "equals," although it does not meet, the listings. There is no attempt to specify what equivalence might mean other than that the malady be equivalent in "severity" and "duration." Finally, the per se, medically *non*disabled end of the continuum has historically been defined simply as those claimants having only "slight impairments," that is, impairments that do not "significantly limit an individual's physical and mental capacity to perform basic work-related functions."

These medical criteria obviously "objectify" adjudicatory standards in varying degrees, but they nevertheless leave considerable scope for subjective judgment. Even the more objective standards, the medical listings, use adjectives like "marked," "sustained," "high," "moderate or repeated." "Equivalent" and "slight" are yet more judgmental.

Pointing to complaints by DDS units about the vagueness of their instructions and to the marked disparities among the states in denial rates and in the percentages of awards assigned as either "meeting" or "equaling" the medical listings, critics urge SSA to provide more guidance.

Use of the more judgmental categories has also been closely associated with growth in the disability program's expenditures. This has led to the belief that SSA's failure to suppress the use of the more judgmental bases for awards—or to more rigorously structure their use—accounts in part for the tendency of program expenditures to always exceed expectations. The shift in the basis noted for awards in the period 1960–75 is, indeed, quite dramatic (see accompanying graph).

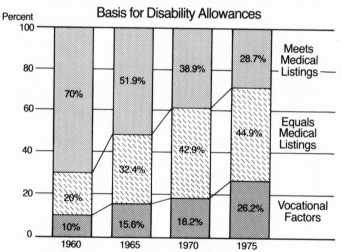

Source: Subcommittee on Social Security, House Ways and Means Committee, 94th Cong., 2nd Sess., "Disability Insurance-Legislative Issue Paper" 17 (1976).

The prima facie merit of the critics' case is obvious but not overwhelming. Medical criteria cannot be more objective and scientific than the body of knowledge and practice on which they rely. Moreover, the weasel words in the listings that call for comparative clinical judgments ("moderate," "characteristic") may often be more informative for the experienced medical professional than for the layman; and each medical finding is reviewed by a consulting physician. (I will take up the question of the effectiveness of that review at a later stage.)

The judgmental elements in the listings may also be necessary both to construct a consensus at the time of their promulgation and to provide sufficient flexibility to permit use of the listings over some considerable period between revisions. The medical community is hardly of one mind, after all, concerning appropriate diagnosis or therapy with respect to any medical condition. Moreover, the practice is remarkably dynamic. Coronary conditions considered severely and permanently disabling a decade ago are now viewed almost as temporary inconveniences. Indeed, the relative objectivity of the cardiovascular listings, combined with the ponderous process of revision, has caused those criteria to be chronically outdated. Softening the hard edges of objective measurement with judgmental adjectives may often be a prudent policy.

The critical commentary has more bite when directed to the questions of equivalence and slight impairment. At the risk of overextending this discussion, an example seems necessary to illustrate the point.

The medical criteria for making an award solely on the basis of degenerative or osteo arthritis provide:

Hypertrophic (osteo or degenerative), gouty, infectious or traumatic arthritis. With:

A. History of pain and stiffness in the involved joints; and
B. X-ray evidence of joint space narrowing with osteophytosis (exostosis) or bony destruction with erosions and cysts, or subluxation, or ankylosis of involved joints and one of the following:
   1. Abduction of both arms at shoulders restricted to less than 90 degrees; or
   2. Ankylosis (fibrous or bony consolidation of fixation) of hip at less than 20 degrees or more than 30 degrees of flexion, measured from neutral position; or
   3. Ankylosis or fixation of knee at more than 10 degrees from neutral position; or
   4. Limitation of flexion of both hips to 50 degrees or less from neutral position (including ankylosis of both hips at any angle); or
   5. Limitation of flexion of both knees to 30 degrees or less from the neutral position (including ankylosis of both knees at any angle); or
   6. Combined involvement of single hip and knee in contralateral extremity, with impairment in each as in 4 or 5 above; or
   7. Reconstructive surgery or surgical arthrodesis of a major weight-bearing joint (hip, knee, ankle, or tarsal region) and return to full weight-bearing status did not occur, or is not expected to occur, or is not expected to occur within 12 months of onset of disability; or

8. X-ray evidence of lumbar spine abnormalities as in B above with motion of dorsolumbar spine limited to 5 degrees or less from neutral position and impairment of single hip or knee as in 4 or 5 above.[1]

This section can yield a mass of medical equivalence issues. Consider only § 1.04(b)(1). Is abduction of one arm at 130° and the other at 50° the equivalent of both at 90°? Would any combination less than 180° suffice? Or is some less mechanical and more "functional" approach to capacity intended? But if so, what is the function by which equivalence is measured? "General usefulness of the arms"—whatever that means? Should limitations with respect to elbows, wrists, and fingers be included in a general functional approach, although they are not mentioned in the listing? If so, how are these latter limitations "added" for purposes of comparing them with the listed limitation?

There is also the common problem of combining the effects of impairments that relate to different body systems. Claimants often have multiple complaints—arthritis *and* cardiovascular disease, an amputated limb *and* psychiatric disorders. Are these complaints cumulative? In what sense? And if an adjudicator is meant to cumulate the impairments, as the DISM suggests, how should he or she go about it?

Obviously these questions could call forth a number of perfectly reasonable approaches to the question of medical equivalence. In discussions with disability examiners, I have been given (not counting shrugs of the shoulders or rolled eyeballs) five plausible definitions of equivalence: (1) the claimant is a "wreck," but doesn't fit any listing; (2) the objective medical evidence approaches the listing's severity and subjective evidence (pain) suggests that the effect is similar to that of the condition described in the listing; (3) the disease is similar to that described in a listing, but no listing actually deals with it; (4) the diagnosis uses different tests from those the listing assumes will be used, but severity seems equivalent; (5) the claimant has two or more conditions that (a) each "approach" the listing or (b) cumulatively have effects equaling one listing. Neither the regulations nor the manual makes the necessary choices among these approaches. "Slight impairments" are similarly unspecified, beyond two examples in the regulations—"slight neurosis" and "slight sight or hearing" impairments—both of which define "slight" in terms of itself.

1. 20 C.F.R. Subpart P, Appendix I, §1.04 (1981).

Recent regulations have altered the term "slight impairments" to impairments that are "not severe." A draft "program policy directive" states that the "unchanged essence of this policy is the absence of significant restriction of work-related functions because of solely medical considerations." The draft then proceeds to discuss the concept in general terms:

The statement "*basic work-related functions*" refers to the abilities and aptitudes necessary to do most jobs. Examples of these include:
(a) Physical functions such as working, standing, sitting, lifting, pulling, reaching, carrying, or handling;
(b) Capacities for seeing, hearing, and speaking;
(c) Understanding, carrying out, and remembering simple instructions;
(d) Responding to supervision, co-workers, and usual work situations; and
(e) Dealing with changes in a routine work setting.

And further,

The expression "does not significantly limit" refers to the extent that impairment limitations (physical or mental) restrict the performance of basic work-related functions. When the ability to perform basic work-related functions remains essentially intact, the impairment(s) does not significantly limit the individual even though the capability for activities involved in work may be affected.

Finally, the draft directive gives five examples of not-severe impairments, such as loss of sight in one eye.

It may be that disability examiners will find this advice helpful. I must confess that I am doubtful. If the "not severe" category is to constrain false positives in the way that the medical listings constrain false negatives, much more detailed guidance is required. And while I do not wish to minimize the difficulty of generating specific criteria, it does not seem implausible to begin by attempting to provide for each per se disabling condition a comparison symptomatology that is, at least by itself, per se not-disabling.

SSA's desire to introduce judgmental flexibility into the listings through the "equivalent severity" notion and to establish some floor under qualifying medical impairments via the "not severe" idea is certainly reasonable. But surely the critics are correct in suggesting that it is both possible and necessary for SSA to provide more specific guidance. Given different but reasonable interpretations of present policy, one could expect to find both very high and very low acceptance rates among the states for nonlisted arthritic (or other) complaints. A generous interpretation of "equals" might lead to many awards in cases not covered by the listings—arthritis affecting the hands, neck, or elbows, for example. A cautious, conservative approach, on the other hand, might view the absence of these impairments in the listings as presumptive evidence that they should be considered "not severe." On the basis of current policy, neither of these interpretations is clearly wrong.

## Vocational Criteria

Historically, the consideration of vocational criteria (residual functional capacity) has been relatively unconstrained by regulations, although some guidance was afforded by the DISM. As has been mentioned, several considerations supported such a passive administrative posture. First, any attempt to routinize consideration of vocational factors in ways that actually control decisionmaking undermines the notion that SSA considers the whole person—and considers him or her on an individual basis—in disability adjudications. There is no responsible way to avoid this problem. The drafters of vocational regulations must confront very difficult choices between overgeneralization and fuzziness. One must either draw sharp lines, for example, between age groups or rely on vague categories like "older workers" and "younger workers." The first technique seems arbitrary; the second ineffectual.

Perhaps more important, an attempt to regulate the consideration of vocational factors reveals that SSA's rationality is bounded in at least two important ways. First, as prior discussion has noted, some of the vocational criteria made relevant by the statute are only marginally relevant to the realities of work capacity. There is much evidence that workers above fifty-five (fifty? forty-five?) years of age have difficulty obtaining employment. There is little (or none) that relates those difficulties to real differences in the adaptability of various age groups to new work environments; and the statutory definition of disability is concerned with capacity, not employability. Second, the information available to DDS decision units at reasonable cost is often very sketchy. They can make a gestalt judgment about a claim that appears reasonable, but that judgment will not necessarily withstand a discriminating analysis that compartmentalizes discrete vocational issues. Crisp regulation of the effects of vocational factors thus invites challenge both in the courts and in the Congress.

The determination of a claimant's residual functional capacity (RFC) provides a major example of SSA's judicial review problem: its potential inability to appear rational in individual decisions if it is very clear about what rationality entails. RFC is in many ways the most crucial issue in deciding claims that cannot be determined on the basis of medical evidence alone. In regulations made effective February 26, 1979, the secretary for the first time elaborated what is (or should be) involved in assessing RFC:

(a) General. . . .
(b) Physical capacities. Assessment of physical capacities (e.g. strength and exertional capabilities) includes an evaluation of the individual and indicates the individual's maximal residual functional capacity for sustained activity on a regular basis. The assessment also includes the evaluation of the individual's ability to perform significant physical functions such as walking, standing, lifting, carrying, pushing or pulling. The assessment includes the evaluation of other physical traits and sensory characteristics such as reaching, handling, seeing, hearing, and speaking, insofar as limited capacity to perform these functions may also affect the individual's capacity for work for which the individual would otherwise be qualified.
(c) Mental impairments. The assessment of impairments because of mental disorders includes a consideration of such factors as the capacity to understand, to carry out and remember instructions, and to respond appropriately to supervision, co-workers and customary work pressures in a routine work setting.
(d) Non-exertional limitations. Any medically determinable impairment(s) resulting in non-exertional limitations (such as certain mental, sensory, or skin impairments) must be considered in terms of the limitations resulting from the impairment. When an individual has a non-exertional impairment in addition to an exertional impairment(s), the residual functional capacity must be assessed in terms of the degree of any additional narrowing of the individual's work-related capabilities.[2]

One need not be experienced in disability adjudication to be skeptical that any administrative record will adequately inform the adjudicator concerning the considerations made relevant by this regulatory language. Batteries of special tests and prolonged observation of the

2. 43 Fed. Reg. 55349, 55363–64 (Nov. 28, 1978).

claimant would often be required to provide even moderately reliable information. But in the overwhelming majority of cases disability claimants have not received the sustained, unified, and expensive medical care that would yield the requisite data. Development of adequate evidence for each claim that requires an RFC evaluation would necessitate a massive investment by SSA in the purchase of medical and vocational workshop evaluations—an investment Congress has shown no desire to fund.

What this may mean tactically is that the knowledgeable claimant can load up the record with descriptions of what he or she can or cannot do; and, unless rendered wholly implausible by available medical evidence, such declarations must be believed. More frequently, regulatory definition of the appropriate approach to evaluating residual capacity will provide claimants' counsel (who usually appear only at the appellate stages) with a multitude of potential evidentiary gaps in the adjudicatory record to be trotted out as a basis for judicial remand of unfavorable decisions. (This potential was, of course, always there. The regulations merely make it obvious to the nonspecialist. In my wilder moments I am tempted to make large wagers that I can get *any* negative disability decision remanded by a federal court.) Breaking the vocational judgment down into its components may, thus, under current conditions, rationalize ultimate judgment less than it exposes interstitial uncertainty.

Notwithstanding these difficulties, SSA has recently adopted detailed vocational regulations that prescribe the effects of the various vocational factors—age, education, and prior work experience—when combined with specific RFCs. The latter are defined in the broad terms employed by the Labor Department's *Dictionary of Occupational Titles* (DOT), that is, "sedentary," "light," "medium," and "heavy" (or "very heavy") work. Indeed, the DOT (along with other publications) was relied upon quite heavily in prescribing the vocational impact of education and prior work experience as well.

These new regulations were adopted after long consideration and after an extensive (and not very productive) process of public comment and public hearings. They are preceded in the Federal Register by a generally excellent and often candid statement of their basis and purpose. This is not the place to discuss the regulations in great substantive detail. But a sense of how the regulations attempt to structure adjudicatory discretion (and the limitations on that structuring) can be obtained by a brief look at one major section. The portion of Appendix 2 (or "grid") reproduced on pages 118–19 specifies the effect of various vocational factors when an applicant's residual functional capacity limits him or her to sedentary work.

A glance at the grid reveals its potentially powerful effects on disability adjudication. The vague considerations of age, education, and work experience are broken down into broad categories, and their relationships to work capability are specified under varying conditions. Moreover, application of the matrix requires a series of discrete findings: not only must educational level be specified, but in many cases the high school record apparently must be examined to determine whether the course of study fits the applicant for direct entry into a skilled, sedentary occupation; not only must prior work experience be classified, but also the transferability of skills must often be determined. Finally, this matrix contains a strong policy judgment concerning age. Workers aged 18–44 who are capable of the exertion levels of sedentary work are not disabled. Workers in this category who are 55 and over *are* disabled unless they possess transferable skills.

From the perspective of an administration concerned with systemic rationality, these regulations have much to commend them. They make possible relatively clear determinations not only of the correctness of results, but also of the appropriateness of evidentiary development. In the context of either appellate review or a quality assurance system, these regulations represent major advances in the system's capacity to detect and correct errors. Moreover, the explicit policy judgments that underlie the grid permit an informed appraisal by the Congress of whether SSA has correctly appreciated its legislative intent. SSA may be wrong but it now at least has a knowable policy.

Herein, of course, lies SSA's political difficulty. The grid approach has been subjected to vigorous challenge because of its potential for overgeneralization. For example, it is quite plausibly argued that people have much more complicated capacities and limits than the definition of sedentary work (or other work classifications) suggests. Skills are *partly* transferable or *sometimes* transferable rather than simply *not* transferable. Transferability depends both on the specific sedentary job one has in mind and on the ability of the individual to make the necessary linkages between past and present tasks. Opponents of the "Grid Regs"

**Residual Functional Capacity: Maximum Sustained Work Capability Limited to Sedentary Work as a Result of Severe Medically Determinable Impairment(s)**

| Rule | Age | Education | Previous work experience | Decision |
|------|-----|-----------|--------------------------|----------|
| 201.01 | Advanced age 55 and over | Limited or less | Unskilled or none | Disabled. |
| 201.02 | " | " | Skilled or semiskilled—skills not transferable. | " |
| 201.03 | " | " | Skilled or semiskilled—skills transferable. | Not disabled. |
| 201.04 | " | High school graduate or more—does not provide for direct entry into skilled work. | Unskilled or none | Disabled. |
| 201.05 | " | High school graduate or more—provides for direct entry into skilled work. | Unskilled or none | Not disabled. |
| 201.06 | " | High school graduate or more—does not provide for direct entry into skilled work. | Skilled or semiskilled—skills not transferable. | Disabled. |
| 201.07 | " | High school graduate or more—does not provide for direct entry into skilled work. | Skilled or semiskilled—skills transferable. | Not disabled. |
| 201.08 | " | High school graduate or more—provides for direct entry into skilled work. | Skilled or semiskilled—skills not transferable. | " |
| 201.09 | Closely approaching advanced age. 50–54 | Limited or less | Unskilled or none | Disabled. |
| 201.10 | " | " | Skilled or semiskilled—skills not transferable. | " |
| 201.11 | " | " | Skilled or semiskilled—skills transferable. | Not disabled. |
| 201.12 | " | High school graduate or more—does not provide for direct entry into skilled work. | Unskilled or none | Disabled. |
| 201.13 | " | High school graduate or more—provides for direct entry into skilled work. | " | Not disabled. |

Residual Functional Capacity: Maximum Sustained Work Capability Limited to
Sedentary Work as a Result of Severe Medically Determinable Impairment(s) (continued)

| Rule | Age | Education | Previous work experience | Decision |
|------|-----|-----------|--------------------------|----------|
| 201.14 | " | High school graduate or more—does not provide for direct entry into skilled work. | Skilled or semiskilled— skills not transferable. | Disabled. |
| 201.15 | " | " | Skilled or semiskilled— skills transferable. | Not disabled. |
| 201.16 | " | High school graduate or more—provides for direct entry into skilled work. | Skilled or semiskilled— skills not transferable. | " |
| 201.17 | Younger individual age 45–49 | Illiterate or unable to communicate in English. | Unskilled or none | Disabled. |
| 201.18 | " | Limited or less—at least literate and able to communicate in English. | " | Not disabled. |
| 201.19 | " | Limited or less | Skilled or semiskilled— skills not transferable. | " |
| 201.20 | " | " | Skilled or semiskilled— skills transferable. | " |
| 201.21 | " | High school graduate or more. | Skilled or semiskilled— skills not transferable. | " |
| 201.22 | " | " | Skilled or semiskilled— skills transferable. | " |
| 201.23 | Younger individual age 18–44 | Illiterate or unable to communicate in English. | Unskilled or none | " |
| 201.24 | " | Limited or less—at least literate and able to communicate in English. | " | " |
| 201.25 | " | Limited or less | Skilled or semiskilled— skills not transferable. | " |
| 201.26 | " | " | Skilled or semiskilled— skills transferable. | " |
| 201.27 | " | High school graduate or more. | Unskilled or none | " |
| 201.28 | " | " | Skilled or semiskilled— skills not transferable. | " |
| 201.29 | " | " | Skilled or semiskilled— skills transferable. | " |

argue that the regulations represent inappropriate "pigeonholing," that they will induce as much or more error than they correct, and that Congress has not authorized this generic approach.

The critics surely have a point, but two considerations suggest that SSA's regulations are nevertheless reasonable. The first is the system's potential for inaccuracy absent the grid. To instruct thousands of deciders to decide millions of claims on the basis of a value matrix with unspecified weights is simply not to be serious about systemic rationality. It will be impossible to label erroneous any decision that indeed "considers" all the factors and contains no obvious internal contradiction.

Second, the new regulations contain more than the grid. They contain the principles and policies that include some significant exceptions to its applicability. The (edited) language of the regulations puts the matter concisely:

Since the rules are predicated on an individual's having an impairment which manifests itself by limitations in meeting the strength requirements of jobs, they may not be fully applicable where the nature of an individual's impairment does not result in such limitations, e.g., certain mental, sensory, or skin impairments. In addition, some impairments may result solely in postural and manipulative limitations or environmental restrictions. Environmental restrictions are those restrictions which result in inability to tolerate some physical feature(s) of work settings that occur in certain industries or types of work, e.g., an inability to tolerate dust or fumes.

In the evaluation of disability where the individual has solely a nonexertional type of impairment, determination as to whether disability exists shall be based on the principles of §§404.1505–404.1511, giving consideration to the rules for specific case situations in this Appendix 2. The rules do not direct factual conclusions of disabled or not disabled for individuals with solely nonexertional types of impairments.

However, where an individual has an impairment or combination of impairments resulting in both strength limitations and nonexertional limitations, the rules in this subpart are considered in determining first whether a finding of disabled may be possible based on the strength limitations alone and, if not, the rule(s) reflecting the individual's maximum residual strength capabilities, age, education, and work experience provide a framework for consideration of how much the individual's work capability is further diminished in terms of any types of jobs that would be contraindicated by the nonexertional limitations. Also, in these combinations of nonexertional and exertional limitations which

cannot be wholly determined under the rules in this Appendix 2, full consideration must be given to all of the relevant facts in the case in accordance with the
definitions and discussions of each factor in §§04.1505–404.1511, which will
provide insight into the adjudicative weight to be accorded each factor.[3]

The regulations also give examples of circumstances in which the grid
would not preclude a finding of disability for workers younger than 45
who cannot do the full range of sedentary jobs:

Example 1: An individual under age 45 with a high school education can no
longer do past work and is restricted to unskilled sedentary jobs because of a
severe medically determinable cardiovascular impairment (which does not meet
or equal the listings in Appendix 1). A permanent injury of the right hand limits
the individual to sedentary jobs which do not require bilateral manual dexterity.
None of the rules in Appendix 2 are applicable to this particular set of facts,
because this individual cannot perform the full range of work defined as
sedentary. Since the inability to perform jobs requiring bilateral manual dexterity significantly compromises the only range of work for which the individual is
otherwise qualified (i.e., sedentary), a finding of disabled would be appropriate.
Example 2: An illiterate 41 year old individual with mild mental retardation (IQ
of 78) is restricted to unskilled sedentary work and cannot perform vocationally
relevant past work, which had consisted of unskilled agricultural field work: his
or her particular characteristics do not specifically meet any of the rules in
Appendix 2, because this individual cannot perform the full range of work
defined as sedentary. In light of the adverse factors which further narrow the
range of sedentary work for which this individual is qualified, a finding of
disabled is appropriate.[4]

In short, it is still possible to individualize when the grid classifications
are appropriate. Indeed, one might wonder whether the exceptions will
swallow the rules.

But the interplay of exceptions and rules is a question more of the
dynamics of decisionmaking, to which I will soon turn, than of the
formulation of decisional guidelines. The basic point remains: SSA has
made substantial progress toward establishing one of the necessary
preconditions for the pursuit of transparent and (systemically) rational
adjudication: sufficiently detailed and knowable substantive policies.
To be sure, its behavior has not been above reproach. But by comparison

3. *Id.* at 55367.
4. *Id.* at 55368.

with some other federal agencies that deal in large-volume adjudication, SSA's present posture is exemplary.

Consider, for example, the polar positions of the National Labor Relations Board (NLRB) and the Occupational Safety and Health Administration (OSHA). The NLRB literally has no substantive rules. Neither the fulminations of commentators[5] nor the prodding of courts[6] has convinced it that any of its vague adjudicatory doctrines can bear particularization or objectification in regulatory form. This posture may be wise. But critics who pay close attention to NLRB policy believe much of it to be inconsistent and/or wrongheaded.[7] And some suggest that exclusive reliance on adjudication has seriously inhibited the development of sensible labor policies.[8]

At the other extreme, OSHA has historically operated on the basis of a rule book of staggering particularity.[9] "The rules," moreover, so channel and constrain the discretion of its inspectors that they are virtually precluded from attending to the general purposes of the statute—to provide workers with a reasonably safe place to work. This "rulish" behavior so annoys employers—even plant safety engineers— that OSHA gets little voluntary cooperation. More importantly, there is impressive testimony to the effect that attention to the rule book screens out relevant information about hazards that are much more significant than the ones covered by the rules. Enforcing the rules thus produces underenforcement of the statute, which, when combined with destruction of employer cooperativeness and employer initiative concerning safety and health matters, may mean that OSHA's implementing technique has reversed the intended effects of the statute.

This is not the place to investigate whether these conclusions about the NLRB and OSHA are correct or the degree to which the problems identified have been remedied. But if the critical literature is accurate,

---

5. *See, e.g.,* Note, *NLRB Rulemaking: Political Reality Versus Procedural Fairness,* 89 Yale L.J. 982 (1980) and authorities therein cited.

6. NLRB v. Wyman-Gordon Co. 394 U.S. 759 (1969).

7. J. GETMAN, S. GOLDBERG, AND J. HERMAN, UNION REPRESENTATION ELECTIONS: LAW AND REALITY (1976).

8. *See, e.g.,* Bernstein, *The NLRB's Adjudication–Rulemaking Dilemma Under the Administrative Procedure Act,* 79 Yale L.J. 571 (1970).

9. For an excellent commentary *see* E. BARDACH AND R. KAGAN. GOING BY THE BOOK (1982).

SSA's hesitant, incremental, but progressively more detailed approach to elaborating the definition of disability looks quite sensible and responsible by comparison.

# 6 · Designing Decision Processes

We have already outlined the administrative stages of disability decisionmaking. Claimants present themselves to SSA district offices (or, in some Supplemental Security Income [SSI] programs, to state welfare agencies), where intake workers collect basic information concerning the claimant's medical problems, work history, and current employment or earnings. The claims file is then transferred to a state agency for development and decision by a claims examiner. A denied claimant may seek reconsideration—a new decision by a different claims examiner—and thereafter may obtain a de novo, personal hearing before an ALJ and an appeal, on the hearing record, to a panel of the multimember Appeals Council.

The general issue at each level of decisionmaking is whether the claimant is disabled. But as that general question has been unpacked to reveal more particularized and objective inquiries, so the information-seeking and decisional tasks of administrators have been routinized and structured to produce systematically accurate decisionmaking at an acceptable cost. And while much that appears in the formal procedural instructions to claims examiners (who will be the main focus of our discussion) is explicable wholly in terms of the goal of establishing a bureaucratically rational organization, much also responds to broader concerns with the potential fairness costs or demoralization costs of bureaucratic routines.

At the examiner level the decision process occurs literally within one head. An examiner may consult with colleagues, supervisors, or medical staff and perhaps have telephone contact with the claimant or a treating or consulting physician. But ultimately the examiner must decide by applying the regulatory criteria to the facts in the claims file as he or she has constructed it. Instructing examiners how to build a file is thus the essence of designing the decision process.

## PURSUING THE FACTS

### Sequential Development

If a substantive regulatory strategy of making criteria more objective and limiting expensive errors is to be effective, it must be accompanied by routine decisionmaking that gives priority to the resolution of claims on an objective basis. SSA has long had an established sequence for addressing the development and decision of disability cases. It is set out concisely in the background statement accompanying the new vocational regulations:

The criteria are considered in appropriate sequence in the context of the overall disability sequential evaluation process. This sequence, conforming to existing social security regulations, and left substantially unchanged by the amendments, is applied in the following manner.

1. Determinations based on an individual engaging in substantial gainful activity.

   Where an individual is actually engaging in substantial gainful activity, a finding will be made that the individual is not under a disability without consideration of either medical or vocational factors.

2. Determinations based solely on the medical severity of impairments.

   a. Medical considerations alone can justify a finding that the inidividual is not under a disability where the medically determinable physical or mental impairment(s) is not severe, e.g., does not significantly limit the individual's physical or mental capacity to perform basic work-related functions.

   b. On the other hand, medical consideration alone would justify a finding of disability where:

      (i) The impairment meets the duration requirement (i.e., is expected to last at least 12 months or result in death);

      (ii) The impairment meets or equals the severity of a listed impairment published in the Appendix (now designated "Appendix 1") of the disability regulations; and

      (iii) Other evidence does not rebut a finding of disability, e.g., the individual is not actually engaging in substantial gainful activity.

3. Determinations based on vocational as well as medical considerations.

   a. Where an individual with a marginal education and long work experience (e.g., 35 to 40 years or more) limited to the performance of arduous unskilled physical labor, is not working and is no longer able to perform such labor because of a significant impairment or impairments, the individual may be found to be under a disability.

b. Where a finding of disability (or its absence) is not made under any of the foregoing steps, the individual's impairment(s) is evaluated in terms of physical and mental demands of the individual's past relevant work. If the impairment(s) does not prevent the performance of past relevant work, disability will be found not to exist.

c. If an individual cannot perform his or her past relevant work but the individual's physical and mental capacities are consistent with his or her meeting the demands of a significant number of jobs in the national economy and the individual has the vocational capabilities (considering his or her age, education, and past work experience) to make an adjustment to work different from that which the individual has performed in the past, it will be determined that the individual is not under a disability. However, if the individual's physical and mental capacities in conjuction with his or her vocational capabilities (considering his or her age, education, and work experience) are not consistent with making an adjustment to work differing from that which the individual has performed in the past, it will be determined that the individual is under a disability.[1]

Thus, an examiner begins with a relatively straightforward indicator of disability—current earnings. If the claimant's statement, wage-postings, or other evidence (usually unavailable) do not reveal earnings greater than the SGA standard, it is time to turn to the medical evidence. If that evidence fails to resolve the case, the examiner proceeds to the analysis of so-called vocational factors.

## Collecting Evidence

SSA's sequential development instructions are so obviously sensible that their statement is a sufficient evaluation. But an orderly progression from relatively objective to relatively subjective criteria only begins to structure developmental discretion. The disability examiner must answer a series of other questions in the course of collecting data on a claim. They include at least the following: (1) what "quality" of evidence is required? (2) what responsibility does the examiner have to generate the requisite data? (3) how much time per case should be spent on development? (4) how much money should be spent to acquire evidence about a claimant's condition? Moreover, these questions are obviously related: quality has to be traded off against the constraints of time and money; money can be substituted for time, and vice versa.

1. 43 Fed. Reg. 55349, 55351–52 (Nov. 28, 1978).

Examiner–claimant allocations of responsibility will depend in part both on the claimant's ability to produce evidence of the requisite quality and on the time and resource constraints of the examiner.

Developmental guidelines can only hope to provide principles with respect to discrete developmental issues and a sense of priorities when trade-offs are inevitable. There is no way to determine a priori, for example, whether a claimant's complaint to the district office intake interviewer of "nervousness" should actuate development of psychological evidence through the purchase of a psychiatric consultation. That judgment depends on an assessment of all the other facts surrounding the case. It may not even be possible to establish general guidelines such as quotas for the purchase of consultative examinations (CEs). A 1979 study,[2] seeking to establish a consensus of expert examiners on the appropriate CE rate, found that in the ten states studied the expert consensus ranged from a 23 percent rate to a 56 percent rate. These variations are not necessarily evidence of interpretive differences. The variance from state to state in the quality of the medical evidence of record (without a CE), and perhaps also the projected quality of a CE, if ordered, may also be substantial. An examiner who works with good consultative specialists but an uncooperative hospital will order many more CEs than an examiner facing the reverse situation.

## Developmental Priorities

As in most bureaus, regulations may codify policy, but the line personnel work from a more discursive biblical source—the manual. The primary goal that emerges from the DISM's developmental guidelines is the protection of the claimant's interest in full development and consideration of his or her claim. Although there is a technical sense in which the claimant has the burden of proof, that is, of producing evidence that will establish a disability, it seems clear from the manual that this burden is very modest, indeed. If the claimant or some other source provides sufficient information to give direction to a search for relevant evidence, the disability examiner is expected to follow up every reasonably pertinent lead. Any doubt concerning the willingness of a claimant to provide information is to be resolved in favor of the

2. SSA, Bureau of Disability Insurance, Program Evaluation and Appraisal, "The Consultative Examination Study" (mimeo, January 1979).

claimant's inability to do so, and development of that information becomes the examiner's responsibility. Where there is a reasonable prospect that missing evidence can be provided by purchasing a CE, it should be purchased.

The development of "high quality" (that is, highly reliable) information is a close second among the DISM's developmental injunctions. Medical evidence is to be sought from qualified sources; it is to include objective clinical data wherever possible (EKG tracings, for example, not just their interpretation by a treating physician); and it is to be descriptive of the claimant's condition, not conclusory as to his or her work capacity. To the extent that evidence must be subjective or evaluative, it is to be obtained from the most qualified source. Thus, a description of the claimant's residual functional capacity (RFC) (ability to stand, stoop, lift, and climb stairs, stamina, etc.) should come, if possible, from a treating or consulting physician who has had an opportunity to observe the claimant's capacities. RFC may be evaluated by a DDS consulting physician only if clinical evidence already in the file permits an adequate evaluation. If both the above sources are inadequate, the claimant should be sent for evaluation by a vocational consultant or a vocational workshop.

Time and cost are not ignored. The manual offers many suggestions for saving development time, establishes timeliness goals, and makes clear that an inquiry will be made from the central office concerning any case that stays in the DDS longer than four months. Examiners are also urged not to buy information that is available free and not to consider CEs a routine part of case development. But the general message of the DISM is that client protection and quality evidentiary development come first.

One may question whether these developmental priorities represent a sound policy. Is it sufficiently clear that pursuit of the best available evidence contributes sufficiently to error reduction to justify its costs in delay and in direct administrative expense? Isn't the ready substitution of examiner development effort for claimant development effort a substitution of high-value for low-value resources? (Claimants are after all otherwise unemployed, and their claims implicitly assert that their services are worth less than $250 per month.) And isn't an emphasis on claimant protection a tilting of the system toward the avoidance of false negatives, when in principle there is no reason to believe that that type of error is more costly than false positives?

Last (and easiest) questions first. The pro-claimant orientation of development does not entail resolving doubts concerning the interpretation of the evidence in favor of the claimant. The DISM and all the regulations studiously avoid presumptions one way or another on the ultimate substantive issue. Moreover, there is a sense in which the insistence on high-quality evidence entails a systemic skepticism concerning the claimant's contentions. While there is no a priori reason to believe that pursuit of objective and reliable evidence will systematically disadvantage (or advantage) claimants, the subjective and opinion evidence that the developmental guides instruct examiners to avoid will normally be supplied by the claimant and those who are interested in supporting his or her petition for benefits—including the family doctor.

This last observation is connected, of course, to the first question: is high-quality evidence worth its cost? To the extent that pursuit of objective medical evidence tends to neutralize an otherwise inherent "tilt" toward false positives, it may substantially reduce error costs. And while one cannot know that there is a net benefit—induced false negatives plus administrative costs may outweigh the savings—it is difficult to propose a more neutral, less (administratively) expensive counterweight to the tendency for soft evidence from the claimant and the claimant's supporters to overstate the vocational effects of medical impairment. Claimants do not apply after all (or rarely apply) unless they believe that they are disabled. That belief is usually supported by advice from some source—a doctor, social worker, minister, family member, or friend—that the claimant cannot or should not work.

Better medical evidence apparently moderates "anti-claimant" or "conservative" bias as well. In the previously mentioned study of the use of CEs,[3] federal reviewers, who presumably are imbued with SSA's contemporaneous fiscal concerns, were asked to decide a random sample of cases twice—first on the medical evidence of record and then by considering a CE report. Consideration of the consultative report changed the result in 24 percent of the cases. Moreover, the change was from a denial to a grant in twice as many cases as from a grant to a denial.

The calculus of costs and benefits from quality evidentiary development is nevertheless awkward. *Changes in results that derive from the*

3. *Id.*

*pursuit of medical evidence are not the same as error corrections*. The evidence from the CE study also suggests that purchasing a CE in a case that has medical evidence of record sufficient to permit a judgment has a very modest payoff in decreased error rates—from 1 to 4 percent. Even this slight improvement may overstate a CE's error-reducing properties. Because the tests for error employed by the study were a subset of the usual quality assurance criteria, which define documentary deficiencies in the medical evidence as errors, the test may assume the necessity of the evidence whose effect on error reduction is purportedly being tested.

The pursuit of objective evidence also risks confusing objectivity with reality. Objectivity can be a fetish, and evidentiary requirements that insist on objective evidence may have unfortunate effects on outcomes. Pain is, obviously, subjective. But an attempt to limit subjectivity by concentrating on some objective indicator, such as tissue atrophy in the affected area, may simply disadvantage the courageous claimant who has continued to exercise in the vain hope of overcoming his or her impairment. Even more poignantly, insistence that clinical evidence of a metastasized carcinoma be available to support a favorable judgment may foreclose all but posthumous awards in certain classes of cases where the spread of the malignancy is, as a statistical matter, almost certain.

The DISM's demands for quality evidence are not limited to medical evidence or to objective data. And its other approaches to "quality" are also quite problematic. The guidelines on RFC, for example, seem to reintroduce a preference either for potentially unreliable evidence (the evaluation of a treating physician) or for a potentially very expensive bit of evidence from outsiders (vocational specialists or a vocational workshop), who in the final analysis will to able to offer only an opinion. To be sure, the treating physician has had an opportunity to observe the claimant, and an RFC questionnaire can limit the physician's flight into vague and conclusory generalities; but the prospect of bias—either to support a continuing relationship, help a friend, or buttress prior medical advice—is everpresent.

An even more extensive system for improving the quality of the evidence in DI cases can be imagined. In the late 1960s Saad Nagi[4]

4. S. NAGI, DISABILITY AND REHABILITATION (1970).

conducted an elaborate experiment designed to test the effects of multiprofessional assessments on claims adjudication. Specially trained medical, psychological, social service, and vocational personnel examined, evaluated, and discussed each claim. These assessments were then provided to state-agency adjudicators. On the basis of this "professional" evidence, adjudicators revised the decision in 30 percent of the sample cases. Two-thirds of these changes were in the claimants' favor. Unfortunately, while the Nagi study strongly indicates that evaluation of the workshop type tends to support claims, it gives us no idea how much such development costs nor any assurance that these costs are exceeded by benefits measured along other dimensions of system quality.

Our final developmental concern, the problem of substituting high-value examiner time for low-value claimant time, is probably a non-issue. Quite apart from normative doubts concerning whether market prices should be determinative, the substitution decision is, after all, left to the examiner. Whatever the DISM says, one has difficulty imagining that examiners systemically make inefficient substitutions of their effort for anyone else's. The dynamics of what happens in DDS offices is not necessarily captured by the manual.

This latter remark should, moreover, cause us to be skeptical about the efficacy of the manual's emphasis on quality evidence and claimant protection at the expense of delay and cost. The regulations and the manual are not the only management techniques available for guiding the exercise of developmental discretion. Budgets, training, supervisory feedback, and general work environment all influence examiner behavior. It is certainly possible that these influences will urge timeliness and cost consciousness at least as effectively as the DISM supports other values. If so, the policy skew apparent in the DISM may merely reflect the need to counter known and all-too-immediate work place concerns with the articulation of the ideals of service and accuracy. An appreciation of the operational balancing of developmental values must be sought in the dynamics of ongoing administration as well as in attempts to structure discretion by regulation or manual. We confront some of these questions in the next chapter.

## PROTECTING DIGNITARY INTERESTS

Many opportunities exist for claimants to feel alienated, abused, or disadvantaged in the DI decision process—or, for that matter, in any adjudicatory process. Persons seeking to obtain favorable judgment on claims relating to important interests always wonder whether they really understand what needs to be done to activate a favorable judgment, whether they have drawn a sympathetic "judge" who will pay close attention to their case, or whether politics might somehow be involved. No decision process can wholly eliminate these all-too-common reactions to the stress and uncertainty of adjudication. I have already expressed some skepticism of any process designer's capacity to generalize about questions that bear on individual preferences and self-definitions. Yet there are surely better and worse ways of promoting confidence and security, rather than their opposites, when constructing an adjudicatory process.

In order to make the discussion of these methods more manageable I will limit my inquiry to four "fairness" issues: (1) protection of claimant privacy; (2) equality of access to the decision process; (3) claimant control over the processing of a claim; and (4) the existence of appropriate legitimating symbols. Each of these issues is important to the development of an adjudicatory process that maintains or fosters dignity and self-respect. But, while some of the questions unearthed by a discussion of these topics have relatively nonproblematic answers and implications for the adjudicatory process, others are quite resistant either to conceptual or to programmatic resolution.

### Privacy

Certain types of incursions on personal privacy are both highly objectionable and easily controlled. Claimants should be assured that information supplied to the government for one purpose is not put to other, previously unannounced, purposes, and that personal data will remain inaccessible to the outside world save by the claimant's consent or direction. These basic privacy concerns are quite easily honored, with no significant interference in the effective operation of the disability adjudication process. Long before the passage of the Federal Privacy Act afforded general protection,[5] SSA had established elaborate safeguards against the misuse or improper release of identifiable information concerning its claimants, beneficiaries, or the "insured" population generally.

Protecting privacy in the pursuit of information necessary to decide a claim is more difficult than it is in merely handling information already

5. 88 Stat. 1897, 5 U.S.C. §5529 (1974).

collected. Examiners cannot perform their duty of developing the facts either effectively or expeditiously if they rely only upon data submitted by claimants. But independent development by the examiner always risks the collection of information that the claimant would have preferred not to submit. SSA attempts to guard against this possibility in two ways. First, the blanket authorization form, which permits SSA access to medical records and is routinely signed by claimants when they apply for benefits, segregates certain classes of sensitive medical evidence—treatment for mental illness, alcoholism, or drug abuse—and requires a separate authorization to collect such information. Second, the claimant may always preempt the examiner's development by declaring that he or she will produce evidence from a particular source.

More cannot prudently be done. To secure a new authorization for each treatment source discovered would cause significant delay. And even then the risk remains that a request for evidence of record from a hospital or physician will produce information that is both irrelevant and potentially embarrassing. The additional step of allowing claimants to screen all reports before they are included in the case file would be enormously time-consuming and would risk exposing claimants to information that *they* do not wish to have.

Other aspects of claims development are also regretably, but necessarily, intrusive. Questions about earnings, about skills and education, about family and other personal relationships, about bodily functioning, and about daily activities may all be intensely embarrassing, but they are not needlessly intrusive. The information sought is pertinent, and sequential development assures that it will be requested only if needed. Indeed, a process like SSA's that in merely asking for information provides the claimant an opportunity to decline to furnish it is much less intrusive than alternative processes that might be provided, such as surveillance, questioning of family and neighbors, or adversary cross-examination. Respecting privacy while securing personal data is an inherently awkward business. Given the obvious difficulties, SSA policy structures the process of data collection in relatively sensitive ways.

## Equality

SSA clearly attempts, through its development guides, to assure that each case gets the development that it needs for a sound judgment on eligibility. The demand for objective or other high-quality evidence, for example, is in equality terms a demand for a uniform level of developmental *results*, whatever differential costs of developmental *effort* those results may entail from case to case. The manual also makes clear that examiners are intended to apply their energies to the development of claims based not on some notion of equal expenditure of time and money but on the basis of the difficulty of accumulating needed data and of the claimant's need for assistance in developing the claim. (To the extent that developmental policies produce systematic inequalities in the availability of needed evidence—for example, the underdevelopment of subjective evidence—these are effects of the emphasis on documentary evidence at the initial and reconsideration levels of decision. I will discuss these and other equality problems of the multi-tier structure in more detail below.)

A policy mandating uniform developmental results is justifiable to a substantial degree only by fairness considerations. A developmental policy concerned exclusively with error costs would attempt to allocate development effort in terms of the probability that a case would fall at the high-error-cost tails of the disability continuum. These cases, of course, tend to be those in which a judgment can be made on the medical evidence alone. Yet under current directions the middle-run or marginal cases, where error costs are presumably modest, always get additional effort devoted to vocational development *after* the medical evidence has been collected. And it seems highly likely that these cases will often also benefit from greater-than-average medical development: examiners will order CEs in an attempt to clarify or resolve conflicts in the medical evidence of record and thereby avoid moving to more judgmental criteria. SSA's approach to developmental equality, to attempt to give each case the development it needs for sound judgment, thus seems consistent with the distributive purposes of the Social Security Act. It also suggests an investigative decision process that has a service orientation as well as a bureaucratically rational one.

There is, however, one glaring exception to SSA's exemplary official posture—the treatment of cases involving congressional inquiries. Under existing policy these cases are entitled to expedited processing, and the inquiring congressman receives first notification of an award (presumably in order to permit him to telegraph the results to his constituent, thus associating himself with a favorable outcome). Although examiners uniformly testify that congressional interest almost never expedites a case and has no effect on outcome, both policies are preposterous. There is no justification for expediting 100,000 "sensitive inquiry" cases per year at the expense of additional delay in the more than 1 million remaining disability filings. And the suggestion that there is a "political" avenue to favorable judgment undermines the apparent integrity of a decision process that has been so carefully constructed and defended in other ways.

The level of congressional inquiries may nevertheless be an important indicator of claimant dissatisfaction with the adjudicatory process, particularly with unexplained delay. If nearly one in twelve claimants writes his or her representative expressing the fear that his or her claim has somehow been lost in the bureaucratic shuffle, then the decision process is not inspiring confidence in a substantial portion of its clientele. I will return to this issue momentarily.

The general policy "develop each case according to its needs" is a necessary condition for developmental equality, but it is not alone sufficient to limit or eliminate systematic disadvantages in the claims process. Nor is it the end of SSA effort. Responding to greater need for prompt payment and to greater difficulty and therefore longer delays in developing SSI claims, SSA has devised categories of "presumptive" disability that permit payment before all the evidence is in. In addition, special studies have attempted to validate various evidentiary requirements and thereby to avoid unnecessary disadvantages to claimants who cannot produce customary documentary evidence.

Nevertheless, there is always the possibility of doing more. And given the suggestions in prior studies that the decision process may systematically disadvantage the uneducated, the unintelligent, racial minorities, and women,[6] there has been surprisingly little attempt by SSA to validate the complaints or to take corrective action.

Plausible reasons for this "default" are not too difficult to generate. First, validation is not easy. To detect bias, including developmental bias, outcomes must be evaluated as a function of one variable, say race, while other variables—particularly what might be called "real claim strength"—are either held constant or accounted for. This entails both the development of a quasi-objective and mathematically manipulable

---

6. See the authorities in chapter 2 note 2. See also, Institute for Community Studies, "Case Facilitator Project" (mimeo, undated) SSA-71-3409; M. Bendick, "Why Do Persons Eligible for Public Assistance Fail to Enroll?" (mimeo, Urban Institute Working Paper, August 1979).

index of the various factors affecting claim strength and the use of a sampling procedure that does not rely on the documentary record produced by potentially biased prior development. The first task is conceptually difficult and the second is very expensive.

Second, if a "racial" or "sex" or "intelligence" or "education" factor were to be found in development or decisionmaking—one that could not be accounted for by other closely linked variables—it is not clear that anything could be done about it. Having confirmed the critics, SSA might then be in the position of having no clearly effective and acceptable means of solving the problem. For if these biases exist they may be more a reflection (in the disability program's inherently judgmental decisionmaking) of deep-seated cultural stereotypes than a result of the program's structures or processes. That would mean that the agency would confront a choice between a weak and possibly ineffective response (consciousness raising) and a strong but undesirable remedy (elimination of subjective judgment).

Given these problems and pitfalls, the commissioner is unlikely to believe that a massive study of the fate of disadvantaged persons in the DI process should be a high-priority item. But fear of exposing a problem that, if it exists, should be considered serious is hardly courageous management. And despair of a solution to an as yet vaguely defined potential problem may well be misplaced. Doubts, in my view, should be resolved in favor of investigation.

Similar and equally difficult equality problems beset the multi-tier decision structure. As previously mentioned, the oral ALJ hearing process is substantially different from the documentary state agency decision process. Moreover, ALJs grant nearly 50 percent of the claims they hear, whereas state agencies grant less than 30 percent. And, of course, the very severely disabled will generally have been granted benefits at the state agency level and will, therefore, not be seen at the hearing level. The questions are whether this substantial change in the chances for success on a marginal claim is merely a reward for pursuing a claim to a third decision; and, if so, whether that "perseverance bounty" is in some way discriminatory.

Two possible views of the purposes of hearings and of the nature of appealed cases would suggest that an increased success rate from moving to a different decision process raises no serious equality concern. One view is that the hearing process is designed to emphasize subjective evaluation of the claimant's situation and that appealed cases represent those in which a more intuitive and personal approach is necessary to understand the claimants' residual capacities for productive work. If this were the situation, there would be no prejudice to non-appealing claimants. Claimants who are successful at the hearing would be disadvantaged only by the delay entailed in having to appeal twice to get to an oral hearing. While that disadvantage may be substantial, it may be outweighed by the costliness of installing a hearing procedure earlier in the decision process.

A second apologetic view is that hearings and subsequent stages of the process are concerned with legitimizing the resolution of a conflict in which neither side can be said to be correct. This view further asserts that these additional efforts at legitimation (a hearing before a judge) are actuated by those who are most dissatisfied with earlier dispositions of their claims. From this perspective, nonappealing claimants are satisfied claimants and no disadvantage to them inheres in the provision of a different and potentially very beneficial decision process to those who do preserve to an appeal.

These descriptions of the (alternative? dual?) purposes and operations of the hearing process have both plausibility and appeal. Yet they are hardly persuasive to those who believe that appealed and unappealed claims do not differ either in their strength or in the satisfaction of those who hold them, and that the requirement of persevering to the hearing stage in order to get an approximation of the current hearing process disadvantages the ignorant, the incompetent, and the demoralized. Some data on the characteristics of appellants in 1970 and 1975 suggest that they are disproportionately white, middle-aged males with relatively more recent and higher earnings than those who do not appeal.[7] The appealing and nonappealing claimants have virtually indistinguishable subsequent job histories (few return to work) and mortality rates. And a pretest of the broad 1978 National Survey of Disability and Work, which included the question, "Why didn't you ask to have your case reviewed?" found only 4 percent willing to admit that they thought their denial had been correct.[8] The existing data thus give some grounds for concern but do not permit comparison of the appealing and

7. Ralph Treitel, "Disability Claimants Who Contest Denials and Win Reversals Through Hearings," DHEW, SSA, Office of Research and Statistics Working Paper Series, Division of Disability Studies, no. 3 (mimeo, 1979).

8. *Id*. at 19.

nonappealing claimants along the important evaluative dimensions of claim strength and satisfaction. Although obtaining the information needed to make such evaluations would be difficult and costly, assuming the power of the appeals process to sort claims and claimants in appropriate ways is not costless.

## Claimant Participation and Control

Major features of the disability decision process combine to divest claimants of control over or participation in the processing of their claims. The basic criteria for judgment are opaque. The critical medical evidence is technical and often incomprehensible to the lay person. The state agency as decisionmaker is a faceless, formless, and presumably inaccessible bureaucracy. At least until the hearing stage of the process, there are no well-organized groups who provide guidance or assistance to claimants. The claimant makes an application, signs a release form for medical evidence, and waits for the decision to arrive in the mail some months later. The manual urges examiners to write concise, informative decisions, but the reality seems to be that neither denial nor grant letters are comprehensible to their recipients.

To be sure, there are points of contact and choice in the process, but they are not likely to be very meaningful as devices for involving claimants in claims processing. Information is initially taken by someone in a Social Security district office, but this potential "contact person" has virtually no involvement in the case after the file has been transferred to the state DDS. The claimant may or may not receive requests for further information from the examiner handling the claim, but such communications respond to the examiner's judgment about the purposes and usefulness of a contact and provide only the reassurance of a disembodied voice at the other end of a telephone line. The claimant chooses either to submit the requested evidence or undergo a CE; but given his or her knowledge of the system, that choice is almost of necessity delegated to the examiner.

Impersonality and lack of control are to a degree remedied at the hearing level. There, claimants encounter a decider face-to-face, are invited to review the evidence of record, may say or ask what they will about their claims, and are assisted in obtaining outside representation should they desire it. Too much can easily be made of these features of hearings. The operational reality is that the hearing process, and much of the claimant's participation in it remains firmly within the control of the ALJ. But by comparison with the level of claimant participation in the prehearing levels of decisionmaking, the ALJ hearing resembles an encounter group.

Proposals abound to incorporate one or another participatory aspect of the hearing process into earlier stages of DI decisionmaking. While it is difficult to be against providing claimants with a greater sense of participation in and control over their claims—thereby, hopefully, giving them a stronger belief that they have been fairly treated in the claims process—the question remains whether, and in what ways, increasing claimants' knowledgeable participation and sense of control is a useful and prudent strategy. Other reforms, after all, might have a greater positive impact on the claimants' sense of the system's fairness and might be implemented at substantially less cost. Moreover, the "participatory" proposals—better information, use of adversary process, provision of representatives, face-to-face interview—subsume a variety of techniques.

If we puzzle for a moment about how participation or control contributes to one's sense of fairness, perhaps the path to improvement will become clearer. Participation and control might promote a sense of fairness in two principal ways. The first is cognitive: participation may produce an understanding on the claimant's part of the substantive adjudicatory norms and of the decision process. This understanding may rationalize both the otherwise apparently random events leading to a decision and the decision itself. Similarly, participation in or control over the collection and presentation of evidence inspires confidence that sufficient efforts (the claimant's or his or her representative's) have been made to inform the decisionmaker about the case. The second function of participation is, thus, monitoring. In addition to increasing the claimant's confidence in the level of development effort, participation may help to ensure that the adjudicator "really listens" to what the claimant thinks is important and that disadvantageous evidence is not accepted without close scrutiny.

Yet the chances seem very slim that claimants can, at acceptable cost, be brought to understand the disability standard sufficiently (1) to participate effectively in collecting and presenting evidence and in monitoring the decision process or (2) to rationalize for himself or herself why a decision is unfavorable. Information about the system is not easily or quickly transmitted. Disability examiners, for example, all of whom have college degrees, are given six weeks of special training, are reviewed intensively for their first six months, and are generally considered experienced or expert only after several years on the job. Without understanding, participation or control becomes an obvious and cruel joke rather than an assurance of fairness.

If this conclusion is correct, then several things seem to follow. First, inexpensive attempts to increase the flow of information to claimants, such as the Congress's recent instruction to the secretary to provide better explanation of unfavorable determinations, are not likely to have major effects on levels of satisfaction with the process. These communications remedies confront the intractability of the human materials. How much more effective district office explanations, brochures, examiner contacts, and decision writing can be made is deeply problematic. We should remember that the vagueness, ambiguity, and incoherence of carefully crafted statutes, regulations, and judicial opinions provide the minor premise for a massive critical literature, the output of the nation's law reviews. That literature finds much of the contemporary expression of legal rules less than fully legitimate because much less than fully rational. Beautifully crafted disability opinions and fulsome explanations of the process of decision seem destined for a similar fate. They must contend in addition with the difficulties of communicating to an audience that has modest interpretive skills and a strong incentive to feel aggrieved.

In addition, attempts to convince claimants of the rationality of their initial or reconsideration denials may overshoot the mark. Does SSA *want* to convey the notion that decisions are correct, and implicitly that appeal is fruitless, when in fact appeal is quite fruitful? Would intensive and self-conscious projection of rationality reflect reality? Or would it be a pose? Is there not a sense in which SSA relies on claimant dissatisfaction to complete a process of institutional decisionmaking that cannot conform to all the dimensions of rational adjudication at any one decision point?

The appropriate calibration of claimant acceptance and skepticism is obviously a subtle business. It requires knowing what claims *ought* to be appealed and how to structure communications in ways that foster the productive and deter the unproductive pursuit of claims. Given the dim probability that these things will ever be known, it is perhaps comforting that efforts at legitimizing decisions through better communication concerning the systematic and rational character of bureaucratic decisionmaking will almost certainly have but modest success. A sense of illegitimacy, even outrage, may also have its value in promoting bureaucratic justice.

Expensive changes in the decisional structure—the use of face-to-face hearings at the reconsideration level, for example—may also have an insubstantial impact. (Indeed, tests of face-to-face reconsideration suggest that it has only a modest impact on the desire to go on to a hearing.)[9] A better candidate for "participatory" reform might be the provision of independent representatives who can become knowledgeable about the system, substitute themselves for claimants as participants in the adjudicatory process, and act as information mediators between the adjudicatory system and its clientele.

Such a proposal has a number of drawbacks—cost, the problematic relationship between representation and participatory satisfaction, problems of "institutionalizing" or "professionalizing" claims representatives—but it seems worth exploring. The Veterans Administration has fostered a high level of representation of claimants in its comparably sized disability program. And while there are many other contributing factors, the VA seems to have managed to maintain an acceptable level of satisfaction with its process without significant use of oral hearings, without employing independent ALJs, and without subjecting its judgments to judicial review.[10] Moreover, broadened or universal representation is one technique that has not been given serious study at SSA.

## Appropriate Symbolism

The preceding discussion foreshadows the conclusion that the DI process, at least prior to the hearing level, lacks an effective legitimizing symbolism. At the level of general policy choice, we may view bureaucratic rationality as a legitimate, indeed (all things considered) a just decision process. But from the perspective of a denied claimant, the suggestion that SSA is generally well-structured, rational, and efficient

9. DHEW, SSA, Division of Field Disability Operations, "SARIS. State Agency Reconsideration Interview Study" (mimeo, October 1971). A later study of a similar procedure (RIS Reconsideration Interview Study) found a somewhat larger impact—one sufficient to offset the increased administrative costs of the reconsideration interviews.

10. *See generally,* S. LEVITAN AND K. CLEARY. OLD WARS REMAIN UNFINISHED: THE VETERANS BENEFITS SYSTEM (1973).

is rather cold comfort. That bureaucratic rationality adequately defines justice may be persuasive, to use John Rawls's mellifluous phrase, as a "considered judgment" in "reflective equilibrium."[11] But that is a posture more easily assumed by the economically secure and physically sound. Moreover, it requires the appreciation and assessment of much that fails to appear in a disembodied decision letter.

The technical soundness of medical and vocational judgments is not particularly meaningful to people who have concluded from concrete and often bitter and demoralizing experience that they cannot work. A denial will seem unjust both as implicit moral commentary on the claimant's plight and by comparison with the situations of others who have been given benefits. Moreover, given the claimant's exposure to the decision process, it may also seem to have been reached mysteriously, if not whimsically or arbitrarily. The internal workings of the process that might inspire confidence—interpretive and developmental guides, sequential processing, utilization of professional expertise, training, management supervision, quality assurance activities—are invisible.

At the hearing, on the other hand, the claimant is provided a "day in court" that seems to have a substantial impact on acceptance of an ultimate denial. Appeals from hearing decisions occur with much less frequency than do appeals to the hearing stage. This may be due, at least in part, to the symbolic power of the judge or the legal hearing to promote acceptance of the legitimacy of a disappointing judgment. Even at the hearing, however, the symbolism is mixed. The judge is statutorily independent, but nevertheless an employee of SSA. The day in court may resemble a business conference or social services consultation more than a trial. The ALJs are themselves divided as to whether they should project the formality and dignity associated with the courtroom or the informality and concern associated with the helping professions. The Office of Hearings and Appeals (OHA) encourages informality, believing both that it reduces delay and also that it limits the exasperating tendency of ALJs to construe their independence to mean that they are a substantive law unto themselves. No serious attempt has yet been made to discover the effects of changes in the format of hearings on claimant perceptions of legitimacy.

11. J. Rawls, A Theory of Justice 20, 48–51 (1971).

No other legitimizing symbols strongly support the SSA judgments emerging from the current decision structure. The disability decision can hardly be described as a social or community judgment. No jury of peers or committee representing affected interests gives its imprimatur to SSA decisions. Professional medical judgments are imbedded in the process, but they are somewhat hidden from the claimant's view. The SSA consulting physician who signs off on a decision never sees the claimant, nor does he or she provide a separate written medical opinion. Physicians who do CEs do not report their findings to the claimants, and unless an appeal is taken the claimant will almost never see the CE report. The potential legitimating effects of medical professionalism are often impaired or wholly subverted in any event by the denied claimant's prior medical advice to stop work.

Nor is it likely that the present process will gain legitimacy by its obvious concern for the claimants' interests. As social caseworkers will amply attest, the prospects of inducing acceptance of undesired advice or control through identification with the client's concerns are limited even where institutional arrangements are designed specifically for that purpose. And, while disability examiners may care deeply about fair treatment of claimants, their concern is mediated by a bureaucratic structure whose attempts to institutionalize empathy are submerged by its need to manifest orderliness and control.

It is perhaps the fate of SSA to be misunderstood. But fate and duty should not be confused. The agency can explain itself better; it can make reliance on medical expertise more transparent; it can institutionalize concern through representatives or other mediating structures; it can begin to investigate carefully claimants' perceptions of its process. I will return to these themes in chapter 10, which proposes some reforms for SSA's brand of bureaucratic justice.

# 7 · Exercising Hierarchical Control

Translating statutory policy into operational norms and processes for decisionmaking is a necessary administrative task. But it is only the beginning of good public sector management. SSA must also attempt to ensure that regulatory and manual instructions control—or at least influence—the concrete events of disability adjudication. This managerial task includes (1) an "oversight" function—determining whether low-level actions (disability decisions and procedure) are consistent with the policies enunciated—and (2) what I shall refer to as a "cultural engineering" function—putting the pieces of the decision process together so that the interaction of policy, process, personnel, and structure yield desirable outputs: in this case, rational, efficient, and fair disability adjudications.

The two tasks are, of course, connected; and there are many other ways to conceptualize SSA's exercise of hierarchical control. But these two categories respond to two of SSA's major administrative problems. The first is how to develop useful information for managerial evaluation and action in a system of this scale. If the secretary of Health and Human Services is to be responsible, as the Social Security Act says he or she is, for the more than 1 million disability decisions made each year, how is that official to know what he or she is doing and deciding? Less abstractly, how can SSA, acting for the secretary, find out whether those disability examiners are getting and doing things right? The second problem embraces and transcends the first: how is SSA, assuming that it can get relevant information, to exercise authority over decisional personnel who are not only widely dispersed but also not its own? Examiners and all of their immediate—indeed, all of their direct—supervisors are state employees.

145

In this chapter I will discuss the problems SSA faces when perform-ing these managerial tasks and the methods by which it has begun to improve its capacity to control the adjudicatory system. Yet, as we shall see, these "improvements" introduce a sense of unease about a hierar-chically controllable structure. Control, as chapter 8 argues, has its own imperatives—imperatives that may inhibit rather than enhance the attainment of bureaucratic justice.

## OVERSIGHT

SSA might learn about and evaluate disability adjudications by monitor-ing the cases or by monitoring the state agencies. In fact it does both. Cases are reviewed by SSA administrative law judges and by the SSA Appeals Council, and they are separately scrutinized in the quality assurance (QA) program. The state agencies have a continuing relation-ship with SSA regional offices, which review the usual mountains of paper reporting associated with federally funded activities, make on-site inspections, and serve as an intermediary between the states and the SSA central office.

We will not concern ourselves extensively here with the role of the regional office in monitoring state agencies. Such an analysis leads into too dense a thicket of federal-state relations, a tangle whose subtleties and complexities would justify another book. We will content our-selves, therefore, with a mere sketch of the reasons for believing that exercise of hierarchical supervision or control is not an apt description of regional office functioning.

Ideally, regional offices might be viewed as necessary communication links between federal and state cultures, translating the former into a vernacular that is useful and effective in the latter. But the reality is surely more complex. I suspect that the position of regional offices is rather like that of U.S. embassies abroad. Strategically located in the flow of information, uniquely situated to understand what neither state nor central office officials can readily appreciate, the regional office develops its own perspectives on appropriate administration in the federal–state mode. It seeks to mediate inevitable conflict and misun-derstanding rather than to facilitate hierarchical supervision or control.

The case for a unique regional office perspective can certainly be oversold, but in the disability program at least there is reasonably solid evidence of it. State agencies customarily ask for interpretations of policy from their regional contacts rather than from Baltimore. And these letter or memorandum instructions are not consistent from region to region, nor are they necessarily the same as those that Baltimore would issue if it were consulted on the same question. Heads of state agencies constantly complain about this diversity: it is perhaps their favorite "you-see-what-I'm-up-against" story. The states also note inconsistency in the QA feedback from their regional office (Title XVI and concurrent cases) as compared with that from the central office (Title II cases). Not only do sharply differing rates of errors appear in the statistics, but also different types of errors are found. No one believes this represents differences in the handling of virtually identical cases, from identical geographic areas, by identical examiners, in identical state agencies.

After extensive staff interviews and reviews of internal documents in one regional office and several of its (client? subordinate?) state agencies, two of my students conclude:

Evidence is mixed as to the effectiveness of the Regional Office in helping the disability program to achieve its objectives. On balance, the RO helps modestly to promote program objectives. . . . [T]he problem appears to be the virtual impossibility of the RO's task resulting from both structural difficulties inherent in the federal/state relationship and lack of clear national policy directives about the role and responsibilities of the RO. Examples of factors which impede the RO's performance of its assigned tasks are the following: conflicting bureaucratic objectives (e.g., accuracy and timeliness); monitoring responsibilities without direct enforcement power; system-wide quality assurance responsibility without authority for making system-wide corrections; responsibility for negotiating federal/state agreements when national policy permits no real negotiating; tension between the RO's watchdog and facilitator roles.[1]

I will therefore focus attention on the monitoring of cases. As I mentioned, there are two separate techniques: appeals and quality assurance. At a conceptual level, the use of these two techniques need entail only the difference between review initiated by disappointed participants in an adjudicatory proceeding (appeal) and the agency's review of its own work product to appraise and improve the quality of adjudicatory performance (quality assurance). In the context of the SSA decisional system, however, the two approaches generate significant

1. Krome and Levenson, "The Social Security Disability Program Regional Office: Help or Hindrance?" (Sept. 15, 1980) (unpublished paper).

differences in what gets reviewed, what information concerning performance is fed back to adjudicators, how that information is interpreted, and what positive or negative sanctions are available to correct poor performance.

## Appeals

Appeals in private civil litigation have a series of characteristics that may make them important checks on adjudicative accuracy. First, appeals are universally available to losers or even to partial winners. Every decision is potentially a subject for appellate review. Second, appellate review is based on the factual record and normative claims previously made—review on appeal is of the same case that was tried below. Third, limitations on the scope of appellate review direct attention to whether a clear error was committed below and thereby reduce the possibilities for the introduction of new errors on appeal. Fourth, the reasons for believing that an error has or has not occurred are specified in an opinion of the appellate body—an opinion that of necessity is communicated to the trial court, which retains control over effectuation of the ultimate judgment. Fifth, accurate adjudication is sanctioned by the obvious effects on professional reputation of a large number of reversals in a judicial system that emphasizes personalized responsibility for decisions.

Appeals in civil litigation do not provide a perfect system for the elimination of error. Yet by comparison with SSA appeals the customary structure of civil appeals has major advantages. First, in the DI system appeals are only from denials, not from grants; roughly half the caseload is outside the appellate review system. Second, appeals are de novo; they therefore do not focus on the existence of errors at the prior adjudicative level. Indeed, the hearing process, which employs live testimony, substantial redevelopment of the documentary record, and vaguer criteria for judgment, so transforms cases that DDS and ALJ adjudicators could be said to be dealing with different cases. Third, "appellate" determinations generally do not become known to first-level adjudicators. A hearing grant is directly effectuated through the national office and will return to the state agency only if the case is diaried for redetermination at a later date. (Even if known to state examiners, ALJ decisions are viewed as deciding the case anew; they contain no clear information on the quality of the initial adjudication.)

Finally, no public, professional appraisal based on the ability of decisions to withstand review continuously constrains individual adjudicative performance by state DDS personnel.

If appeals make any contribution to the pursuit of high-quality adjudication at the state agency level in the DI program, it is very limited. This is not necessarily a condemnation of the structure of Social Security appeals. There may, indeed, be quite sensible bases for the features of that structure that limit its usefulness as a general oversight mechanism. The preceding discussion merely highlights the necessity for a strong QA program, if accuracy is to be subject to systematic evaluation and hierarchical control.

## Quality Assurance[2]

The basic idea of a quality assurance system is quite simple: performance standards must be developed; performance data are then evaluated in accordance with those standards; and actions are taken to improve performance where it fails to meet the predetermined goals of the system. Virtually all organizations of any size, in both the public and private sectors, have supervisory systems that respond to this basic structure. Indeed, the importance of the QA function has so permeated the consciousness of consumers in our mass production economy that manufacturers find it worthwhile to feature their quality control programs and personnel in television advertising. Each aspect of the QA structure—standards, evaluation of data, and action—will, however, vary with the organization involved and the type of activity it undertakes. Adjudication of disability claims is no exception.

*Standards*  If the quality of performance is to be judged, there obviously must be some standard against which to judge it. The more specific and objective the goals of the organization can be made, the easier it will be to determine whether or not performance meets expectations. In this sense, the problem of setting appropriate standards in QA replicates the problem of developing appropriately specific and objective norms. There are, however, other complications. The first lies in determining

2. For more extended discussion of these techniques *see*, Mashaw, *The Management Side of Due Process*, 59 Cornell L. Rev. 772 (1974); Chassman and Rolston, *Social Security Disability Hearings: A Case Study in Quality Assurance and Due Process*, 65 Cornell L. Rev. 803 (1980).

when adjudicative behavior should be classified as erroneous or inappropriate. The norms of the system will necessarily leave some area for discretion or judgment, and a QA system might be seen merely as a device for second-guessing the first-line adjudicators. To some degree this problem can be solved by limiting the QA analyst's scope of review. An error is assigned only if it is "clear."

The difficulty with this approach is that in a system involving a substantial degree of adjudicative judgment, there are likely to be very few clear errors. Yet it may be the case that certain decision-makers consistently exercise their "judgment" in ways that the responsible managers of the system would consider inappropriate, albeit not clearly erroneous. If the QA mechanism is to be very useful, it must have some technique for dealing with these judgmental deficiencies. This problem can be at least partially solved by giving the QA analyst an opportunity to assign a "judgment deficiency" in cases where there is no clear error, but where the analyst believes nevertheless that discretion was improperly exercised.

Another problem is the possibility that deficiency assignments alone would not generate reform. The QA system must attempt to identify the underlying causes of judgmental deficiencies and to mold the exercise of discretion in an appropriate form. One means of accomplishing this is an increasingly fine-grained analysis of the inputs to decision-making. The system can concentrate, for example, on the completeness of the evidence collected, the degree to which appropriate use was made of specialists in either medical or vocational factors, whether rules concerning the weight to be accorded different types of evidence in case of conflict have been followed, and so on. While process never wholly determines outcome, attention given to the information collection and processing aspects of decisionmaking should certainly foster the pursuit of correct adjudication.

QA standards must not only specify expected behavior but also include some notion of how good individual adjudicative performance should be in order to be acceptable. SSA must decide both what an error is and how many of them are too many. As a management tool, the specification of a zero error rate would be useless. That goal, which cannot be met within sensible cost constraints, would be either irrelevant or demoralizing. This much is clear, but choosing a number larger than zero can be quite difficult. A historical error rate might be based on experience. Alternatively, the error rates of the best state agencies might be used. Beginning with either of these normal rates, the acceptable percentage of erroneous decisions might be reduced over time as the capacity to meet specified targets is realized.

A third problem in developing standards for administrative adjudication in the disability program has to do with one's interest in record errors as against real world errors. A QA analyst who reviews the output of first-line adjudicators will, in a system as massive as SSA, necessarily rely on the administrative record that was before the adjudicator. But that record may not represent the real world characteristics of the claimant. Hence, a decision that is correct on the record might well be incorrect if the true facts were known. Obviously, QA is intended to provide correctness, not a facade of correctness.

Addressing this dilemma from a QA perspective, we can see the importance of concentrating on inputs; assuring that the record is complete is of the highest importance. Furthermore, it is necessary to buttress the review of the record with a program for redeveloping cases from the ground up to determine whether the input controls are sufficient to make the records reveal, or approximate, reality. In this way the QA program can feed back into policy formation.

*Data Gathering and Evaluation* If we assume a QA system that specifies standards, then information must be collected concerning the conformity of individual adjudicative judgments with those standards. That information must then be evaluated to determine whether the overall performance goals of the system are being met, and, if not, why not. Given the availability of well-understood statistical techniques for sampling the universe of disability adjudications (or other universes), there will of course be cost advantages to statistical (or sample) review methodology. Moreover, the fact that review is limited to a sample of claims reinforces the notion that QA is a device for identifying errors for management purposes. The goal is to identify trends in the adjudication process and to take action that remedies the underlying causes of erroneous decisions.

Statistical analysis, of course, also has disadvantages. QA analysis may not sample a sufficient number of decisions by any one adjudicator to analyze his or her work product reliably. Information will be aggregated to a more general organizational level, such as the state agency as a whole. Moreover, in order for the data from the QA program to be manipulable electronically, the information cannot be very subtle. The analyst will be asked to look for relatively objective factors in the decision process and to record them in some binary way, as existing or not existing, or as being right or wrong. Both of these disadvantages may undermine the ultimate usefulness of the QA information. Hence, statistical analysis must be combined with other more fine-grained management techniques for the collection and evaluation of performance information.

*Action* The rationale for setting behavioral standards and gathering information on compliance with those standards is obviously to provide the basis for management control of performance. That control equally obviously entails action based upon the information that is collected and analyzed. Perhaps the most straightforward action that can be taken to improve performance is to disseminate the information collected in the QA enterprise among the deciders whose performance is being appraised. To be effective, the feedback on trend analysis and on the causes of erroneous decisionmaking must be timely (that is, related to behavior patterns that still exist) and detailed enough to enable adjudicators or adjudication units to perceive how their performance should be improved. Because information feedback and reliance on efforts at self-correction are the principal supervisory techniques in virtually every management system, general respect for the integrity of the QA data is critical.

Management reaction to QA reports could take any number of additional forms. Maybe performance can be improved only by improving the specificity of the normative directions that the SSA statute, regulations, and handbook material give to individual adjudicators. Difficulties may emerge that require changes in the decision process (including alteration of evidentiary requirements) or in the use of professional staff. Further studies may be necessary to determine the causative elements that underlie trends identified by the QA data. And ultimately it may be necessary to apply some sanctioning mechanisms (required training, more intensive review, or even changes in federal–state contractual relationships) in order to improve performance. I will return to these action themes in a moment, when I take up SSA's cultural engineering function.

*SSA's Performance* Since 1974, SSA has had a quite elaborate three-tier QA system. The first tier is a preadjudicative review conducted by QA units within the state agencies. It functions almost like an automatic appeal of a percentage (at least 15 percent) of examiner decisions. Cases that are "bounced" are sent back for redevelopment or redetermination before a decision is transmitted to the claimant. The second tier consists of a 5 percent postadjudicative sample review by the SSA central office for Title II claims and a 7 percent regional office review for Title XVI (including concurrent Title II) claims. The third tier of the system is an end-of-the-line review and appraisal by the SSA central office that uses a subsample of the second-tier review cases to monitor and evaluate the entire claims process.

The system, despite its thoroughness, was strongly criticized by the General Accounting Office (GAO) in its 1976 study of SSA's management of the disability claims process. In the words of the report:

The quality assurance system is not fully effective because: The system is not properly established or functioning in all state agencies. The feedback to the three levels within the system has been inadequate or non-existent. The trend analysis and special studies intended to correct system-wide problems are non-existent. The criteria for returning cases to the states for reconsideration or review may be too restrictive. The present quality assurance system provides little or no assurance that problems related to the disability determination process are identified and appropriate action taken.[3]

In its memorandum commenting on the GAO's findings, SSA in effect admitted that the QA program had, at that time, a great many shortcomings. The list of the actions that SSA was prepared to take "along the lines of GAO's recommendation" indicates the degree of ineffectuality then existing with respect to all elements of the system. SSA promised to:

1. Issue a comprehensive message to regional offices on strengthening DDS quality assurance related activities and functions.
2. Prepare a summary of quality assurance surveys of selected state agencies.

3. Office of the Comptroller General, "The Social Security Administration Should Provide More Management and Leadership in Determining Who is Eligible for Disability Benefits" (Aug. 17, 1976, unpublished report).

3. Establish a series of "quality pars" (performance goals) for measuring state agency quality.
4. Strengthen DDS quality assurance organization.
5. Further refine the standardized classification system for defining errors and/or deficiencies.
6. Redesign reporting format to provide users more definitive date.
7. Develop procedures for implementing flexible review and for coordinating statistical and narrative feedback.
8. Complete work on mechanical selection of DI and SSI samples.
9. Complete development and implementation of the quality review system for determinations of continuing disability.

The GAO looked at SSA quality assurance activities again in 1978. In that report, the GAO merely recounted what SSA had said it would do and added that, according to its conferences with state agency and regional office officials, the latter believed that SSA's actions would help to improve quality and to provide better feedback throughout the system. However, these same state and regional officials believed that SSA's actions to that time would not correct all the problems and that it was too early to tell whether the system had in fact been improved.[4]

SSA's reforms are, on paper, sufficient to establish all the basic elements of a properly functioning QA program. Among other things, SSA gave new impetus to the regional office approach to QA by holding a series of high-level meetings and by demanding regional action plans for reforming deficiencies. It issued new instructions to the state agencies that reorganized their QA effort and set out in greater detail points that they seemed to have misunderstood. SSA redesigned and redrafted its QA forms and the instructions for their use. It successfully implemented an automated QA data collection and retrieval system that permits QA information on various aspects of the process to be retrieved by regional offices at any time. SSA has finally established processing goals for both timeliness and accuracy of decisionmaking. It has initiated "staged federal response" to low-performance states. And it has expanded review projects both to test the differences between 100-percent preadjudicative on-site federal review and the QA program

---

4. Office of the Comptroller General, "A Plan for Improving the Disability Determination Process by Bringing it Under Complete Federal Control Should be Developed" (Aug. 31, 1978, unpublished report).

and to determine the cause of chronic low performance in three state agencies. Perhaps most important, SSA reorganized itself to unify the programmatically dispersed QA staff into a single appraisal branch for monitoring adjudicative performance in all its programs—and gave that new office a prominent and high-level position on the SSA organizational chart.

Congress, however, was unwilling to await the results of these efforts. In the 1980 amendments it mandated an eventual 65 percent preeffectuation review of all state agency *awards*. In so doing, it seems to have expressed a legislative view that the primary function of QA review is cost containment. It has thus introduced a skewed perspective into a monitoring system whose previous design had treated errors, wherever occurring, as equally worthy of interest, correction, and prevention. How seriously one should be concerned about skewing, of course, depends in part upon one's view of whether certain existing program features or operational realities, bureaucratic ease and one-sided appeals among others, give the system a proaward bias that needs correction by a skewed QA effort. Concern about skewing should also be mediated by an appreciation of the functional effectiveness of any QA effort, indeed any SSA *managerial* effort—a topic to which we now turn our attention.

## ENGINEERING AN ADJUDICATORY CULTURE

The history of QA at SSA yields competing conclusions. That history might be thought to demonstrate that a QA system has little prospect of making a real impact on the quality of decisionmaking at the initial stage. On the other hand, it may simply represent a shakedown phase in the implementation of an increasingly sophisticated and effective system for controlling and improving performance. In the absence of definitive data, we can only speculate about the program's effects and about how those effects reflect the broader environment of state agency decisionmaking.

One might predict that the collection, organization, and feedback of QA data would be both too weak and too powerful in shaping adjudicatory behavior. Too weak because the chances of any particular case being caught by the QA net would counsel examiners to "play the numbers," that is, to treat QA review as irrelevant to their task; too powerful because the easily objectifiable aspects of review, for example, clinical documentation, may come to define quality to the detriment of more subjective, but equally important, dimensions of claims processing. The power or frailty of QA signals depends upon their interpretation.

To be more concrete, let's imagine an identical QA return (for better documentation) from SSA's second-tier review to four different state agencies. In state agency A the return occasions critical comment by the affected examiner's supervisor and a memo from the agency director reminding all examiners to be sure to secure the particular bit of clinical data whose absence prompted the return. In state agency B the return is delivered to the offending examiner with commiseration about the "★?+0!" federal reviewers, "who have probably never decided a case," and a promise that the agency head will protest the return. In agency C the file is returned to the examiner with no comment. In agency D the examiner, his or her supervisor, and perhaps someone from the agency QA staff discuss the return to ensure that its rationale is understood, try to assess whether the return is justified or should be protested, and consider whether the point made by the return warrants an instructional memo to the staff.

These four responses (based loosely on my interviews with state agency personnel) seem symptomatic of remarkably different agency environments—environments that might be expected to color not only the interpretation of QA returns, but also the interpretation of regulations, manual issuances, advice, or anything else emanating from SSA's central or regional offices. Our imaginary return therefore raises an important question: are there ways not only of overseeing but of engineering this system so that it produces predictable and acceptable responses? If the answer is No, much of our previous talk about appropriate policies, as well as whatever hopes we have for improving the capacity of the disability decision process to be rational, fair, and efficient, may be exposed as the naive musings of armchair reformers.

The answer to our question is in part provided by the GAO's 1976 inquiry. Because of weaknesses in the overall structure of control, including the QA program, SSA action on all fronts was having differing effects (when it had any effect at all) at the state agency level. The problems seemed to lie not just in the design or implementation of an obviously important policy function like the QA program but in the general design of the adjudicatory system. In the view of the GAO management study, the essence of the problem was how to make the system responsive to SSA direction and control. But, as we shall see, that way of putting the issue has its defects. It may suggest the need for a degree of hierarchical control that is unachievable without a forfeiture of important programmatic and adjudicatory values. I prefer to put the question, therefore, as a broader question of systems or cultural engineering and to explore from that perspective the use and abuse of various management tools.

The notion of "engineering" a "culture" is jarring. Culture exists: it can, perhaps, be described with some accuracy, and cultural changes over time can be noted; but it is not something that one thinks of as being subject to the conscious design, adjustment, repair, or fabrication. To put the task as one of engineering an appropriate adjudicatory culture thus suggests that at best its performance can be only partially successful.

Yet the attempt is inevitable. The ability to make "sound" decisions of any sort requires an appreciation not just of the many facts and decision rules bearing directly on the decision but also of the context within which the decision is to be made. Without a sense of context— what will here be called the culture of decisionmaking—the relevant and cogent cannot readily be distinguished from their opposites. Conversely, decisionmakers who function within a strong and identical decision culture should exercise their interpretive discretion to apply norms and evaluate facts in much the same way. In establishing management control of the adjudicatory process, cultural unity can thus, to some degree, serve as a substitute for centralized or unified decisionmaking. Moreover, the response at operational levels to other management efforts at direction from the top down, such as the feedback and initiatives based on the QA system, will depend importantly on cultural context.

Several questions must, therefore, be addressed: (1) what, in general, are the organizational tools at the disposal of the cultural engineer? (2) what are the predictable obstacles encountered in shaping an adjudicatory culture? (3) how has SSA used its available engineering techniques? (4) how successful have these efforts been in developing a culture of decision that is responsive to the normative framework that we have previously elaborated? By addressing these questions we can in some measure appreciate the peculiar managerial difficulties that face the disability program. But, more important, we shall begin to see how the frustrations of federal–state relations and fiscal stress combine with the technological demands of statistical QA techniques and a rational bureaucracy's quest for hierarchical control to shape the program. It is this interaction of politics, managerial technique, and normative aspiration that defines the DI program's brand of bureaucratic justice.

### Basic Techniques of Cultural Engineering

Without attempting a detailed account, we can nevertheless specify the basic techniques for cultural engineering in an adjudicatory system. We have encountered them all before. First, there is the normative element, the prescription and reinforcement of the values that should inform adjudicatory effort. Second, personnel policies can be employed to establish the educational, personal, or professional characteristics of the cultural actors attached to the bureau (examiners, physicians, QA staff). These characteristics should obviously be those that are thought to induce or to support appropriate habits of thought and action. Third, modes of operation—bureaucratic structures and processes—can be designed to establish appropriate relationships among the relevant norms and actors (including the actors outside the bureau—claimants, representatives, consultants). The contours of the adjudicatory culture are thus established by its distinctive values, personnel, and operations. The current structure of the DI program creates obstacles to the pursuit of cultural unity along all these dimensions.

### Obstacles

*Normative Ambiguity* We have discussed at length SSA's many efforts to develop the norms of the adjudicatory culture. Without rehearsing those efforts, we can isolate a critical feature of the program that substantially limits the possibility for cultural unity in the DI decision process—the ambiguity of cautious benevolence. The norms of this system do not say to adjudicators, "Be generous!" or "Be stingy!" They say instead, "Be right!" Yet they say, "Be right!" in a system that is so inherently judgmental that a slight "tilt" toward generosity or stinginess has dramatic effects on outcomes.

Moreover, the system does not say that "rightness" flows exclusively from adherence either to the injunction "Be systematic!" or to its opposite, "Be intuitive!" Rather, the demand, at least as described by the regulations and the DISM, is to attempt to be systematically rational while recognizing the necessity for intuitive leaps and "sound" judgment. In specifying developmental norms, the system does not say either, "Treat each case as a work of art" or, "Produce X decisions a week at a cost of $Y per case." It says, "Give each case the development it needs, remembering the general requirements of timeliness and fiscal responsibility."

The point here is not to criticize the normative instructions that the system employs—we have previously considered them generally appropriate—but to note the way in which this "balanced" or "neutral" approach inhibits promotion of a stable cultural unity. A normative framework that specifies overriding goals—"Protect the innocent!", for example—has obvious advantages. It provides an unambiguous rule for resolving inevitable doubts about what should be done. The possibilities for implicit choices by individual adjudicators (or decisional units) of different sets of operational norms from among paired alternatives are thus sharply limited. The rule is easily internalized by the relevant decisionmakers and reinforced by supervisory controls.

To continue the prior example, it is difficult to imagine a modern American trial judge in the criminal justice system who believes that swift vengeance is the overriding goal of the conduct of trials. But one can easily imagine different DI adjudicators plausibly ranking the relative importance of speed, completeness of evidentiary development, individualized treatment of claimants, income maintenance, the fiscal integrity of the program, and so on, in any order. Moreover, there may be strong incentives to make some such choice: the failure to adopt a clear ranking of values may produce sufficient psychological stress for many examiners or their supervisors that maintenance of a balanced posture is insupportable. The system must therefore constantly struggle with whatever tendencies toward imbalance this stress generates, while at the same time remembering that efforts to reinforce a value that seems to be submerged may quickly make that value preeminent. In a consciously ambiguous value structure, the attempt to redress the balance of values must confront the (perhaps unconscious but nevertheless destabilizing) demand of decisionmakers for certainty.

A recent example is instructive. SSA, concerned for some time with the comparative generosity of several state agencies, undertook a review of all of the *grants* in these states for a six-month period. As might be expected, the review resulted in a flood of error returns to the affected state agencies, all of them, of course, concerning awards. Not surprisingly, these states got the message that they had been too generous, and that message may well have been appropriate. But instead of merely redressing the balance between generosity and fiscal conservatism, the action seems to have reversed the previous bias. One reviewed state's award rate dropped 20 percent in the six-month review period. That shifted its position from near the top of the award-rate table for the country to near the bottom. Moreover, the examiners that I interviewed in that state seem convinced that they are now required to interpret *all* policies in the most stringent fashion. They are wary of ever using the judgmental and ambiguous "equals the listings" classification. They also insist that they must find virtually anyone who fails to meet the medical listings not disabled, because the *Dictionary of Occupational Titles* lists nearly two hundred job classifications for unskilled sedentary workers. A massive rejection of prior exercises of discretion has produced rigidity—examiners cling to the security of combining the "objective" medical listings and a negative presumption where they are not met.

*Limited Management Techniques* The top management of SSA views this response as an overreaction. But dramatic effects are predictable when one takes up cabinetmaking with a sledgehammer. SSA may be faulted for employing such a blunt instrument, but its tool kit runs to jewelers' appliances and blasting equipment—plain old carpenters' implements are in short supply. SSA can attempt to elicit appropriate conduct by refining its instructions, by calling conferences between state agency heads and regional and central office personnel, and by processing routine QA returns. But these informational devices (the jewelers' appliances, to play out the metaphor) may have little or no effect. On the other hand, SSA can conduct an intensive review of some aspect of claims processing, backed by the implicit threat of replacing the state agency for poor performance (the blasting equipment). What SSA cannot do is make midrange management moves that would reinforce or generalize an appropriate adjudicatory culture—selection, training, assignment, and promotion of personnel; rotation of staff from state to state or into and out of regional or central offices; and the like (carpenters' tools). The state agency device may tend to fuel an insularity that both resists subtle management and overreacts to (because it misinterprets) dramatic confrontation.

*Varying Institutional Cultures* Yet, again, generalization is difficult. Agencies react diversely to different managerial initiatives, producing yet another obstacle to cultural unity. Something as simple as differences in bureaucratic attachments at the state level may have substantial effects on the personnel available for disability adjudication and ultimately on agency performance. Consider two state agencies in which I spent some time. The first operates as part of the state welfare department. It therefore classifies its personnel in accordance with the general state scheme applicable to eligibility technicians in other welfare programs. Pay scales and entry-level qualifications are low. The second is part of the state department of education. It classifies examiners as "counselors" and requires that they hold or work toward a master's degree in vocational counseling. The attachment to the education department thus produces not only a better qualified, better paid, and, therefore, more stable organization, but also one whose members have a more "professional" outlook toward their jobs.

These differences in outlook or internal agency culture have effects on responsiveness to managerial direction as well as on the quality of any response. Professionalism in the second agency seemed to translate into preferences for quality products. Examiners were thoughtful about their work, resourceful and energetic in developing claims files. There was continual discussion among examiners and with supervisors and medical consultants about ongoing cases and problems. The agency's management was also resistant to SSA directives that it thought detrimental to the continued professionalism of its staff. It was always in trouble because of its long average processing time, but had one of the lowest QA error rates in the country.

The welfare agency's personnel were quite different. The QA staff and supervisors seemed quite professionally oriented, but the line examiners, to be uncharitable, seemed merely to prefer doing DI work to driving a taxi. They took paths of least resistance. Cases were decided quickly (delay is the easiest thing for supervisors to spot), the award rate was generous, and the QA error rate was atrocious. The director was reminiscent of harassed welfare officials everywhere. As a part of the state bureaucracy that is the favorite punching bag of many politicians, he tried desperately to conform to each role suggested by potentially powerful outside political forces, including SSA. But because the roles conflicted he was most energetically engaged in bobbing and weaving, fancy footwork, and when on the bureaucratic ropes, the creation of defensive paper trails.

These descriptions are to some degree caricatures; and the behavior and attitudes reported have more than one cause. But the essential point remains: state agencies and the people in them define themselves, in part at least, in terms of their separate state political organization. This is evidenced by their careers. There is little movement from state to federal employment (or vice versa). State officials advance within the state institutional environment. They replicate themselves through their power to hire and acculturate their own personnel. In obvious ways this lessens SSA's power to develop a unified decision culture.

Why not "federalize" the state agencies, thereby increasing the opportunity for using carpenters' tools and eradicating the inappropriate institutional cultures? Moreover, whatever the original rationale of state agency expertise, the reality is now firmly established: even if formally a part of a vocational rehabilitation service, state agencies have specialized branches for administering disability benefits, and they are not generally staffed with persons trained in vocational counseling or placement. Their specialty—and it is quite a special position in American government—is giving away 100 percent federal dollars under 100 percent federal guidelines, being paid with 100 percent federal funds, and yet remaining state employees. Yet the impeccable logic of federalization has not triumphed. The absence of federalization from the 1980 amendments signals that proposal's most recent defeat. How is this to be explained?

One explanation is obviously political. The state disability examiner may have an almost unique status, but his or her political value is the same as that of many state and local officials—they permit programmatic expansion at the federal level without either increases in the federal bureaucracy or the disruption of state political arrangements based on patronage in the form of employment or procurement. The current SSA organization for adjudicating DI claims may be administrative nonsense, but it contains a conventional brand of political wisdom.

Political convenience might be overcome if SSA thought the game worth the candle. It apparently does not. One reason for that view, perhaps, is also political. If the operation were federalized, but similar problems persisted, what could be blamed but ineffective SSA management? The suggested motivation is, of course, scurrilous and so far as I know unfounded, but it suggests an issue of moment for our current analysis. Would federalization produce a unified decision culture?

It might help, but there is a residual intractability to the human materials. People come from somewhere and are attached to a set of cultural symbols concerning work and the receipt of public benefits that will confound training and institutional allegiance unless all discretion is purged from their judgments. The differences are not just in the politics of Minnesota and Mississippi; they are also in the religious beliefs of Shreveport and New Orleans, and in the economic and social climates of Richmond, Norfolk, and the Southwest Virginia coal country. People recruited to be *federal* disability deciders at different locations *within* one state will have different award/denial rates that reflect, in part, their own local culture.

Even with federalization, the problems of cultural diversity that we have been describing will persist. It might yet be necessary to maintain a middle tier of regional offices as a mediating resource. The conventional administrative problems of span of control and coordination will not be erased by changing the employees' classification nor necessarily by exercising the powers of hiring, firing, training, and transfer that such a change would allow. The logic of hierarchical control is not just the logic of unified administration; to be fully effective it also demands objectivity, that is, the elimination of discretion.

## THE INABILITY TO BORROW A CULTURE

Ambiguity of norms, the limitations on "ordinary" management techniques, the competition from divergent state agency and even from regional, SSA-decisional subcultures, all are obstacles to the creation of a unified culture (or environment) of adjudication. These difficulties and others sometimes call forth the suggestion that decisionmaking be unified around an existing culture—the medical profession. Why not hire rotating boards of physicians to decide DI cases, perhaps in every case with direct examination of the claimant by the board?

Indeed, the Congress and SSA have used medical professionalism as a device for insuring appropriate decisionmaking. As we have seen, the Social Security Act requires that disability result from a condition determinable by medically acceptable clinical and diagnostic techniques; that certain awards be based wholly on medical factors (the medical listings); and that state DDS units obtain the "medical judgment" of "a physician in the[ir] employ . . . or engaged for this purpose"[5] on the issue of medical equivalence.

Yet the special features of disability adjudication require that SSA remain skeptical of medical judgment. Physicians are hardly fungible. Diagnosis by "clinical" or "laboratory" techniques may cover a host of divergent approaches—approaches that may respond more to the physicians' economic context, location, and tastes for risk than to a unified notion of what is good medicine. More important, the doctor's professional culture is often dominated by a concern with maximizing the long-term health of patients. Activities that might impair health or recovery—including, frequently, work—are "contraindicated," and patients are advised accordingly. Treating physicians have so often advised DI claimants not to work that SSA has adopted the following regulation:

The function of deciding whether or not an individual is under a disability is the responsibility of the Secretary. A statement by a physician that an individual is, or is not, "disabled," "permanently disabled," "totally disabled," "totally and permanently disabled," "unable to work," or a statement of similar import, being a conclusion upon the ultimate issue to be decided by the Secretary, shall not be determinative of the question of whether or not an individual is under a disability. The weight to be given such physician's statement depends on the extent to which it is supported by specific and complete clinical findings and is consistent with other evidence as to the severity and probable duration of the individual's impairment or impairments.[6]

State agencies even find that they must frequently "rebut" the RFC evaluations included in CEs they have purchased because the interpretation of functioning is markedly dissimilar from that of RFC reports in most cases having similar clinical findings.

When SSA must rely on physician judgment—in making the medical equivalency decision, in explaining the import of raw clinical data, or in providing missing diagnostic data for medically ambiguous cases—it attempts to remove the physician, by instruction in the DI program and by contract or employment, from his or her inappropriate treatment culture. Where the physician's report is used as evidence, attempts are

5. 42 U.S.C. §§423(d) & 1382c(a) (1976 & Supp. IV 1980).
6. The new "plain language" version of this regulation is at 20 C.F.R. §404.1527 (1981).

made to confine that evidentiary contribution to the descriptive evaluation of the medical aspects of the case. By combining this technique
with careful selection and utilization of consulting or advising physicians, SSA can make some progress toward harnessing an appropriately
modified professional medical culture to the disability determination
process.

In practice, however, even this approach breaks down. In many areas
high-quality consultative physicians in a large number of specialities are
unavailable. Moreover, consulting physicians may have any number of
undetectable biases that color their judgment once they are removed
from their usual context of personal responsibility for treatment. Doctors who view work as therapeutic and welfare as demoralizing will have
quite different perspectives on cases than physicians holding the opposite views. I have talked to SSA consulting physicians who fudge clinical
findings to meet the medical listings ("because they [the listings] are so
strict *live* patients don't have those symptoms") and doctors who
surreptitiously observe disability claimants entering and leaving their
buildings ("to catch the rip-off artists"). And, given the independence
and intellectual toughness characteristic of treating physicians, they
could be expected to be considerably less malleable and therefore considerably less manageable than the usual run of DI examiners. The
desirability of transforming physicians from consultants and witnesses
into DI decisionmakers is, thus, far from clear.

The other professional culture that is incorporated into the SSA
decision process, the vocational specialist, compounds the problems of
disunity and inappropriateness encountered with the medical profession. There is, indeed, no clear definition of what a vocational specialist,
or expert, is, although many courts require SSA to include the testimony of such a person in the hearing record in cases in which the
claimant cannot return to his former work. The profession is in some
sense a legal invention and includes persons whose training ranges from
rehabilitation therapy through psychology to high school counseling.

In addition, vocational experts' judgments are often highly colored by
their institutional affiliation. Rehabilitation counselors, for example,
vary enormously in their perception of the work potential of similarly
impaired individuals. Those employed in overburdened public sector
programs, whose success is measured by the ratio of job placements to
accepted clients in a given period, tend to be skeptical of the employ-

ment potential of seriously impaired persons. They will find many more persons "disabled" than will counselors in private rehabilitation clinics, who have, in general, much greater resources to expend in the rehabilitation and placement of each of their clients. SSA can thus place little reliance on the professional culture of vocational specialists or experts. As it does with physicians, here too it must attempt to structure the role of the vocational specialist, both as a witness and as a decisionmaker, to supply the appropriate common decision culture.

In practice, SSA has gotten control over vocational specialists at the state agency level by avoiding them. The DOT and physician judgments on RFC are substituted for an "expert" vocational evaluation. There are no requirements that a vocational specialist agree with any examiner findings, and the DISM's directions concerning the need for vocational workshop evaluations are not followed or enforced. The reasons for this deemphasis of vocational analysis by vocational experts are not difficult to fathom. Without a workshop-type evaluation (an extended set of tests using several vocational settings that demand differing skills, stamina, and mental acuity), the opinion of a vocational expert is probably not much better than the opinion of an experienced examiner. Sending claimants out to a workshop approximates delegating the disability decision to the workshop. And incorporating vocational workshops into the DDS structure, thus making them better attuned to the DDS decision culture, may be very expensive.

## SSA INITIATIVES

Lest the preceding section be taken to indicate that chaos reigns in the DI adjudicatory structure, that the cultural symbol is the black flag of anarchism, we should hasten to note that a view of the system that sought common features would produce a quite different picture. The DI examiner attached to the state welfare agency behaves more like the DI examiner attached to an education department than like his or her counterpart in an AFDC office. One finds, going from office to office, a basic similarity in routine and structure, language and perspective. Every examiner's copy of the medical listings is dog-eared and dirty. Examiners uniformly take the seemingly contradictory position that the disability judgment is highly discretionary or judgmental, but that they *personally* suffer very little subjective uncertainty concerning the correctness of their decisions. They generally know a startling array of medical and pharmacological facts and have a sufficiently low regard for the reliability of various types of medical findings that they are willing to exercise independent judgment.

These and many more unifying characteristics do not occur by chance. If SSA suffers in its attempts to unify the decision culture from necessarily ambiguous goals and the intractability of diverse human materials, it can at least in large part control the structures through which decisions are made and to that degree the relationships among the actors and among the norms of the system. All examiners are required to use the same terminology and rating scales, to go through identical sequences in decisionmaking, to collect and evaluate the same types of evidentiary materials, to seek a medical opinion with respect to certain findings of fact or legal conclusions.

Recent management attempts to further unify the decisional culture abound. The "grid regulations," the redesign and emphasis of the QA program, the 100 percent review of poorly performing states are obvious examples. In addition, during the year that I did field research, SSA (1) issued a four-inch stack of (hopefully) clarifying instructions amending the DISM; (2) developed a new, unified training package for DDS use; (3) provided a common work-flow model for state agencies; (4) developed a "staged response" system for bringing pressure to bear on states whose performance is out of line; (5) began an attempt to renegotiate state contracts around a model that would place state agencies under greater federal control; (6) held numerous regional and national conferences to deal with troublesome issues. The list could go on and on. Most of the significant managerial activity since the mid-1970s has been directed at increasing federal control and oversight of the state agency process. As we have noted, these initiatives have been provoked or supported by the GAO, congressional oversight committees, and the 1980 amendments to the Social Security Act.

Moreover, these efforts to reengineer the decision culture have effects. SSA is gaining more and more control over the process. Our earlier question should surely be answered, "Yes, substantial divergences that impair centralized direction and control currently exist in the decisional culture. But the situation is remediable—indeed, is being incrementally and steadily remedied." The opportunities for state agencies, disability examiners, medical consultants, or others to run their own disability program are being squeezed out by more objective rules, standardized routines, and effective monitoring of outputs to ensure that rule and routine have been followed.

We are left with a final question: is effective management control of the type that is being attempted a good thing? that is, is it likely to contribute to rationality, fairness, and efficiency—our complex definition of administrative justice?

# PART IV · GETTING THE BALANCE RIGHT

# 8 · Bureaucratic Justice and Bureaucratic Imperatives

## BUREAUCRATIC JUSTICE

The process of adjudication that we have been discussing is justice in a bureaucratic mode. Several aspects of that mode or model are worth highlighting. First, the bureaucracy has a positive program responsibility; to pay worthy claims and to reject unworthy ones. Because claims adjudication is the basic device through which that responsibility is exercised, the agency as adjudicator is not neutral with respect to who wins and who loses. Its mission is to pay the eligible and reject the claims of the ineligible.

Second, and closely linked to the first, the approach to deciding an individual claim is active and investigatory. The agency does not act merely on the basis of whatever information comes in; it seeks information sufficient to its decisional task.

Third, there is a fundamental political presumption that the agency is responsible for the adjudicatory performance of its employees. A coordinated system of management must be instituted to ensure (or attempt to ensure) that subordinate actions are indeed premised on the policies or goals of the program and on a common understanding of the relevant facts. Only effective management can connect the customary, but otherwise preposterous, statutory direction that the *secretary* decide the cases with reality.

Fourth, the establishment of hierarchical control over the adjudicatory process requires a "systemic" perspective. Each managerial initiative disturbs some equilibrium of forces within the adjudicatory system. Systems managers must be sensitive to how those forces regroup and reinforce or counteract each other. The development of substantive standards, the designing of the decision process, the training and

171

supervision of personnel, the structuring of monitoring systems, the provision of supportive services, and many other management activities are steering mechanisms for affecting the direction and speed of claims processing. To summarize with a string of adjectives, the bureaucratic model of administrative justice is an accuracy-oriented, investigatorily active, hierarchically organized, and complexly engineered system of adjudication.

The quality of the justice provided in such a system depends primarily on how good the management system is at dealing with the set of conflicting demands that define rational, fair, and efficient adjudication. It must translate vague and conflicting statutory goals into administerable rules, without losing the true and sometimes subtle thrust of the program. It must attempt to ensure that decisions are consistent and that development is adequate, without impairing the discretion necessary individualization. It must simplify and objectify the data relevant to adjudication in order to direct action and to monitor outputs, but without so distorting perception that decisionmaking is in fact divorced from a reality that is also complex and subjective. It must deploy appropriate expertise while screening out inappropriate professional bias. It must balance perceptible administrative costs against the less perceptible costs of error, delay, and demoralization.

Given the inherent difficulty of the task, SSA has clearly done a creditable job of managing its complex administrative justice system. The program began with the vaguest of statutory standards and an adjudicatory structure "farmed out" to state vocational rehabilitation agencies and to independent ALJs. In twenty years it has become a program that emphasizes a set of (quasi-) objectively determinable medical impairments and vocational characteristics and that is administered (in the first instance) by state employees who look almost exclusively to SSA, rather than to any branch of their state government, for guidance and supervision with respect to their principal tasks.

Impediments to systematic rationality and hierarchical control—goal ambiguity, developmental inadequacy, ineffective monitoring and feedback, professional and political diversity—have been attacked and, if not wholly conquered, rendered increasingly innocuous. Particularly in the last few years, energized by renewed legislative interest and having recovered from the twin traumas of absorbing the administration of the Black Lung and SSI programs, SSA has moved forcefully to consolidate its managerial position. Its actions respond directly to critics—from the Harrison subcommittee report (1960) through the GAO reports (1976–78)—who have identified lax management as the DI program's major shortcoming.

## BUREAUCRATIC IMPERATIVES

Indeed, managerial success in making the system more controllable raises a different concern: How manageable should the system be? Several considerations caution against ready acceptance of the notion that the best management system would produce disability determinations that seemed to emanate from some controlling collective mind located in the central office.

First, the history of the administration of the program reveals that "the mind," that is, the top management of SSA, cannot focus on all dimensions of the decision process at once. It is concerned (often at congressional insistence) sometimes with delay, sometimes with accuracy, sometimes with administrative costs, sometimes with projected fiscal disasters, sometimes with service delivery. If the normative structure we have elaborated is sound, these are all important dimensions of administrative justice. More crucially, these are value dimensions that must be traded off against each other. The attempt should be to achieve some form of harmonious and consistent balance among competing objectives. A system capable of making this week's perspective an instantaneous imperative would have a tendency to veer unstably from one imbalance to another: some weeks (or months or years) claims would be treated generously and some weeks stingily, some weeks speedily and some weeks carefully and at length.

From this perspective, organizational slack has its advantages. Loose linkages in the chain of command tend to prevent perceptible inequalities in the treatment of different claimants (or the same claimant) at different, but closely spaced, times. More importantly, as management directives filter through the system, there is opportunity to mediate the value of the moment through consideration of the complex of other values imbedded in ongoing modes of operation. Without waxing too lyrical about the virtues of administrative inertia, one can portray it as having a useful as well as a frustrating place in a system of administrative adjudication characterized by a complex value set and by recurrent political pressures to treat one or another value as preeminent.

There is currently much evidence, for example, that SSA, responding to congressional concern, is constraining the supply of disability benefits. The new stringency is reflected both in SSA's normative prescriptions and in its operational and management activities. Consider a few examples.

First, since the late 1970s SSA's policy advice (that is, its interpretations of existing directives) has been almost uniformly in the direction of tightening the eligibility standard. A change in the policy concerning the continuation of benefits in "diaried" cases is typical. Previously a beneficiary who was thought likely to improve over time was reinvestigated periodically to determine whether improvement would justify a cessation of benefits. Under the new Continuing Disability Investigation (CDI) policy each redetermination is a de novo decision on *current* disability. This policy shift, combined with an increasingly stringent approach to eligibility and a surge in the number of CDI reviews conducted, is expected to have dramatic effects. In 1980, 71,500 persons were removed from the rolls pursuant to CDI review. By 1984 the estimate is 360,000 terminations per year.

Second, the data from the second-tier QA review of Title II claims suggest that even before the 1980 amendments QA review was being employed by central office reviewers to reinforce the tilt toward stringency. For the calendar year 1978, for example, "errors" were found in almost three times as many awards as denials.[1] It could, of course, be the case that allowances, neutrally reviewed, have three times as many errors as denials. But that is not the historic pattern of error identification at the central office, and there is no obvious explanation for a pronounced shift toward generosity among examiners. The second-tier review of Title XVI and concurrent cases by regional offices shows no such skew in the errors. Indeed, the regional review operation finds 20 percent more errors in denials than in awards.[2] As we noted earlier,

1. *See generally*, Reports and Analysis Branch, Division of Disability Program Quality, Office of Assessment, Social Security Administration, Quarterly Report of Central Office Review of Title II Initial Disability Claims, April–June 1977, July–September 1977, October–December 1977, January–March 1978, April–June 1978, July–September 1978, October–December 1978.

2. *See generally*, Reports and Analysis Branch, Division of Quality Assurance, Office of Program Evaluation and Appraisal, Bureau of Disability Insurance, Social Security Administration, BDI Quarterly Report of CRS Review of Title XVI Initial Disability Determinations, February–March 1977, April–June 1977, July–September 1977, Octo-

there is simply no good explanation for this divergence other than that there is a more stringent climate in the central office.

Third, the recent 100 percent "disciplinary" reviews of "poor quality" states all occurred in states with high allowance rates, and the reviews concentrated on allowances. Even where the 100 percent review was a "test" and covered denials as well as allowances, intensive supervision by a central office staff dramatically reduced the award rate. (On the basis of a three-month test of 100 percent federal review, the annual budgetary savings from federal preeffectuation review in one small state were conservatively projected to be $30 million.) In an internal memorandum, the study teams attributed the downturn in the award rate to the ability of intensive federal review to make DDS examiners "feel the pulse of the adjudicative climate" at the federal level.

These activities have already produced dramatic shifts in the program's statistics.[3] The state agencies granted 50 percent of the claims submitted to them in 1975. By 1980 the award rate had dropped to 33 percent. Whereas in 1975 only 29 percent of awards were on the relatively "objective" meets-the-listings basis, while 45 percent were based on an equals-the-listings determination and 26 percent on vocational factors, in 1980 the meets-the-listings percentage of awards had doubled, the more subjective "equals" category had been cut in half, and vocational allowances accounted for less than 20 percent of awards. By 1980, the ratio of beneficiaries to covered workers had also dropped from its 1975 all-time high (7.1 per 1,000) to its 1964 all-time low (4.1 per 1,000). On the other hand, persons terminated due to "recovery" rose from 40,000 per year in 1975 to 72,000 in 1980. ("Recovery" is in quotation marks because it refers to persons found not disabled after a CDI. The beneficiary need not have improved or have gone back to work to be terminated. Indeed, the number of beneficiaries becoming reemployed during the 1975–80 period remained unchanged.) The cumulative effect of the new administrative posture is a stable or slightly

---

ber–December 1977, January–March 1978, April–June 1978, July–September 1978, October–December 1978.

3. Source: SUBCOMMITTEE ON SOCIAL SECURITY, HOUSE WAYS AND MEANS COMMITTEE, 97TH CONG. 1ST SESS., STATUS OF DISABILITY INSURANCE PROGRAM (1981). (The subcommittee, while offering no alternative explanation, churlishly refuses to credit SSA's management activities with producing these effects. Having spent a decade berating SSA for lax management, it cannot seem to kick the habit.)

declining beneficiary population, in the face of rapidly increasing application rates.

The point is not that saving money is bad, that too liberal granting of federal monies by state agencies should be continued, or that the nondisabled should remain SSA beneficiaries. The new stringency may be aimed at getting the system back to 1972 levels, before a massive infusion of cases—Black Lung, SSI, and significant increases in DI applications—caused a shift away from careful development and monitoring toward expedition and productivity. Whatever the reason, the problem of maintaining balance remains. No systematic attention is being given to what classes of cases are being caught in the current squeeze, to whether the increased denial rate is in the truly marginal cases, or to the potential inequalities in claims processing and decisional results that occur as ripple effects from a general tightening down of the program.

A valid response to these concerns is that the decline in award rates is merely a secondary effect of the new emphasis on better-quality adjudications. This answer may not be responsive, however, to the normative question. Declining award rates may be the necessary effect of a more "manageable" and "objective" approach to adjudication. But are those adjectives synonymous with "better"?

Consider how the attempt to improve the quality of evidence and the controllability of the system tends to support a substantive move toward stringency. The absence of documentary information to show medical impairment will justify a denial but not a grant. A demand for objective evidence, coupled with increasing time pressures and no substantial increase in funds to purchase CEs, will thus have predictable effects: cases lacking certain required and perhaps producible evidence will be classified as denials so that they may be decided. A demand for objectivity, without changes in the resources devoted to processing, tends to produce stringency.

Indeed, the demand for objectivity alone may tend to squeeze out awards based on combinations of objective clinical evidence and subjective evidence. Cardiovascular cases, for example, abound with objective clinical indicators—EKG tracings, angiographs, X-rays—and with descriptions of pain. Several of the medical listings for angina pectoris require a depression or inversion of the EKG tracing line of at least 0.5 mm. Examiners generally receive xerox copies rather than original tracings, however, and they are well aware that the deviation caused by xerography alone can introduce a 0.2 mm error. And, of course, the EKG machines themselves are not always accurate. Hence, many examiners would rate a case with a 0.4 deviation, plus characteristic pain, as "equaling," perhaps as meeting, the listings. A QA reviewer who takes seriously the injunction to rely on "objective" evidence will bounce that case.

The relationship between objectivity and stringency raises anew the question of the degree of effective management control that should be attempted given the current (perhaps the necessary) structure of the DI program. The exercise of hierarchical control demands one of two strategies: intimate association with subordinates or relatively objective bases for providing negative feedback. Intimate association with the central office is hardly possible for thousands of widely dispersed examiners, even if "federalized." In this context, substantially increasing management control virtually demands that the system be purged of soft data and of subjective, discretionary judgment that cannot be characterized as right or wrong. Vigorous pursuit of this goal will ultimately transform the nature of the disability system. It will become a program focused on medical impairments that are objectively demonstrable. As one DDS official put it, "The current approach causes the human side of claims to be lost in the shuffle." The progressive logic of managerial control makes that effect almost inevitable.

As the criteria become less concerned with judgments about total human functioning, the decision process will become less interested in the involvement of claimants (and their treating physicians) in the decision of claims. The importance of the information that the claimant can supply diminishes, the more "objectivity" is stressed. Claimant descriptions of pain or functioning will not support a decision in the absence of objective medical indicators. And the grid regulations tend to reduce the importance of the most frequent traditional occasion for claimant involvement—description of prior work activities.

To be sure, the loss of human contact in the claims process might be outweighed by an increase in accuracy or consistency. But this is not self-evidently the case. The substitution of good CEs for claimants' subjective accounts of their difficulties has obvious benefits. But to the extent that the CE, because objective, always dominates contextual signals from the claimant, his or her treating physician, and others, examiners are prevented from making holistic judgments that may be better, albeit less "reviewable," than objective ones.

A desire for "objectivity" may also supply a false rationale for policies that are defensible, if at all, only on other grounds. For example, once a determination has been made that vocational factors will decide a case, an evaluation of the claimant's RFC must be made. Assuming that an RFC report is not to be made part of a CE in the case, the examiner has several choices: (1) the treating physician may be requested to fill out an RFC report; (2) the claimant may be sent for a workshop evaluation; (3) an RFC report may be made out by a consulting physician in the DDS on the basis of the medical evidence of record. (A CE might also be ordered, but the administrative budget does not permit this technique as a routine matter.)

The conventional wisdom in the system is that the third approach is better than the former two. Treating physicians vary in quality and may be subjectively involved in the claim. Vocational workshops have differing perspectives on employability and sometimes mushy evaluative techniques; they are also slow and expensive. In-house consultative physicians, on the other hand, know the program and have considerable experience in making RFC judgments.

The only thing wrong with this practice is that it responds more to the logic of controllability than to the logic of quality decisionmaking. As SSA's regulations make clear, RFC includes a number of difficult judgmental variables—exertion levels, stamina, ability to concentrate—that do not routinely appear from the medical evidence. The consulting physician who fills out an RFC form from a claims file is doing something that he freely admits cannot be done with any reliability.

Nor is it really credible to assert that the treating physician's opportunity to observe the claimant over time or the workshop's ability to test his or her functioning multidimensionally and in work situations produce systematically poorer evidence. That evidence is, however, because it comes from outside the bureaucracy, systematically less controllable. In-house consultants can at least "feel the pulse of the adjudicative climate."

There may, of course, be plausible arguments concerning delay and administrative cost that would support the routine use of in-house, consulting physician RFC evaluations. But a careful analysis of those arguments has been submerged by ready acceptance of an approach that maximizes agency opportunity for control. In short, not only does objectification contribute to control, but the desire to have control colors the operative notion of objectivity.

From this perspective, one is tempted to applaud one of the disability examiner's antimanagement tricks. An examiner is supposed to put claims files requiring an RFC evaluation into the ordinary flow of work going to the medical consultants. The medical consultant who will review the file is thus determined (specialization aside) randomly. However, it is accepted practice for examiners to personally deliver a claim to medical personnel when for some reason it has been delayed and needs to be expedited. An examiner who has strong feelings about how a case should come out (often because he or she has "lived" with it) can purposely delay it and then give it to a consultant who will provide an "appropriate" RFC chart. The management system's quest for objective medical evidence can thus be obstructed by a persistent intuition. But how often will an individual examiner's desire to nonconform surface in a system that emphasizes and rewards objective findings and conformity to routine?

There is also the broader question of whether the previously hypothesized opportunities for individualized treatment outside, or under, the new grid regulations will be realized in the adjudicatory climate that is emerging. I previously argued that the opportunities to mediate the potential overgeneralization of the grid, by more specific and individualized considerations, supported the reasonableness of the grid against the complaint that its pigeonholing approach would produce arbitrary decisions.[4] If the operational realities of a controllable disability adjudication process eliminate or sharply constrain these opportunities, the reasonableness of the grid—perhaps even the balance of the whole system—is called into question.

To summarize, the process of gaining management control and thereby avoiding inappropriate discretionary judgments by subordinates requires choices that eliminate possibilities for exercises of discretion that would have been (could they have been effectively monitored) considered appropriate—perhaps even wise. The system of control thus demands that some cases be decided irrationally. Moreover, because the

4. See pp. 116–24 *supra.*

system can be monitored only in terms of its own "objective" redefinition of reality—the existence of specified types of data in a case file—it is not possible to know how many irrational decisions are being made. Controllability also tends to exclude outsiders (claimants, medical professionals) whose participation does not conform to established routines for generating and reporting data and who will, for that reason, produce information that must be considered irrelevant.

We have here, of course, the traditional complaints against bureaucracy: that it tends to be narrow-minded, rigid, and insular; that somehow institutional imperatives begin to dominate program goals; that individualized concerns and dignitary values are lost; that its "expertise" systematically misdescribes reality. And at some level, of course, these complaints begin to undermine the legitimacy of administrative action, that is, they begin to assert that the agency makes policy undemocratically, is a false or misguided expert, and insulates itself from the contributions of relevantly affected interests. In the end, if the complaints are valid, the agency fails in its own terms—it fails to implement "the program" we have in mind.

How are these problems to be attacked? Is the fact that the bureaucracy is imbedded in a traditional set of external legal constraints a sufficient answer to the critic who concludes that the administration of the disability program is characterized more by bureaucratic imperatives than by administrative justice? If not, what reforms in the external constraint mechanisms or changes in the structure or methodology of adjudication can increase the acceptability of disability adjudication? And what can be said about the "new balance" among competing justice perspectives that these reforms might provide?

# 9 · Reform from an External Perspective

There are traditional legal techniques for dealing with the problem of bureaucratic imperatives. Deviation from legislative goals or the popular will may be ameliorated by a better legislative definition of statutory standards, by increased legislative oversight, or, in extreme cases, by judicial invalidation of administrative action. Bureaucratic tunnel vision is sometimes thought to be correctable through a broadening of the statutory value matrix or by requiring that administrative decisions gain the approval of other institutions—including the judiciary—having different perspectives. Myopic administration can also be countered through a variety of techniques that attempt to restructure and thereby "open up" the decision process to outsiders—hearings, advisory committees, required consultations, demands for expert evidence, and so on. Indeed, the SSA adjudicatory context exhibits variations on all these themes. Reforms might broaden and strengthen those techniques. The question is whether those reforms will deal effectively with the problems of administrative justice that we have encountered. Consider the three traditional legal approaches.

## THE DEMOCRATIC CONNECTION

First, it seems clear that a better (more absolute, precise, consistent, or stable) definition of legislative goals is not likely to be forthcoming. The statutory definition of disability and the statutory structures for program administration paper over problems that cannot be resolved crisply in the political arena. Congress has amended the DI program repeatedly and has apparently expressed itself with as much clarity as it can muster.

Moreover, to the extent that our concerns are with regulatory over-generalization, rigidity, or the like, they are the direct result of congressional demands for a controllable and consistent decision process. The tracks of the GAO reports and the reports and hearings of the House Subcommittee on Social Security are clearly visible in the trail of management initiatives and regulatory actions that SSA has taken to bring the system under tighter control. If administrative goals like honoring value complexity and providing individualized judgments are being given low priority in the contemporary administration of the DI program, that result is certainly not contrary to the wishes of the Congress and its relevant oversight organs. Whatever overbureaucratization of claims processing afflicts SSA is largely a function of political responsiveness, not political nonresponsiveness.

The 1980 amendments to the Social Security Act (the first social security legislation to contain significant disability provisions since 1967) formally reinforced a stringency that congressional studies, hearings, and reports had foreshadowed. Disability benefits (including dependency allowances) were limited to the lower of 85 percent of a worker's indexed prior earnings or 150 percent of his or her primary insurance amount (that is, the amount payable on behalf of the worker alone). A number of apparently liberalizing moves in the 1980 legislation—for example, elimination of medical assistance waiting periods for second-time beneficiaries, extended trial work periods, assistance to persons with earnings near the SGA standard, and making SSI-earned income disregards cover sheltered work payments—are also designed to provide work incentives and thereby reduce total payments. We have already noted that the amendments' administrative provisions seek to tighten SSA oversight and control. They require QA review of at least 65 percent of state agency *awards* and make the state administration subject to SSA regulatory power rather than merely to the provisions of federal–state contracts. Controllability and fiscal restraint thus seem to be the current interests of the Congress. That interest politically validates the movement toward hierarchical control that we have characterized as the bureaucratic imperative.

On the other hand, the work incentive and rehabilitation portions of the new legislation could be viewed as pushing in a different direction. In addition to the liberalizing provisions previously mentioned, Congress also permitted payment of benefits to medically recovered beneficiaries enrolled in vocational education programs and allowed a deduction from the SGA amount for extraordinary work expenses. Taken together, these provisions might be viewed as a renewed effort to integrate income support with medical care, rehabilitation, and partial reentry into the labor force. As such, it could form the basis for a modified internal perspective on adjudication of disability benefits—a subject I will return to in the next chapter.

The ambiguities of a cautious benevolence, and the propensity of administration to react thoughtlessly to legislative pressures, sometimes suggest the need for a different approach to reform of the legislative connection.[1] Were categorical assistance programs like DI abolished and replaced by a simple negative income tax,[2] the excruciating indeterminacies of the disability standard would give way to a simple means test. Under such a legislative scheme, bureaucratic rationality would seem at once a realizable goal and a transparently appropriate conception of bureaucratic justice. Moreover, simplicity and objectivity might reduce the opportunities for administration to bend to political pressure expressed in a nonstatutory form.

This is an attractive prospect, particularly to those who worry about the gaps and overlaps in existing programs of income maintenance and who find the complexities of their administration disquieting if not wholly unfathomable.[3] Yet I confess that I find the position unconvincing. It is unconvincing first because it often confuses complexity with incoherence. By specifying a unitary goal—say income support for the indigent—the provisions of any categorical assistance program that are designed to mediate between that goal and others can be made to appear confused and contradictory. The suggestion is then that legislation can be reformed quite simply by making all statutory provisions consistent with the previously specified goal.

I do not recognize the world that this kind of critic describes, in which people seemingly do not differentiate among children, the aged, the

1. *See, e.g.,* Liebman, *Definition of Disability in Social Security and Supplemental Security Income: Drawing the Bounds of Social Welfare Estates,* 89 Harv. L. Rev. 833 (1976).

2. A good basic description is GREEN, NEGATIVE TAXES AND THE POVERTY PROBLEM (1977).

3. *See, e.g.,* JOINT ECONOMIC COMMITTEE, 93D CONG., 2D SESS., INCOME SECURITY FOR AMERICANS: RECOMMENDATIONS OF THE PUBLIC WELFARE STUDY (1974).

disabled, or the able-bodied unemployed as potential donees; in which varying disincentives to productive activity are ignored for purposes of calibrating benefits; and in which all connections between income support and rehabilitative ideas are severed. It is also a world in which there are no "merit goods" and therefore no special in-kind or third-party payment programs to complicate the system by generating complexities concerning access and levels of support. Finally, it is a world in which voters have a unified view of whether transfer programs should be considered charity, insurance, or the means of equalizing wealth. Of course, the legislature in this patent *other*world has made a mistake by adopting categorical assistance programs that have conflicting aims and internal contradictions.

Surely such a position is naive. The electorate has a range of purposes that can be served by explicit redistributions that target a variety of donees. The "patchwork quilt" of the system reformer's nightmare is a function, at least in part, of the inevitable complexity of pursuing multiple goals.[4] Improvements are obviously possible. But they are possible only through an appreciation, not an avoidance, of complexity. We must adjust and compromise among competing goals that are simultaneously pursued.

When conjuring up the comprehensive negative income tax, should we also imagine, for example, that it would be a tax system that ignored differences in living arrangements and competition between the basic social goals of equity and efficiency? Would it ignore economies of scale so that four-person families would receive exactly four times as much as individuals? And, if not, would we not need to develop rules about what constituted a "family," what living arrangements were analogous to families, how earned income is to be allocated among related and unrelated individuals, what differentiates boarders from friends or family, and so on? And what about income? Should earned income and savings income be treated the same? What about implicit income (the homeowner's "rent") or in-kind income (a garden)? Should there be deductions for work expenses? For investments in training? Child care?

4. An excellent survey is provided by SALAMON, TOWARD INCOME OPPORTUNITY: CURRENT THINKING ON WELFARE REFORM (Duke-Ford Foundation Welfare Policy Project, 1977).

In short, if there is to be a negative tax, must there not be a negative tax code?[5] If we consider the equity and efficiency effects of raising revenue, are we not likely to consider those effects when distributing it? And, if so, does that not mean that implementation of the negative tax will be beset by the uncertainties, conflicts, and ambiguities that we have been describing? Does anyone believe that the story we have been telling, with some variation to be sure, could not be told about the Internal Revenue Service?

The legislative standard for disability benefits is obviously the problem. And its reform is just as obviously not the solution—at least in a world having the expressed political preferences of the one we live in. To be sure, the disability judgment can be made less poignant by the addition of a negative tax or demogrant system, or by including benefits for partial disability. But these moves do not make the decisions cognitively less difficult; the latter may, indeed, make them more complex.

## GENERALIST JUDICIAL REVIEW

It is not likely that bureaucratic tunnel vision, induced by attempts to gain control over the adjudicatory process (and reinforced by congressional oversight), will be ameliorated by the necessity for judicial acquiescence. For one thing, the Supreme Court has itself endorsed a narrow definition of the disability judgment as "primarily a medical determination" and has concluded from that characterization that the state agency documentary process is perfectly adequate when followed by an opportunity for an ALJ hearing.[6] But, as we noted in chapter 1, there are more fundamental reasons than the contigency of Supreme Court approval that prevent judicial review from having a major beneficial impact on the quality of administrative justice in the Social Security system.

First, even important substantive policy questions (for example, the adoption of new medical listings or of the grid regulations)[7] seem well

5. An attempt to address some of these problems is made in Asimow and Klein, *The Negative Income Tax: Accounting Problems and a Proposed Solution*, 8 Harv. J. of Leg. 1 (1971); and Klein, *Familial Relationships and Economic Well-Being: Family Unit Rules for a Negative Income Tax*, 8 Harv. J. of Leg. 361 (1971).

6. Mathews v. Eldridge, 424 U.S. 319 (1976).

7. *See, e.g.,* Cummins v. Schweiker, 670 F.2d 81 (7th Cir. 1982); Santise v. Schweiker, 676 F.2d 925 (3d Cir. 1982); Keik v. Secretary, 667 F.2d 524 (6th Cir. 1981). *But, see* Broz v. Schweiker, 677 F.2d 1351 (1982).

within the secretary's discretion. That the wisdom of these policies is disputable does not make them illegal. Judicial invalidation is the fate only of outrageously inept policy choices.

Second the courts have some considerable difficulty making their views effective. Judicial review touches less than 1 percent of the DI caseload and has virtually no impact on the rest. The latter statement is true in part because judicial review of DI claims rarely addresses general questions of law or practice. Thousands of cases are remanded for lack of substantial evidence, but that has little discernible impact on ALJs' development efforts in other cases and no impact at all below the hearing level. Judicial opinions review ALJ determinations, and they are not communicated to state DDS personnel. Nor do the examiners' instructions reflect judicial holdings unless SSA agrees with the judicial interpretation.

The Ninth Circuit Court of Appeals, for example, has twice ruled[8] that the new CDI policy of de novo redetermination conflicted with the Social Security Act. But SSA practice has not changed in the Ninth Circuit or elsewhere except in the cases specifically decided. SSA has "declined to acquiesce" in the Court of Appeals' rulings because it believes them to be incorrect. And, in the words of SSA's general counsel, "the federal courts do not run SSA's programs. . . ."[9]

SSA policy concerning the treatment of judicial precedent is set out in the Office of Hearings and Appeals handbook, sec. 1–161:

While the ALJs are bound by decisions of the United States Supreme Court, they should also make every reasonable effort to follow the district or circuit court's views regarding procedural or evidentiary matters when handling similar cases in that particular district or circuit.

However, where a district or circuit court's decision contains interpretations of the law, regulations, or rulings which are inconsistent with the Secretary's interpretations, the ALJs should not consider such decisions binding on future cases simply because the case is not appealed. In certain cases SSA will not appeal a court decision it disagrees with, in view of special circumstances of the particular case (e.g., the limited effect of the decision).

When SSA decides to acquiesce in a district court decision, or a circuit court

8. Finnegan v. Mathews, 641 F.2d 1340 (9th Cir. 1981); Patti v. Schweiker, 669 F.2d 582 (9th Cir. 1982).

9. Associate Commissioner Office of Hearings and Appeals, Memorandum, "ALJ Policy Council Meeting," p. 2 (Jan. 7, 1982) (unpublished memorandum).

decision, which is inconsistent with our previous interpretation of the law, regulations, or rulings, SSA will take appropriate action to implement changes by means of regulations, rulings, etc. ALJs will be promptly advised of such action.

While it is not clear that SSA's construction of its constitutional position vis à vis the federal courts is correct, that construction is not idiosyncratic. The IRS and NLRB have similar policies.[10]

Moreover, whatever the resolution of this judicial–administrative struggle, the judiciary may be grasping at shadows. The subtle but powerful management actions that shape the adjudicatory culture—the focus of QA review, the budget for CEs, the setting of productivity goals for examiners—have little obvious bearing on the outcome of particular cases, even though they may markedly affect the gross award or denial rates. Even if courts took an interest in these characteristics of administration—what I have called elsewhere "the management side of due process"[11]—it is doubtful that anyone would have "standing" to complain[12] or, once having obtained standing, could convincingly demonstrate that the action was so irrational that it abridged his or her right to due process of law.

Quite apart from the potential unavailability of judicial review in these contexts, the desirability of substantial judicial monitoring of the claims adjudication process is questionable. Particular questions that might be framed for judicial cognizance are by and large too subtle, too connected with other aspects of the system's operations, to permit sure-handed judicial remedies even in the procedural areas where SSA is prepared to follow the judicial lead. Federal judges in several jurisdictions have, for example, imposed time limits on the production of

10. See generally, Vestal, *Relitigation by Federal Agencies: Conflict Concurrence and Synthesis of Judicial Policies*, 55 N. Caro. L. Rev. 123 (1977). See also, Ithaca College v. NLRB, 623 F.2d 224 (2d Cir. 1980).

11. See Mashaw, *The Management Side of Due Process*, 59 Cornell L. Rev. 772, 810–23 (1974); *How Much of What Quality: A Comment on Conscientious Procedural Design*, 65 Cornell L. Rev. 823, 832–35 (1980).

12. See, e.g., Simon v. Eastern Kentucky Welfare Rights Organization, 426 U.S. 26 (1976). The statement in the text oversimplifies a complex question. But the likelihood that, standing attained, the claim would fail on the merits counsels against entering here the arcane world of the federal jurisprudence on standing. As the materials in the preceding footnote reveal, I once held a more sanguine view of the potential efficacy of judicial oversight.

hearing decisions in disability claims.[13] There is, of course, much to be said for reducing delay in DI decisionmaking. But that is hardly the most pressing question facing the commissioner; furthermore, the secondary effect of speeding up hearings may be to reduce the overall quality of the process.

I have observed some of the fallout from the judicial order in one of the states operating under time limits. Because the OHA does not think that the offices subject to injunction need additional permanent manpower, the backlogs are being cleaned up by detailing ALJs from other areas. These judges come in for a day or two and hold a large number of hearings—sometimes *forty or more in a single day*. (The claimant's day in court is here reduced to about ten minutes). More important, because development work must be done locally these cases have been assigned to the local ALJs' hearing assistants—on top of their other work. Predictably, the development effort both for these cases and for all others is reduced. The assistants have to cut corners in order to get the cases ready for hearing—CEs not ordered, hospitals and treating physicians not contacted, records not updated, and so on. In short, merely speeding up processing without making other changes (changes which are not within the court's purview) probably makes the whole process worse.

SSA's single acquiescence in a circuit court opinion, thus making it national policy,[14] tells a similar tale concerning the benefits of judicial review as an antidote to bureaucratic routine. (Besides, the story is so apt an example of the irrelevance–impertinence dialectic that I cannot resist telling it anyway.) Without elaborating the case law in its excruciating technical detail, I will summarize the history briefly. A series of cases plus the 1977 amendments to the Social Security Act have produced an evidentiary principle known as the *Kerner* doctrine.[15] That doctrine requires the secretary of HHS to introduce evidence, once a claimant makes a showing of inability to engage in his or her prior work, to show that there are jobs in substantial numbers in the local or national economies that the claimant could perform.

To carry this burden, SSA has developed a register of "vocational

13. *E.g.*, White v. Mathews, 559 F.2d 852 (2d Cir. 1977).
14. MASHAW ET AL., SOCIAL SECURITY HEARINGS AND APPEALS 140 (1978).
15. *Id*. at 74–76.

experts" who are called by ALJs to testify at hearings in cases in which the claimant's impairments make his or her prior work seem to be unsuitable. These experts do not interview or examine the claimant. Rather, they read the file, sit in the hearing, and respond to "hypothetical" questions put by the ALJ. (The hypotheticals represent possible findings of fact concerning the claimant's skills, education, and RFC.)

Although a real contribution to the understanding of a case can be made by a vocational expert, most ALJs view them as useless and treat them accordingly. If the ALJ fails to get what he believes are sensible and appropriate responses to his hypotheticals, he will continue the questioning through various modifications of the factual hypotheses until he elicits a response that confirms his judgment. The opposite adaptation, that of the timid ALJ, is to ask an open-ended question that permits the vocational expert, in effect, to decide the case. Neither of these results is what the courts had in mind when they sought, in the interest of fairness, to reallocate the burden of proof in disability claims.

Moreover, because the evidentiary reallocation responded to a sense of frustration with the substantive results of disability decisions, many courts have refined the essentially ineffective Kerner doctrine to impose ever higher standards of proof—as to both production of evidence and persuasiveness—on SSA. A recent study of the Fifth Circuit's jurisprudence concludes that the courts are forcing SSA to move toward adversary processes in order to protect its decisions from judicial interference in the form of findings of procedural and evidentiary inadequacy.[16] Indeed, as we noted in chapter 2, SSA recently proposed and then withdrew a test of fully adversary hearings.

In short, judicial review of Social Security disability cases seems to reveal a judiciary impaled on the horns of a now familiar dilemma. It can recognize the complexity and subtlety of the administrative system and exercise a restrained review having little or no statistical impact or precedential significance; or it can wade in with the tools at its disposal, producing sometimes unanticipated and negative dynamic effects on quality, sometimes formal but insubstantial obedience, and sometimes a simple transformation of administrative into judicial process.

In a prior survey of the SSA hearings and appeals process, my colleagues and I concluded:

16. Symposium, *Judicial Review of Social Security Disability Decisions: A Proposal for Change*, 11 Tex. Tech. L. Rev. 215 (1980).

The preceding discussion of judicial review as currently practiced in disability claims does not paint a very cheerful picture. The contribution of court-review to accuracy through its corrective function is modest at best. Only with some rather heroic assumptions concerning the nature of the case load . . . and the willingness of most courts not to second-guess the ALJ in claims having substantial human appeal, can we justify a conclusion that corrective review does more good that harm. Even so, if the net corrections are in a case load of marginal cases, the value of this function cannot be expected to be large.[17]

## HEARINGS

The right to a hearing might well be the answer to our criticisms of the current decision process. A hearing should provide claimants with an opportunity to break out of the bureaucratic routine, to emphasize subjective aspects of claims, to appeal to the complex value matrix that underlies the program, to participate in a direct and meaningful way in the adjudication of their claims. Indeed, hearings are appended to the disability decision process and seem to provide an escape from bureaucratic rationality into another mode of decisionmaking for a growing subset of denied disability claimants. Yet I have previously described the hearing process as contributing to, rather than relieving, stresses that result from the underlying bureaucratic regime. Why should this be the case?

The foregoing account makes the answer obvious. The hearing process and the disability decision process are too radically different not to produce different results. As pressures are brought to bear to control program growth, the divergence in results increases. Although the awards per 1,000 workers in 1980 were at the 1964 all-time-low level, the distribution of awards between state agencies and ALJs had shifted dramatically. In 1964 state agencies accounted for 97.5 percent of all awards, ALJs for 2.5 percent. In 1980 the figures were 79 percent and 21 percent, respectively. Ultimately, the decision will have to be made either to constrain and control the hearing process, thus depriving it of its legitimating power, or to shift the system strongly in the direction of the moral judgment model. By the latter I mean a shift that would view hearings as the primary decisional technique for all cases not subject to award (or denial) on the basis of purely objective criteria.

17. MASHAW ET AL., *op. cit. supra* note 14 at 146–47.

If such a structure were chosen, the proposal to make ALJ hearings adversary has considerable appeal. For here we are entering a world that views reasonably well functioning, bureaucratically rational, administrative systems, such as the SSA disability process, as unacceptable. Or, less dramatically, in such a world such a process can be acceptable *only if* it provides an opportunity for those who loathe the administrative state to opt out of its paradigmatic process (while seeking its benefits) into a moral judgments modality. Under these assumptions, limiting ALJ decisional independence and objectifying criteria are dysfunctional. Instead, the hearing process should be constructed to reflect what is at issue—the festering belief that a morally deserving claimant has been denied. Concern about the budgetary effects of such a system might then be allayed by providing for a vigorous defense.

A vigorous government defense against impaired and largely impecunious claimants may seem inappropriate, but the moral judgment model need not presume that desert is one-sided. Deservingness reflects a synthesis of community values. Putting on a defense both affirms the interests of FICA contributors and keeps faith with denied claimants who, for whatever reason, accept the bad news without appeal.

While hearing outcomes might be less favorable generally for claimants who appeal in an adversary process, there are potential benefits to claimants as well. Some claimants might receive more timely awards, and many might view the process as "fairer" than the current ALJ hearings. If government counsel had the power to pay strong claims without trying them, the more deserving appellants would not have to await hearing. And adversariness might enhance the independence of the ALJ and with it the acceptability of hearing decisions. Although ALJs are functionally independent under the Administrative Procedure Act,[18] it is not clear that they are perceived as independent. The ALJ must develop the "government side" of the case, and this must to some degree limit the claimant's sense of the judge's independence. The ALJ hearing, with no one representing the government, may also appear too good to be true. Surely somebody must be concerned that the claimant is not ripping off the Treasury. Who are they? Is that the ALJ's principal concern? Clinical studies in other contexts have demonstrated that contestants have the greatest trust for a process that has clear adversary

18. 5 U.S.C. §§1305, 3105, 5362, and 7521 (Supp. IV 1980).

roles and a passive decisionmaker. Their confidence diminishes as processes move toward an inquisitorial mode.[19]

But shifting the hearing process toward the ideal moral judgment regime has some unhappy features. Unrepresented claimants would seem disadvantaged, thus perhaps necessitating additional expenditures to provide counsel. More importantly, the dynamics of such a system seem to make it unworkable. Hearings would doubtless last longer than they do now, and the binary nature of the decision would make compromise virtually impossible. The only negotiable items might be the date of onset and the duration of the disability. Unlike most cases "decided" in other adversary processes, these cases would go to trial. The delay and expense entailed by adversariness would be great. Indeed, if there is truth to the widespread belief that settlement (including plea bargaining) is the only thing that prevents collapse in the civil and criminal courts, adversariness here seems a formula for disaster.

A remodeled hearing process would not obviate the need for a prehearing bureaucratic routine, for what Robert Dixon once called an administrative "flushing" process.[20] If the rates of awards in hearings continued to diverge substantially from prehearing, administrative award rates, the hearing process would continue to provide both a powerful source of criticism of the earlier decisional stages and a powerful reason to make further attempts at stringency. Stringency would fuel the appeal rate, and the spiral would continue until the system collapsed in chaos. Moreover, having eschewed accuracy, consistency, and control, we would have to be willing to live with the results, whatever emerged. There is the real possibility, for example, that those in charge of the flush chain in an adversary system, the employees who could pay a claim rather than contest it, would pay off most of the time in order to make their caseload manageable. Settlement is, after all, the norm in most adversary systems. If so, the reservoir would soon be empty. The most likely outcomes of adversary process thus seem to me to be interminable hearing delays or fiscal disaster.

The traditional legal techniques for moderating excessive bureaucratization of decision processes are essentially bankrupt. The legislature

---

19. THIBAUT AND WALKER, PROCEDURAL JUSTICE 67–96 (1975).

20. R. DIXON, SOCIAL SECURITY DISABILITY AND MASS JUSTICE 32 (1973).

seems likely to insist on more, not less, effective bureau control over the claims system. Moreover, to the extent that legislative concern with management control focuses on issues such as speedy processing, consistency, and limitation of the total budget, it may skew management initiatives sharply in the direction of objectification of standards and routinization of process. In short, whether or not the legislature sees clearly what it is doing, legislative action may support bureaucracy in a rather extreme and dysfunctional form.

The courts, as they themselves often maintain, are truly incompetent to deal with the complexities and subtleties of engineering and managing a large administrative decision process. And adversary hearings as *the* administrative process seem destined to cause big trouble. Although the moral judgment model in an adversary process mode can be defended, reform that emphasizes the role of hearings should be contemplated only if one despairs of the acceptability of some modified form of bureaucratic rationality.

# 10 · Opportunities for Internal Reform

Several interpretations might be placed on the foregoing account. A pessimist might describe the DI program as plagued by excessive concerns with hierarchical control and fiscal responsibility. This pessimist would decry the translation of these concerns into an objective, stringent, and impersonal decision process, and the apparent inability of traditional legal techniques to promote corrective action. A sanguine observer, on the other hand, might emphasize the increasing transparency and uniformity of the decision process and note that the existence of active legislative oversight, frequent judicial review, and fulsome opportunities for personalized hearings, far from being a cause for concern, describes the epitome of a legitimate administrative process. The optimist would predict that, over time, changes in legislative perspective, episodic judicial incursions into program management, and the threat of huge increases in hearing requests would correct any momentary tendencies toward excessive bureaucratization.

I do in fact take an optimistic view, but I do so for reasons somewhat different from those offered by our hypothetical optimist. For, as the preceding chapter demonstrates, I take the pessimist's view of the efficacy of conventional legal controls. It is not the subjection of the DI decision process to external constraint that provides our principal assurance of its acceptable operation, but rather the capacity to make its *internal* structure and operation respond to a sensible set of demands for rational, fair, and efficient adjudication. The DI adjudicatory process can obviously be improved, but those improvements lie primarily in the direction of internal changes in managerial approach and decisional technique, not in intensified legal or political control of a traditional sort or in the substitution of conventional legal process—adversary hearings—for current bureaucratic process.

## DIRECTIONS FOR INTERNAL REFORM

From this internal perspective, there seem to me to be two major problems with the current management of the DI decision process—the first is informational; the second, conceptual.

### The Information Shortfall

SSA desperately needs the answers to two questions: are claims correctly decided? is the decision process perceived as fair? These questions are, as we have seen, outrageously complicated. Yet the truth remains that it is not possible to make well-informed decisions about the effects of reform or of retention of current techniques without better information on both. The lack of adequate information undermines the unique claim of a bureaucratically rational system to our support—the promise to exercise power on the basis of knowledge.

The corrosive effect of ignorance is perhaps most evident with respect to the question of accuracy. The disability decision process has been repeatedly studied and repeatedly criticized for (1) interstate inconsistency in both outputs (award rates) and inputs (use of CEs, for example); (2) dramatic variance between state agency–ALJ and ALJ–court decisionmaking; (3) ineffective QA controls; and (4) the structural complexity and delay in the decision process. These same problems have been perceived ever since the Harrison subcommittee's report in 1960.[1] Why, in twenty years, haven't some clear remedies emerged?

The answer lies in the elusiveness of accuracy in the DI program. If state agencies in Arkansas and New York produce different results and use different techniques, SSA cannot simply tell them to be consistent. It must first determine who is right (or whether anybody is). It cannot settle the perennial conflict between state agencies and ALJs without a similar determination. Nor can SSA validate its QA and other management techniques without first defining accuracy and then determining what contributes to its pursuit. Finally, without some reasonably objective definition of accuracy, SSA cannot convincingly answer some critics who assert that the DI decision process disadvantages minorities, women, and persons of modest intelligence and education.

<hr />

1. SUBCOMMITTEE ON ADMINISTRATION OF SOCIAL SECURITY LAWS, COMMITTEE ON WAYS AND MEANS, COMMITTEE PRINT, ADMINISTRATION OF SOCIAL SECURITY DISABILITY PROGRAM, 86TH CONG., 2D SESS. (1960).

In short, a whole series of continuous and vexing problems converge on the question of accuracy. Existing management criteria for accuracy will not satisfy the demand for an evaluative standard. The QA program's error definitions are both relatively gross and inconsistently applied. As we have noted, the 1978 central office QA review identified errors in three times as many grants as denials, while the regional offices found that denials were 20 percent more likely to contain an error.[2] The presence or absence of a QA error is not necessarily a robust criterion of claim strength.

Given these circumstances in a program that decides 1,300,000 cases and spends $32 billion per year, the system fairly cries out for a better definition of accuracy. One technique for getting at the accuracy question would be to identify, through a rather heroic regression (discriminant factor) analysis, the current determinants of claim strength. This index could then be used to obtain a detailed understanding, for example, of how state A differs from state B, ALJs from state agencies, represented from unrepresented cases, and regional from national error identification. The analysis could also provide the basis for sorting claims at least into categories such as strong, weak, and marginal. It could thus begin to answer the continuous controversy over whether inconsistency or "reversals" result from an inevitable judgmental variance in close cases or from basic misunderstandings concerning substantive policy.

This effort would be both very difficult and very expensive. It might fail. And the payoff in terms of politically palatable policy initiatives is not obvious ex ante. Yet credible results would move discussion of what ought to be done about the DI decision process off the center upon which it has rested for two decades. Policy choice on a range of matters might be partly freed from the demoralizing and potentially delegitimizing competition between conventional wisdom and political expediency. And, with such a benchmark, discriminating evaluation of the effects of proposed future decisional changes might be feasible. Any number of

2. *Compare* Reports and Analysis Branch, Division of Quality Assurance, Office of Program Evaluation and Appraisal, BDI, SSA, "BDI Quarterly Report of CRS Review of Title XVI Initial Disability Determinations" (1977–1978), *with* Reports and Analysis Branch, Division of Disability Program Quality Office of Assessment, SSA, "Quarterly Report of Central Office Review of Title II Initial Disability Claims," (1977–1978) (unpublished reports).

more modest demonstration studies could be conducted, as policy development dictated, without studiously avoiding the concededly important questions. Indeed only some such effort can validate a claims structure whose legitimating model is bureaucratic rationality. The basic task of SSA decisionmaking, as that system has defined itself, is to decide cases accurately—to pay worthy claims and reject unworthy ones.

## Conceptual Timidity

SSA also lacks systematic information on the perceived fairness of its operations. This information gap seems intimately connected to a conceptual timidity about the potential variations in processes that might satisfy demands for fairness. Historically, SSA procedural innovation has been confined to refinement of its two distinct levels of decisionmaking; levels whose processes have increasingly diverged. The state agency process has been refined in the direction of objectivity and managerial control; the ALJ process, followed by judicial review, has remained largely unstructured and uncontrolled. The howls of the ALJs notwithstanding, the basic pattern is DDS–ALJ divergence in process and product, coupled with an attempt to limit the impact of hearings and judicial review on the main body of claims determinations. This has been combined with a strategy for managing professional (doctor and vocational expert) inputs that attempts to mend tears in the fabric of bureaucratic rationality without fully utilizing significant clinical intelligence.

This is the stance of a well-intentioned and competent bureaucracy with a guilty conscience. Clearly it must act independently of the traditional forms of legal process and legal control and of professional cultures that have different orientations. Adopted wholesale, these forms would be, to say the least, dysfunctional. Yet the bureaucracy cannot escape the impression it gives that its principal administrative processes—because they do not conform to the hearing model, to the aspirations for transparent rationalization of many reviewing courts, or to the clinical care and fiduciary attachment of service professionals— are a form of second-class justice. Policy analysis is thus cast in a defensive mode. It neither directly addresses the efficacy of the legal or professional "ideal" forms nor develops alternatives to them that might be more effective correctives for bureaucratic myopia or insensitivity. Indeed, the existence of these problems must be denied.

If, on the other hand, the bureaucratic rationality model of adjudication were viewed as a fully legitimate form of administrative adjudication, threatening questions concerning the quality of its justice could be viewed as opportunities for experimentation and reform. Those efforts might in turn produce superior, not eternally second-best, adjudicatory processes. It seems plausible to me, for example, that several different structures for the second stage of the decision process, the current reconsideration stage, might substantially improve the rationality and fairness of the overall adjudicatory system and (if ALJ hearings and judicial review could be eliminated) its efficiency as well.

The discussion that follows is not meant to justify the adoption of these proposals, but merely to render plausible some conceptions whose desirability would be assessable only through refinement, analysis, and testing. The discussion is of opportunities, not blueprints, for reform.

## A MODEST PROPOSAL: BUREAUCRACY WITH A HUMAN FACE

However sensible the bureaucratic model of adjudication may be in general, the problems of perspective that we have identified—the tendency to ignore subjective evidence, the susceptibility to transitory political concerns, the suppression of claimant (and other outsider) involvement in claims processing, the submerging of off-budget costs—are nevertheless real. Moreover, they suggest the need for an effective counterforce. Otherwise, systematic rationality may play out a progressive logic of control and objectivity that satisfies the Nietzschean definition of the ultimate stupidity—forgetting what it is that we were trying to do.

If a counterforce is needed, and ALJ hearings and judicial review cannot provide it effectively, where might it be found? Here, it seems to me, there are two plausible reform strategies. One is to make the claimants themselves the counterforce; that is, to structure the state agency process so that claimants are as real to adjudicators as are the medical consultants, unit supervisors, bureau chiefs, QA staffs, medical listings, DOT, DISM, and disability determination forms that make up their daily work environment. The examiners could be forced to talk to claimants, to treat them as important sources of information, to explain their eligibility decisions.

What would happen as a result of face-to-face contact? To some degree SSA already knows the answer. It has experimented with the use of interviews at the reconsideration stage of the process.[3] Those tests were indeed premised on a series of hypotheses that respond to the concerns we have previously expressed. If presenting one's case or information in person and getting immediate feedback are important elements in the perception of fairness, claimants should be better satisfied with such a procedure. This in turn would presumably reduce appeal rates. If, in at least some cases, seeing the claimant adds important information tending to support a claim, the number of claims granted by state agencies should go up. And this result need not imply a loss of appropriate objectivity. It would occur in part from a change in the interpretive perspective carried to the available documentary materials and in part from pursuit of additional objective evidence in cases that seemed stronger on personal contact than the medical evidence of record indicated.

If the latter effects were true, the reversal rate on appeal should go down. Where personal contact is the key to an allowance, the claim would have already been awarded. And when denying the claims of people who have more than a documentary existence, examiners would probably make a better evidentiary case, one that will be more likely to stand up on appeal.

Program costs could be expected to go up because some claims that would not have been appealed to a hearing would be granted at the reconsideration stage. Administrative costs would probably go up. Each case would take longer to process at the state agency level, and the reduction in appeal rates would probably not offset these costs. On the benefits side, a number of "nonappealing" but eligible claimants, who would not have received benefits at all under the present system, would receive them. Moreover, successful claimants who would otherwise have succeeded only after appeal would be spared considerable delay.

In its experiments with reconsideration interviews, SSA found all these propositions to be true. The information from the experiments is

---

3. The structure and results of these experiments are contained in a plethora of unpublished SSA memoranda, letters, "fact sheets," and the like. Many are undated and have no identifiable authors. A couple of the more significant documents are cited at chapter 6, note 9.

not nearly as complete as one would like. *In particular, the tests did not have a sensitive measure of either claimant satisfaction or of decisional accuracy.* One cannot tell why the interview made a difference in either dimension (satisfaction or accuracy) when it did. Hence it is not really possible to tell from the studies whether the hearing stage could be eliminated with no substantial loss or whether the interview substantially interfered with management control of the system. SSA's opinion on the latter question must have been that it did not, for in 1976 the administration recommended adding a reconsideration interview to the current process nationwide. Until recently, however, this position has not been supported at the departmental level (Health and Human Services), and the costs of moving to the proposed system have never been included in the HHS budget.

A second counterforce idea is representation of claimants, an attractive notion for several reasons. First, neither the present system nor the personal interview process really comes to grips with the limitations on claimants' understanding of the program. A system that provided claimants with specialized representatives whenever they were initially denied benefits could instill somewhat more confidence both that informed choices were being made concerning whether to request reconsideration and that relevant evidence was not being overlooked. Representatives could also be expected to filter out frivolous claims. Representatives who viewed themselves as participating in the system over an extended period would be discreet. Rather clear "losers" would be counseled to accept defeat, and energies would be devoted to worthier claims. The number of claims persisting past an initial denial might well decrease.

If properly constructed, representation could also play a mediating role between the claimant's perceptions of distress and the program's policies. Much of what lawyers do in civil and criminal claims can quite properly be viewed as educating the client about the legal system rather than educating the legal system about the client. Both the availability of relevant expertise and the counseling of a personal representative should increase claimants' sense of fair treatment.

There are obviously problems with structuring representation into the reconsideration process. First, who would these representatives be? In my view there is no need for them to be lawyers. Not only are there few, if any, legal issues involved, most lawyers do not understand the disability system well enough to be of much use to the claimant (or to the decisionmaker). The VA system of claims representatives, operating through veterans' organizations, is an attractive model; but there are no obvious representational substitutes for veterans' organizations such as the VFW or American Legion. Nevertheless, it seems critical that, as in the VA situation, representatives have essentially the same qualifications and training as disability examiners. Indeed, they might *be* disability examiners who sometimes work as deciders in the state agency and sometimes as claimants' representatives in a separate bureau established for that purpose.

But if the representatives are also government employees, how can they be given the proper incentives to provide vigorous assistance to their "clients"? In part, I would suggest, through the same devices currently used to monitor examiner behavior. If examiner development and judgment can be supervised, so can a representative performing a similar task. To be sure, there are additional functions and problems involved, but they hardly seem insurmountable. Moreover, we should not forget that the current system is one in which claimants, save for a tiny percentage who are represented at hearings (say 60,000 out of 1,300,000 claimants entering the system each year), are now almost totally at the mercy of government employees (examiners, ALJs) who have no personal obligation to them for the development of their cases.[4] Assigning a government employee the explicit role of representing claimants will certainly increase the incentives to protect the claimants' interests. It might also be possible to generalize the representation idea by establishing a separate bureau of paraprofessional claims representatives (perhaps as an offshoot of the Legal Services Corporation) to handle other types of benefits claims as well.

In my view, a combination of face-to-face reconsideration interviews and representation provided at the time of any initial denial notice is worth trying in a carefully controlled test. By "carefully controlled" I mean a test that is sensitive to the need for data on correctness and satisfaction and that will, therefore, provide a basis for well-informed policy choice. My intuition is that on most of the dimensions of adjudicative quality, the combined method would yield results so supe-

---

4. These officials have obligations to develop the cases, but they are owed to the Social Security Administration, not to the claimants.

rior to the current system that the costs of the change could be partially recouped by eliminating ALJ hearings and judicial review. If this were the case, there would have been developed a bureaucratic model of administrative justice that substantially improves upon both the traditional adversary process model and the existing model of bureaucratic rationality that has emerged as a response to SSA's need to obtain control over the disability decision process.

For the interview-plus-representative idea responds both to the shortcomings and to the strengths of the bureaucratic model. Although bureaucratic rationality deemphasizes intuitive judgment and personalized concern, it also seeks continually to improve upon its technical or scientific mode of thought. Merely introducing the claimant into the process without providing him or her with access to technical resources is to introduce a foreign body that is likely to be rejected by the host organism. The claimant's participation in the development of a claim must be structured in a way that orients the facts of his or her functioning to the stylized reasoning process of a manageable, and managed, adjudicatory system. That orientation requires expertise about the system, as well as sympathetic association with the claimant's situation.

The interview-plus-representative proposal can also be uncoupled. Claimants who prefer privacy to personal contact can be content with the aid of a representative and a decision based wholly on the claims file. The fiercely independent could represent themselves or reject SSA's offer of a representative in favor of employing their own.

## SOME MORE RADICAL PROPOSALS: PROFESSIONAL JUDGMENT

In chapter 2 we explained the initial rejection of professional judgment as a justice model for disability adjudication primarily because of its poor fit with the disability program's objectives and the unpredictable, potentially uncontrollable nature of income support judgments harnessed to a private, professional–therapeutic regime. An additional factor is the not insignificant opposition of the medical profession to the integration of medical diagnostic and treatment functions in a more comprehensive program of publicly administered health care, vocational rehabilitation, and income support. We have also noted physicians' varying conceptions both of medical practice and of income support in relation to therapy as grounds for doubting the existence of a unified professional medical judgment concerning disability claims.

Thus, to propose a mode of disability adjudication that would rely on professional judgment as its primary adjudicatory technique is to suggest that we are somehow talking about a different program and a different political era. Indeed, I believe that we now are. The 1980 amendments may be viewed, in part, as an effort to rebuild linkages between medical care, income support, and vocational rehabilitation. Moreover, I suspect that most contemporary doctors would view the equation of federal involvement in the provision of medical care with "socialized medicine" as quaint.

It is going much too far, however, to view the disability program, even after the 1980 amendments, as an open-ended treatment- or service-oriented program. SSA has not been converted into a comprehensive health and social service agency that can "treat" disabled clients for their multiple health, training, placement, and income security problems.[5] And the hazards that attended the use of professionals as adjudicators for such a limited program have not vanished. Even a *mildly* utopian approach to reform will not suggest converting the dominant income-maintenance-via-bureaucratic-implementation modality that we have discussed into a structure dominated by professionals—health, vocational, or other—and their combined treatment cultures.

Rather, the question is whether some of the intuitive professional judgment of relevant disciplines can be insinuated into the adjudicatory structure in ways that protect professional judgment from the corrosive logic of bureaucratic routine. The idea is to increase the acceptability of decisionmaking by harnessing decisions to some approximation of the service ideals and fiduciary relationships that generally support quality control through professionalization, and yet maintain the accountability and efficiency of bureaucratic organization. Much that has gone before suggests that such a system is impossible. Yet in the world of 1980, when twenty years' experience with administration in a compromised bureaucratic–legal mode has produced less than universal acclaim and mounting systemic stress, a different unhappy compromise might at least be explored. Consider the following.

5. For a powerful conceptual argument that it should be, *see* S. NAGI, DISABILITY POLICIES AND PROGRAMS: ISSUES AND OPTIONS (unpublished interim report to the Office of the Assistant Secretary for Planning and Evaluation, DHEW, May 1977).

## Medical Examination

We have discussed suggestions that the DI program shift its decision process to a professional judgment model employing physician-deciders. One variation on such a system, for example, might use a panel of three physicians who would personally examine the claimant and decide the disability question at the reconsideration stage. The process might be organized around existing hospitals and clinics or special diagnostic centers that could provide all the basic tests that the physician panel would require. Vocational information and other data not available from the initial development, including prior medical findings, would be gathered and supplied by a development staff. If the staff's development suggested that a grant would be appropriate, it might also be authorized to remand cases to the initial stage prior to submitting the case to the medical panel. The specialist composition of the medical panel would respond to the claimant's medical condition or conditions, and the panel physicians would be trained in the basic policies of the DI program and in the demands of major categories of work.

This model has a number of attractive features. It applies a more consistent level of medical expertise to cases by eliminating significant reliance on treating physician reports or the findings of a single consultative physician. The claimant would have personal contact with the decisionmaker, which would permit the evaluation of subjective factors but at the same time harness that evaluation to direct clinical observation and to the trained diagnostic intuition of medical professionals. The combined opinions of three doctors who had personally examined the claimant would also presumably have a strong symbolic effect—hopefully, strong enough to counteract both prior medical advice and the desire to get yet another opinion (appeal).

There are, of course, problems as well: Administrative costs might be substantial. Physicians' aptitudes for assessing vocational factors or applying other program policies are unknown. The dominant medical culture might overwhelm the adjudicatory function. Floating panels might produce substantially inconsistent results. In some areas of the country the medical manpower to run the process may simply be unavailable.

Yet, in my view, these do not seem to be determinative objections. There would be cost savings from the elimination of multiple decisional layers, and two-doctor panels could be the norm, with a third called in only to break ties. Clear grants and nonmedical denials would be culled prior to submission to the medical panels. There is no obvious reason why physicians with some special training should do worse in dealing with vocational factors than BAs in English literature. Furthermore, multimember panels tend to decide cases more consistently than individual adjudicators. Nor is there any reason not to make medical panel judgments subject to a QA system that would tend to support consistency. Were such an approach found to be markedly superior to the current system, it is not clear that instituting it wherever feasible would be unsound, even if universality should prove impossible.

A priori, then, I do not see solid reasons for rejecting the medical examination model. To be sure, we know much less about how it would function than we know about the current system. Obviously there are variations on the theme that would have to be carefully considered—panel composition, collegiate versus individual decisionmaking, staging of the decision process, degree of physician independence from SSA oversight, relations between the panels and treating physicians, and the like. But this seems to me to argue for careful design and subsequent testing, rather than for rejection.

## Multiprofessional Panels

The 1969 Nagi study[6] provided a variation on the medical panel examination that is responsive to the medical-vocational character of the disability standard—a multidisciplinary evaluation, including the testing of functional capacity under simulated work conditions. The Nagi study group put teams of specially trained persons in three state agencies for a substantial period of time. Immediately following the initial determination by state agencies, these teams took a sample of claims and redeveloped them extensively. For each claimant the team did six evaluations: (1) social and economic—information on the individual's background, social relations, and economic situation; (2) medical, including medical histories, physical examinations, laboratory and radiological tests, and consultations as needed; (3) psychological, performed by clinical psychologists on the basis of interviews and a battery of psychometric tests; (4) occupational, conducted by occupational thera-

6. *Op. cit. supra* chapter 6, note 4.

pists and considering work capacities, limitations, and skills under work conditions (applicants were asked to perform a variety of tasks requiring the use of various tools and equipment, and their performance was evaluated for quality and quantity of work; (5) vocational, performed by vocational counselors and assessing the rehabilitation potential of each claimant based upon interviews and a study of the claimant's work history; and finally (6), a panel evaluation in which all of the specialists involved in the prior appraisals jointly discussed the claimant and his or her condition and prospects.

The information generated by these evaluations was then transmitted to the state agency personnel who had made the initial decisions. As one might expect, better information tended to have an impact on decisionmaking. Interestingly, this impact seemed disproportionately to verify claimants' disability rather than negate it. Overall, if we consider the experience in all three of the state agencies studied, initial denials were changed to awards in 21 percent of the cases, whereas initial awards were changed to denials only 8 percent of the time. Moreover, a comparison of the cases in which there was a change favorable to the claimant with various characteristics of claimants and their medical conditions reveals that better development tends primarily to aid (a) persons who are disadvantaged by low IQ, low educational levels, or low socioeconomic status, (b) claimants who have combinations of unlisted impairments (that is, impairments not included in the medical listings that established per se disabilities), and (c) those who have adverse vocational factors but only modest medical impairments.

The Nagi study also casts light on the problem of "close" cases. In addition to developing evidence and providing it to the state agencies, the study teams also classified the cases in eight categories ranging from slightly impaired to completely disabled. When the teams then compared their classifications with the assignment of "disabled" or "not disabled" by state agencies, they discovered that the cases they had consigned to the middle categories turned up with equal frequency in awards and denials. This finding tends to confirm the conventional wisdom in the Social Security system that there is an irreducible category of marginal claims that will never be consistently decided.

The tendency of the Nagi professional team approach to aid the disadvantaged claimant is an attractive feature. It is hard to imagine a case for leaving the handicapped to their own devices in a program in aid of the disabled. Moreover, this model specifically addresses the critical RFC issue from all sides—physical, psychological, cognitive—with specific focus on work and work-related activities. If the puzzle of what a claimant can do is to be put together, this seems the way to do it. And should it appear that changes induced by the Nagi panels' evidence indeed resulted from a "better" approach to the RFC mystery, multiprofessional evaluation would have a strong claim to consideration on rationality grounds alone.

The multidisciplinary approach might also provide a powerful legitimating symbol. The claimant would be exposed to persons whose expertise would permit a much more detailed and therefore more believable description of the requirements of various jobs and comparison of the claimant's capacities with those requirements. It might be possible, in the workshop setting, to give every denied claimant a list of several jobs for which he or she is fitted along with the description of any training or rehabilitative therapy necessary to insure the claimant's capacity to function in those positions.

There are plausible objections to the Nagi technique. One is that it looks very expensive. The Nagi teams employed six specialists, each of whom saw the claimant; all of them had a conference concerning each claim. This expense may seem disproportionate to the increase in knowledge provided by the multiprofessional format. DDS personnel have a low opinion of the quality of evidence supplied by existing multiprofessional vocational workshops. As one leaves the medical profession and enters the domain of "vocational specialists," one encounters a much greater variety of educational backgrounds and professional perspectives than are to be found in the medical profession. There may well be much greater variance among multiprofessional panels than among medical panels or DDS decisionmakers, although restricting the panels to evidentiary rather than decisional functions perhaps would reduce this problem. And it seems even less likely that multiprofessional evaluations can be provided universally than that medical panels could be.

The Nagi approach would also be much more intrusive than the present decision structure. The claimant would have to submit to numerous interviews and batteries of tests. It would also be difficult to gloss over crucial questions of credibility. If the claimant flunked various capacity tests, the medical or vocational specialist would have to decide whether the claimant's efforts were credible. From this perspective, the evaluation begins to approximate surveillance.

Notwithstanding these difficulties, the model seems sufficiently attractive to warrant a serious test.[7] The current low prestige of workshop evaluations may relate to the current structure and staffing of vocational workshops. Most are in the business of providing either sheltered work environments or rehabilitation for a narrow range of jobs available in the local market. Not surprisingly, the evidence coming back from these sources does not fit the needs of the DI program. If the objection, on the other hand, is that workshops tend to place too much emphasis on subjective factors, the response may be that current SSA approach places too little faith in that form of evidence. And if some contemporary workshop evaluations are, indeed, too subjective, that may merely be a function of their position outside the DI system. It is certainly not proof that appropriate structures for and controls on multiprofessional panel judgments cannot be devised.

Although this model looks very expensive, there is no obvious reason to use six specialists in every case. A basic physician–vocational counselor panel that might attach to itself other medical or vocational specialties as necessary seems adequate to the task. And, as in the medical panel model, it should be possible to limit the number of cases that get to the panel stage.

Finally, it is not possible to predict in the abstract how accurate or consistent such panels would be or how claimants would react to them. In particular, one would like to know how often the RFC evaluation turned out to be problematic or seemed to turn on questions of credibility. It may be that a multidisciplinary workshop approach will not provide greater confidence that this critical finding is appropriate. But it would at least turn the spotlight on a dark corner of the current process and permit a more reasoned judgment concerning whether the RFC evaluation must be left in the shadows.

7. At least one such study has been conducted and others are planned. Unfortunately, the methodology of the reported study prevented it from answering the many basic questions concerning effects on adjudicative quality that are necessary for reasonable policy judgment. (The report nevertheless makes the experiment sound like a breakthrough of gargantuan proportions.) The study is reported in SUBCOMMITTEE ON SOCIAL SECURITY, COMMITTEE ON WAYS AND MEANS, 95TH CONG., 2D SESS., DISABILITY ADJUDICATION STRUCTURE, "ANALYST-MEDICAL CONSULTANT EXAMINATION PROJECT—STATE OF CALIFORNIA DISABILITY EVALUATION PROGRAM" 52–92 (1978).

We have, then, at least three proposals for a second, and perhaps final, stage of disability adjudication: (1) the current reconsideration process with the addition of face-to-face interviews and the assistance of representatives; (2) the medical examination panel; and (3) the multidisciplinary "workshop" approach. How can we choose among these models? On the basis of current information, I cannot choose and SSA should not. Plausible hypotheses connect each proposal either to the production of relevant evidence or to the satisfying of various fairness and legitimation concerns. Careful design and testing, including evaluation against a sophisticated index of claim strength and claimant satisfaction, should precede policy choice. For, again, that is the promise of bureaucratic justice—to exercise power on the basis of knowledge. By comparison with the DI program's annual expenditures, the costs of seeking the requisite knowledge are negligible.

# PART V · GENERALIZATIONS

# 11 · Bureaucracy, Justice, and the Rule of Law

Whatever the prospects for reform or change in the Social Security disability program, it is time to return to the more general theme with which we began. What has the intervening discussion told us of the structure of American administrative law or of the nature of the quest for justice in an increasingly administrative state? Can an internal orientation generate both images of administration and means of control that will satisfy our demands for legitimation of the exercise of administrative power?

We obviously cannot say too much on the basis of a single observation. But it seems fair to claim that SSA's implementation of its disability benefits programs has generated an *internal* law of administration. That the law is internal is true in the superficial sense that it consists primarily of unpublished written instructions and interpretations combined with standard bureaucratic routines and with developmental and decisional practices. For our purposes, this law is internal in the more significant sense that it has remained largely unaffected by traditional external legal control through judicial review and, at the examiner level, by the forms of external legal process.

That these documents and practices should be considered *law* is problematic only from a legal perspective that takes as its rule of recognition the existence of rights enforceable in court. But that internal law exists in the form of norms backed by sanctions and that these norms are recognized and acted upon by the relevant officials seems relatively nonproblematic. Our concern, however, has been not just whether (on some plausible conception) internal administrative law exists, but whether that law can make persuasive claims to provide an acceptable system of administrative justice.

## A PANGLOSSIAN SUMMARY

From among conceivable models of administrative justice in benefits adjudication, SSA has chosen bureaucratic rationality. The elaboration of that model reveals the complexity and ambiguity of the system's principal goals, rationality and efficiency, the necessary trade-offs between them, and the operational difficulty of realizing either goal in an organizational setting. The justice of the system thus resides in the operational balance achieved by the combined methods of normative prescription and managerial control.

While we have had much to say about the inherent and contingent difficulties of pursuing justice in the bureaucratic mode, we should not allow that discussion to obscure SSA's considerable success. The general norms of accuracy and efficiency have been elaborated and operationalized to direct activity at the examiner level toward achieving diligence, developmental comprehensiveness, expedition, and high-quality outputs. This orientation is supported by a supervisory system that makes examiners internally accountable for their adjudicatory product. Indeed, one might describe the "compleat examiner" as a productive, detached, persistent, institutional conformist—characteristics that should provide claimants and taxpayers with accurate, efficient, and fair adjudication. Moreover, competing models of justice retain institutional significance and serve as constant reminders of the values that would be foregone by a single-minded pursuit of bureaucratic rationality. SSA has succeeded remarkably well in embracing both the neutrality, expertise, and efficiency that are the promise of bureaucracy and the concern for individual circumstances and well-being that is promised by systems oriented toward moral entitlements and professional treatment.

## A CLOUD OVER CAMELOT

Yet surely this vision of ideal administration is too sanguine. We have also noted how external pressures from the Congress have begun to move the system toward new goals, such as fiscal restraint, consistency, and manageability, that may undermine—at least distort—the accuracy, efficiency, and fairness norms that the system has tended to pursue. Nor is SSA free from internal stress. Unifying state agency approaches has been a continual difficulty. More important, the compromise decision structure, appending relatively uncontrollable hearings and judicial review to bureaucratic adjudication, has seemed both to contradict the fairness and accuracy of state agency decisionmaking and to supply the necessary predicate for greater stringency and control in first-level adjudication. The external forms of legal control thus criticize a stringency that their profligacy promotes. In addition, the system's necessary concentration on medical and vocational findings, while remaining detached from the operational context of professional therapy (and often rejecting professional therapeutic advice) is a source of constant tension.

There is also a troubling gap in our story to this point—troubling at least to those whose experience or learning suggests that much of the reality of bureaucratic behavior has been omitted. For we have been describing a system that is relatively bloodless. It supposedly exalts abstract values like accuracy and efficiency, which on reflection are subtle, complex, and the products of compromise. Yet it operates in a stressful environment. The historic SSA technique of placing itself above politics has begun to wear thin; legal validation via hearings and judicial review threatens to transform the system rather than support it; professional values—particularly those of the medical profession— contradict as well as support decisionmaking; and federal administration must contend with the fifty-odd political cultures that compete for the attention of its front-line adjudicative staff. Have we really explained how SSA managers or examiners adapt to the stress of uncertainty and the pressures of macro (legislative) and micro (bureau) politics? Can we really believe that they do so while maintaining a balanced normative outlook and pursuing complex normative goals?

## A DESK-LEVEL VIEW

It is true that our focus has been on the development, expression, and implementation of norms within SSA, with only some attention to the conditions that might confound the concrete realization of those ideals. That focus has hardly been accidental. I cannot now begin a different story on games bureaucrats play. I can, however, say something about my reasons for believing that a study focused on the behavior and adaptation of managers or examiners would not render the preceding account irrelevant.

## The Managers

We have already made the case-in-chief for the management at SSA. The evidence of balance is almost everywhere in our prior discussion. A number of factors make it possible to sustain this posture. First, the basic operations of the agency are technocratic and apolitical. It exercises primarily a bookkeeping, actuarial, and management function. "Bloodlessness" is built into the basic organizational mission. To be sure, Social Security is a part of ideology of social justice that permeated the New Deal. But that ideology is translated into reality at SSA not by effective social work but by the accurate and efficient processing of claims.

Moreover, external pressures for fiscal restraint should not be oversold. By comparison with most agencies, SSA has been insulated from partisan politics. The general program has wide acceptance. Only recently have indexing, shifts in age cohorts, and phenomenal growth in Medicare and disability expenditures caused concern with the cost of social insurance. With its basic social goals clear and generally approved, Social Security has remained largely a program where policy issues are defined in managerial and technocratic terms. And on that level outsiders pose a modest threat.

This is not a program like drug regulation, for example, in which the FDA's recurrent institutional nightmare—a thalidomide tragedy—forces a single-minded preventative orientation.[1] Nor is it like wage and price controls, whose success or lack of it is obvious to all, and whose implementers must therefore eschew balance and hew to stringency when interpreting their mandate.[2] There is no short-term, visible, and politically significant occurrence that SSA must avoid and, therefore, no obvious incentive to define the task or mission in single-minded terms.

Finally, SSA is run by careerist civil servants who identify with the agency. Indeed, SSA is a rather paramilitary organization. It has a band, a chorus, an anthem, and a flag. Many of its top-level administrators have worked nowhere else. Its headquarters on the outskirts of Baltimore constitutes almost a separate city. Three generations of families are sometimes employed there. Social Security employees do not view

1. *See, e.g.*, Mashaw, *Regulation, Logic and Ideology*, 3 Regulation 44 (1979).
2. *See generally*, R. KAGAN. REGULATORY JUSTICE (1978).

the *Washington Post* as a local newspaper; many don't even think it a particularly important or interesting one.

These are not administrators imbued with the norms of an alien or even closely related profession[3] or political entrepreneurs seeking to parlay highly visible action into the next move up some external bureaucratic or political ladder.[4] There are, of course, the usual problems of "turf," internecine struggle, middle-management doldrums, and the like that beset every bureaucracy. But these have modest effects on policy and performance. If a bureau can maintain a balanced approach to morally ambiguous and technocratically complex goals like accuracy and efficiency, the external politics, location, and managerial structure of SSA have historically provided a hospitable environment for the effort.

Sustained political commitment to stringency, continual crises in the trust fund accounts, and loss of widespread political acceptance may, of course, over time irretrievably alter SSA management's historic commitment to cautious benevolence. Defensiveness and the imbalance that such a posture implies may come to describe the managerial reality. Although the SSA's size, division of labor, and loose-jointed state–federal structure tend to protect it against systematic skews in program administration, the agency is certainly not impervious to political direction at the managerial level.

## State Agency Examiners

Yet, if the managers are somewhat protected from politics, imbued with the complex mission of a technocratic bureaucracy, and insulated from the realities of individual claims adjudication, there is no obvious reason to imagine that state agency disability examiners have a comparable environment. The examiner must, after all, decide. And the complexity, indeterminacy, and poignancy of disability claims, as we have described them, must make a balanced professional detachment hard to maintain. How much easier it would be to define the mission as "helping the

3. Robert Katzman, for example, has described FTC antitrust policy as essentially a vector sum of the professional interests of lawyers and economists within the Bureau of Competition: REGULATORY BUREAUCRACY (1980). *See also* S. WEAVER, DECISION TO PROSECUTE (1977) (discussing parallel policy in the Justice Department's Antitrust Division).

4. The classification of bureaucrats into careerists, professionals, and politicians follows James Q. Wilson's in THE POLITICS OF REGULATION (1980).

handicapped" or "keeping benefits-oriented claimants from taking a free ride," or perhaps in wholly operational terms as "meeting this week's production quota."

Moreover, we have already noted that examiners are employed by state administrative agencies that structure their functions in ways that range from viewing them as indistinguishable from the state welfare agency to including them as a part of the state's complex of education programs. The appropriate mission communicated to the examiner by these exemplary (and other) structures may be radically different, and both may deny the examiner the relatively detached political position of the SSA manager. How can we imagine that the complex vision of administrative justice that bureaucratic rationality entails will be a controlling, even a major, influence on the behavior of claims examiners?

The conditions necessary for control are obviously dual: a vigorous and well-conceived effort by SSA; and an operational reality that does not defeat the best efforts of management. We have discussed the first in some detail previously. The management program for specifying norms and operations and maintaining performance was both praised and criticized from various perspectives. But one thing seemed clear— SSA currently has both a commitment to achieving management control and a reasonably well-designed system for doing so.

From the state agency perspective, the federal presence is being felt. The most common complaint about SSA by state agencies is, indeed, further evidence of a balanced approach. The states complain that there is unremitting pressure to do everything at once—fully develop claims, meet QA accuracy standards, keep up productivity, and render all decisions in a timely fashion. If you improve your accuracy and development at the cost of some increase in processing time, the feds immediately start harping on timeliness, and vice versa. The states also complain that even the regional offices don't understand or respond to local problems. This is, of course, as it should be. It indicates that the federal managers closest to the states are also making the federal presence felt, even if the regional people view themselves (as they do) as playing a mediating and resource role rather than merely a monitoring and enforcement role—and even if the central office thinks (which it does) that the regions are too understanding of local problems.

Moreover, the federal managerial presence in a sense extends into the state agencies themselves via that agency's QA personnel. One finds in state agency offices a clear division, sometimes a marked tension, between examiners and the QA staff. Members of the QA unit view themselves both as an elite review group *and* as a group that is misunderstood and unfairly resented by line examiners. The examiners, for their part, often complain that the QA people are arrogant, aloof, and as compulsively oriented to statistics as the SSA central and regional offices. This again is as it should be. The QA unit's job is to criticize and constantly seek to upgrade performance. Moreover, because the internal state-level QA unit sees a large percentage of an examiner's product, state QA people believe that they have accurate information on the quality of every examiner's adjudications. Some assert that they can tell from their QA review when an examiner has a cold or trouble at home.

But what of the examiners themselves? Can they beat the system by avoiding review? Or does managerial supervision as it affects examiner behavior skew their efforts in directions that defeat rather than support the program's normative goals—accurate, fair, and efficient adjudication? Much of the literature on bureaucracy—particularly bureaucracies that deal with large caseloads—suggests that the answer to both of these questions is probably yes. James Q. Wilson's study of FBI and narcotics agents, for example, concludes that the task of those investigators is inherently uncontrollable by management.[5] He finds that statistical and other bureaucratic routines either have no relation to behavior or shape it in ways that are dysfunctional, given the ostensible goals of the organization.

Bardach and Kagan's more recent study of attempts to promote aggressive and uniform enforcement by the food, housing, and workplace "inspectorate" argues that the necessary concomitants of managerial control—objective rules and minimal discretion—have caused the underlying goals of health and safety to be partially lost.[6] Moreover, the authors suggest that the reaction of the regulated to this bureaucratic phenomenon actually reduces health and safety by comparison with a more discretionary enforcement regime.

Lipsky has generalized the investigator-and-inspector-control problem to all "street level bureaucrats."[7] Particularly as concerns social welfare bureaus, Lipsky emphasizes the deflection of the bureau's

5. J. Q. WILSON, THE INVESTIGATORS (1978).
6. E. BARDACH AND R. KAGAN, GOING BY THE BOOK (1982).
7. M. LIPSKY, STREET LEVEL BUREAUCRACY (1980).

performance that results from the attachment of the street level official to the demands of the bureau's clients. In this, Lipsky replicates Blau's early study of rehabilitation and employment referral agencies— agencies in which statistical performance indicators also tended to skew effort away from the achievement of some of the explicit social purposes for the bureau's existence.

Equally disturbing is Malcolm Feeley's study of the lower courts in two Connecticut towns.[8] Feeley roundly criticizes the notion that controlling the behavior of adjudicators supports an adjudicatory system's explicit normative goals. Feeley discovered that if one looked at what the judges did and how legal norms and adjudicatory routines affected their behavior, one would miss nearly 100 percent of the explanation for the output of the system. All the cases are resolved by other participants on the basis of criteria that sometimes support but often diverge radically from the definition of justice in the formal legal regime. The decisions of those in formal command of the adjudicatory process were virtually irrelevant to the system's output.

This literature may make us skeptical, if we were not so already, of the ability of hierarchical systems to implement their ostensible norms. But the context of managerial control burdens SSA with few of the problems these studies identify. Because the claims are all-or-nothing, they must be adjudicated. Control does not pass from examiners to other participants except through the development of claims. Even there, because examiner development is both active and reviewable on the record in the claims file, the participation of other parties cannot dominate the decision matrix. Moreover, because the cases are decided on documents that are fully reviewable by QA analysts, the client- or task-orientation of examiners can neither avoid review nor sharply skew adjudicatory results.

Examiners are desk-bound bureaucrats who work elbow to elbow with their peers and their supervisors and within a few yards of the QA unit. They contact claimants, physicians, and others by phone or by mail. They make no snap judgments "on the street" under the pressures of threat or supplication. The problems of managing street-level, and therefore uncontrollable, bureaucrats do not beset this agency.

Indeed, examiners do not have enough contact with their clients to develop the conflict of interest that a client advocacy posture would

8. M. FEELEY, THE PROCESS IS THE PUNISHMENT (1979).

imply. We therefore previously suggested accentuating the participation of claimants and professionals in the decision process as an antidote to the external pressures that seem to be deflecting SSA's operations toward the limited goals of objectivity, manageability, and stringency. The argument was that we should be concerned that the system may be becoming too manageable. A loss of perspective at the top might rather too quickly reshape examiner behavior. The value complexity that results from an internal competition among visions of justice might be in danger of being lost.

Of course, these points can be pressed too far. SSA managers do sit astride a bureaucracy having many characteristics that aid control in the interest of system goals, but they cannot squeeze out all the variance in examiner behavior. Nor should they. In part, this variance responds to objective differences in the external environment and, when kept within bounds, supports program goals.

For example, consider Examiner X and Examiner Y. Both confront similar cases that are missing medical evidence and a deadline of six weeks to decide the case (before the tickler file in the central office computer starts sending out "stale case" memos). X orders a CE; Y pursues medical reports from treating hospitals and physicians. Obviously this divergence in their actions may have effects on the eventual outcome. They will get different evidence. The decision to order a CE also affects the costliness of state agency decisionmaking.

Yet, depending on the circumstances, both may have made the proper decision. If, for example, the consultants available to X for the body system in question are prompt and well qualified, but the treating hospital is unresponsive and provides poor clinical records, then X's decision promoted accuracy and timeliness. Reverse the facts and Y's decision is equally sound. Moreover, both claimants get the best development achievable within the objective constraints of the system.

The judgments of X and Y may not, of course, have been so faultless. But if either begins systemically to favor one form of development over the other, contrary to the objective circumstances of the local medical context, that fact will show up either in the QA process, as poor development or delay, or in the budgetary process, as an unreasonable drain on the funds available for CEs. Virtually every dimension of examiner behavior has a statistical check, and statistical aberration can be evaluated against both particular files and the collective experience of an office that repeatedly uses the same external information sources.

There is, of course, looseness in the supervisory scheme. Examiners can sometimes beat the system. But enough has been said to support our basic point. The internal law of administration that we have seen emerge in the disability program is more than Thurman Arnold's law as comfort. It is also a guide to behavior because it is integrated into a system of hierarchical control that operates under structural and environmental conditions that permit success.

## THE PROMISE AND THE THREAT

My conclusion is that bureaucratic rationality—at least as practiced by SSA in the disability program—is a promising form of administrative justice. It permits the effective pursuit of collective ends without inordinately sacrificing individualistic or democratic ideals. It can accommodate competing visions of justice within a staged decision process that also has a high degree of division of labor. Yet, as we have also seen, this system of administration is politically vulnerable. Our individualistic and democratic ideals, embodied in courts and legislatures, symbolically contradict the basic thrust of bureaucratic rationality. The external legal order provides not only inadequate remedies for bureaucracy's ills, but also symbols of justice or legitimacy that challenge the basic premises of the bureaucratic ideal.

Thus, looking at the administration of the disability program through the judicial symbols of the rule of law—due process hearings and judicial review—we might denounce SSA's attempts to manage the ALJ corps as the destruction of the claimant's guarantee of due process. If we took seriously the democratic symbolism of meaningful public participation in the development of administrative policy, we would decry the adoption of the grid regulations over the objections of virtually all the participants in the rulemaking process, and perhaps urge the invalidation of the regulations on that ground alone. We would therefore lament both the failure of SSA administrators to follow the lead of reviewing courts and the failure of reviewing courts to take a more aggressive stance in reshaping SSA administration in its own image, or some quasi-legislative image of participatory democracy.

I obviously believe that these external modes of "reform" are wrongheaded. They can only divert SSA from the administrative-managerial tasks (such as developing. a baseline analysis for claim strength, carefully inquiring into claimant's perceptions of the disability process, and integrating clinical techniques into the adjudicatory process) that might make important differences in the quality of bureaucratic justice. Yet the images of justice that the external legal order evokes are difficult to dislodge. The complicated struggles of the SSA bureaucracy to produce accurate decisions at a reasonable cost have none of the drama of trial; they evoke none of the usual images of popular democracy at work. Indeed, as Thurman Arnold put it in 1935, "Bureaucracy is probably the most important of our negative symbols."[9]

Not much has changed. Forty years later Jimmy Carter ran against the Washington bureaucracy and won. Yet in only four years he created two new cabinet level departments, thus providing Ronald Reagan the campaigner with his principal specific promise in domestic affairs—to abolish the departments of Education and Energy. And in his inaugural address Reagan promised more generally to "get the government [meaning *bureaucrats*] off our backs." The negative symbol of bureaucracy still has force in American politics, the ever-expanding size and functions of administration to the contrary notwithstanding.

*Bureaucracy* is, of course, closely related to *technocracy*, and from there the symbolic shift to *undemocratic*, *elitist*, and *secretive* is but a short hop. Martha Derthick, writing recently of the legislative development of the Social Security system, describes the process as if it were a conspiracy.[10] Why? Because the principal actors were the people whose professional careers have been devoted to the system. In her view, the bureaucrats and their allies have taken an inappropriate role—or at least had inappropriate political influence. By definition, it would be "better" to have policy formulated in a more "democratic" forum.

Well, perhaps. But if *bureaucracy* in the pejorative sense of *insular*, *rigid*, and *insensitive* is the problem, then, as we have seen, reform in the image of democratic ideals is not the solution for a program like the DI program. It is responsiveness to the democratically constituted legislature that has pushed SSA in "bureaucratic" directions. The contemporary demand for managerial control was generated by the efforts of the House Ways and Means Committee, Subcommittee on

9. SYMBOLS OF GOVERNMENT 209 (1935).
10. M. DERTHICK, POLICY FOR SOCIAL SECURITY (1979).

Social Security and by the research reports of the General Accounting Office done at that subcommittee's request. The skewing of the QA effort toward payments errors was accomplished by legislation. And the single-minded pursuit of stringency in CDIs, including quotas for review and target percentages for terminations, is again the product of budgetary politics at the legislative level.

There can be little doubt that this combination of legislatively inspired and directed actions has, at least temporarily, seriously undermined the integrity of rational bureaucratic administration. For, in addition to being insensitive to the complex goals and subtle dynamics of the disability program, these initiatives may only deflect costs into different governmental units and into different time periods.

An unpublished analysis by William Copeland, a former top administrator in the DI program, for the Study Group on Social Security, suggests the following ripple effects from CDI stringency: first, the unavailability of DI payments is pushing large numbers of former recipients into state programs. Moreover, some of those programs, because they involve institutional care, are much more expensive than the DI program. For all anyone now knows the total governmental costs, state and federal, of caring for impaired persons may be increased by CDI stringency. Second, the deflection of funding to state budgets has become so serious that a number of states have enacted special statutes to fund private attorney representation of terminated disability recipients. These state representation programs are almost surely cost-effective, for 80 percent of the terminated DI beneficiaries who are represented on appeal are eventually reinstated. Thus, if all states respond in this way, enormously increasing the number and costs of SSA and federal court appeals, the CDI program will result in net increases in the combined payments and administrative costs of the federal DI (and SSI) program, even before costs deflected to the states are taken into account.

In view of this congressional action, it is difficult to credit Derthick's notion that more "democratic" control is what is needed in the DI program. She might, of course, approve of the new stringency that the Congress has introduced, because the principal problem that she attributed to insider control in her study was the explosive growth of the program in the 60s and early 70s. But that attribution itself seems peculiar. The statutory history does not support it, and besides, since when has Congress been good at avoiding buy-now-pay-later legislative schemes? Indeed, if Copeland is correct, the legislative tilt toward CDI stringency has merely adopted that technique again.

Improving the democratic connection as a device for administrative reform thus seems to imagine a politics that we do not have. Studies of regulatory dysfunctions seem increasingly to feature not the bureaucratic bogeyman but our elected representatives. Presumably the great advance of the environmental safety and health legislation of the 1970s for example, was its action-forcing specificity. But, as we feel the effects of legislation that *chooses*, that puts decisionmaking firmly in the representative assembly and thereby limits administrative discretion, we may develop a fonder view of vague legislative mandates.[11]

Where, then, is the political symbol of bureaucratic competence that can inspire, direct, and defend reform that is also instrumentally significant? When a particular bureaucracy sometimes fails, as it inevitably will, how can we refrain from saying, "Aha! That's because bureaucrats don't act like courts (or are not following their advice), or because the legislature left too much policy choice to the agency." Or, alternatively, stop saying, "Aha! That just goes to show that anything *worth* doing by way of regulation or social welfare can be done via the common law in a minimal state." Must we strive forever within a conceptual framework that either denies its own underlying reality or compares it deprecatingly with institutional and legal structures that our substantive public policy long ago abandoned?

I trust that we will not. The troublesome lack of a positive symbol of bureaucracy may result merely from the nonexistence of a symbolic bureaucratic institution in our constitutional scheme. Courts of Common Pleas gain some majesty from the existence of the Supreme Court, the shabby dealings of state assemblies from the democracy-reaffirming ritual of elections. But the president, as the head of the executive branch, symbolizes not bureaucratic competence, in fact, not bureaucracy at all but its opposite—the charisma of leadership. Our constitutional myth is that liberal democracy requires political leadership tied to electoral politics, with individual rights guaranteed by judicially administered law. Bureaucratic wielding of power is deviant; there is no constitutional office upon which it can be modelled. And from this perspective, "reform" means attempting to cure the deviance by giving

---

11. *See, e.g.,* B. Ackerman and W. Hassler, Clean Coal/Dirty Air (1981).

citizens rights either to force administrators into judicial molds or to make them conform to the democratic will expressed by the legislators. Chapter 1 argued that these "rights" are largely irrelevant or impertinent in the contemporary administrative state. After our close examination of the administration of the disability program, I would hope that the argument now carries conviction. There is something of legal, indeed constitutional, significance going on in administration. But the quality of administrative justice will not be improved significantly by the substantive or procedural interventions of courts responding to claims of individual legal or constitutional rights. Litigants would have to show up asking to be given a well-administered program—a claim that the foregoing chapters have suggested (if nothing else) would raise questions that range from the moderately complex to the ineffable.

Indeed, we seem to face a gap in our constitutional order of both symbolic *and* functional significance. We need to be able to think somehow of a "right" to good administration, without thinking merely of a transformation in the style of litigation.[12] Such a "right" would have to be "enforced" through a mechanism that promised technical competence plus the comfort of legitimating symbolism.

Suppose, for example, that there were a superbureau: an institution that combined a "judicial chamber" with something like the functions of the General Accounting Office, the Office of Management and Budget, the Administrative Conference, the Justice Department's Office of Legal Counsel, and the (now defunct) Regulatory Council. Functionally, this bureau would supervise the drafting of administrative legislation, review the competence of agency policy analysis, audit administrative performance in the field, provide binding counsel on managerial technique, and hear in the final instance complaints of maladministration. And suppose this bureau became the aspiration of the crème de la crème of the public managerial class and was also populated occasionally by academic students of administration and highly regarded private managers; that it gained a reputation for competence and integrity as well as for ultimate deference to the statutory expression of democratic political power. In short, a symbol of ideal administration.

12. See, e.g., Chayes, *The Role of the Judge in Public Law Litigation*, 89 Harv. L. Rev. 1281 (1976). But cf., Eisenberg and Yeazell, *The Ordinary and Extra-Ordinary in Institutional Litigation*, 93 Harv. L. Rev. 466 (1980).

Is there any reason that such an institution could not become the model for ordinary bureaus? And, if it did, would that not reorient administrative activity and the evaluation of the fairness of administrative judgments and processes toward an analysis of the internal structure of administration and ultimately toward the adequacy of the internal structure and functioning of particular agencies? And might not that "law" develop general principles—unifying normative ideals— that would yield a body of doctrine at least as coherent and, because more instrumentally effective, more symbolically persuasive than our current genuflections to an external conception of justice and the rule of law? A conception that is thin to the point of transparency. Is it possible that if we embraced the administrative state, that if we could demand bureaucratic justice without a wink or a sneer, we would find much to do and little to fear?

Again, perhaps. But we have as yet no clear vision of such a superbureau or how its symbolism might reorient the meaning of justice or the rule of law. The story we have told of the implementation of the disability program is suggestive. There is some evidence that the executive branch is tending in the direction of integrated, if not unified, oversight and toward hierarchical coordination, if not control. For the president to take seriously the constitutional command to "see that the laws are faithfully executed" virtually demands such a movement. But how these tendencies might work themselves out and what legal norms might then emerge to explain institutional developments remains highly speculative. Proposal of what such a structure *ought* to look like is a topic for another day.

# Index